£14

A Strange World0
by Mary Elizabeth Braddon

Copyright © 2019 by HardPress

Address:
HardPress
8345 NW 66TH ST #2561
MIAMI FL 33166-2626
USA
Email: info@hardpress.net

Braddon

COLLECTION
OF
BRITISH AUTHORS

TAUCHNITZ EDITION.

VOL. 1480.

A STRANGE WORLD BY M. E. BRADDON.

IN TWO VOLUMES.
VOL. I.

TAUCHNITZ EDITION.
By the same Author,

LADY AUDLEY'S SECRET	2 vols.
AURORA FLOYD	2 vols.
ELEANOR'S VICTORY	2 vols.
JOHN MARCHMONT'S LEGACY	2 vols.
HENRY DUNBAR	2 vols.
THE DOCTOR'S WIFE	2 vols.
ONLY A CLOD	2 vols.
SIR JASPER'S TENANT	2 vols.
THE LADY'S MILE	2 vols.
RUPERT GODWIN	2 vols.
DEAD-SEA FRUIT	2 vols.
RUN TO EARTH	2 vols.
FENTON'S QUEST	2 vols.
THE LOVELS OF ARDEN	2 vols.
STRANGERS AND PILGRIMS	2 vols.
LUCIUS DAVOREN	3 vols.
TAKEN AT THE FLOOD	3 vols.
LOST FOR LOVE	2 vols.

A STRANGE WORLD

A NOVEL.

BY

M. E. BRADDON,

AUTHOR OF "LADY AUDLEY'S SECRET," ETC.

COPYRIGHT EDITION.

IN TWO VOLUMES.—VOL. I.

LEIPZIG

BERNHARD TAUCHNITZ

1875.

The Right of Translation is reserved.

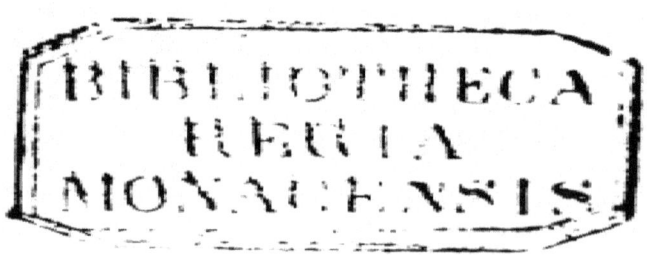

CONTENTS

OF VOLUME I.

			Page
CHAPTER	I.	Poor Players	7
—	II.	Behind the Scenes	28
—	III.	Éveillons le plaisir, son aurore est la nuit	39
—	IV.	"Love's a mighty lord"	49
—	V.	"Il ne faut pas pousser au bout les malheureux"	60
—	VI.	"There is no life on earth but being in love"	69
—	VII.	"Let the world slip; we shall ne'er be younger"	77
—	VIII.	"Have the high gods anything left to give?"	89
—	IX.	"Other sins only speak; murder shrieks out"	101
—	X.	"Nothing comes amiss, so money come withal"	111
—	XI.	"What, then, you knew not this red work indeed?"	127
—	XII.	"Brave spirits are a balsam to themselves"	132
—	XIII.	"My love, my love, and no love for me"	142
—	XIV.	"Truth is truth, to the end of time"	153
—	XV.	"They shall pass, and their places be taken"	164
—	XVI.	"There is a history in all men's lives"	171
—	XVII.	"Death could not sever my soul and you"	177
—	XVIII.	"What great ones do, the less will prattle of"	189
—	XIX.	"Farewell," quoth she, "and come again to-morrow"	205
—	XX.	"O'er all there hung a shadow and a fear"	215

CONTENTS OF VOLUME I.

		Page
CHAPTER XXI.	"He cometh not," she said.	222
— XXII.	"And I shall be alone until I die"	240
— XXIII.	"Surely, most bitter of all sweet things thou art"	250
— XXIV.	"We are past the season of divided ills"	261
— XXV.	"The drowsy night grows on the world"	273
— XXVI.	"Good night, good rest. Ah! neither be my share"	278
— XXVII.	"Such a lord is love".	287
— XXVIII.	"Then streamed life's future on the fading past".	296

A STRANGE WORLD.

CHAPTER I.

Poor Players.

A FAIR slope of land in buttercup-time, just when May, the capricious, melts into tender June—a slope of fertile pasture within two miles of the city of Eborsham, whose cathedral towers rise tall in the blue dim distance—a wealth of hedgerow flowers on every side, and all the air full of their faint sweet perfume, mixed with the odorous breath of the fast perishing hawthorn. Two figures are seated in a corner of the meadow, beneath the umbrage of an ancient thorn, not Arcadian or pastoral figures by any means;—not Phillis the milkmaid, with sun-browned brow and carnation cheeks, not Corydon fluting sweetly on his tuneful pipe as he reclines at her feet;—but two figures which carry the unmistakable stamp of city life in every feature and every garment. One is a tall, slender girl of seventeen, with a pale, tired face, and a look of having outgrown her strength, shot up too swiftly from childhood to girlhood, like a fast-growing weed. The other is a man who may be any age from forty to sixty, a man with sparse grey hair crowning a high forehead, bluish-grey eyes, under thick dark brows, a red nose, a mouth that looks as if it had been made for eating and drinking rather than oratory, a heavy jaw, and a figure inclining to corpulence.

The girl's eyes are large and clear, and changeful, of that dark blue-grey which often looks like black. The delicate young face possesses no other strong claim to be admired, and would be a scarcely noticeable countenance, perhaps, save for those grey eyes.

The raiment of both man and girl is of the shabbiest. His threadbare coat has become luminous with much friction, a kind of phosphorescent brightness pervades the sleeves, like the oleaginous scum that pollutes the surface of a city river; the tall hat which lies beside him in the deep grass has a look of having been soaped. His boots have obviously been soled and heeled, and have arrived at that debatable period in boot-life when they must either be soled again or hie them straight to the dust-hole. The girl's gown is faded and too short for her long legs, her mantle a flimsy silken thing of an almost forgotten fashion, her hat a fabric of tawdry net and ribbon patched together by her own unskilled hands.

She sits with her lap full of bluebells and hawthorn, looking absently at the landscape, with those solemn towers rising out of the valley.

"How grand they are, father!"

The father is agreeably occupied in filling a cutty pipe, embrowned by much smoking, which he handles fondly, as if it were a sentient thing.

"What's grand?"

"The cathedral towers. I could look at them for hours together—with that wide blue sky above them, and the streets and houses clustering at their feet. There's a bird's nest in one of them, oh! so high up, squeezed behind a horrid grinning face. Do you know, father, I've stood and looked at it sometimes till I've strained my eyes with looking? And I've wished I was a bird in that nest, and to live up there in the cool shadow of the stone; no care, no trouble, no work, and all that blue sky above me for ever and ever."

"The sky isn't always blue, stupid," answered the father contemptuously. "Your bird's nest would be a nice place in stormy weather. You talk like a fool, Justina, with your towers, and nests, and blue skies; and you're getting a young woman now, and ought to have some sense. As for cathedral towns, for my part I've never believed in 'em. Never saw good business for a fortnight on end in a cathedral town. It's all very well for a race week, or you may pull up with a military bespeak, if there's a garrison. But in a general way, as far as the profession goes, your cathedral town is a dead failure."

"I wasn't thinking of the theatre, father," said the girl, with a contemptuous shrug of her thin shoulders. "I hate the theatre, and everything belonging to it."

"There's a nice young woman, to quarrel with your bread and butter!"

"Bread and ashes, I think, father," she said, looking downward at the flowers, with a moody face. "It tastes bitter enough for that."

"Did ever any one hear of such discontent?" ejaculated the father, lifting his eyes towards the heavens, as if invoking Jove himself as a witness of his child's depravity. "To go and run down the Pro.! Hasn't the Pro. nourished you and brought you up, and maintained you since you were no higher than that?"

He spread his dingy hand a foot or so above the buttercups to illustrate his remark.

The Pro. of which he spoke with so fond an air was the calling of an actor, and this elderly gentleman, in threadbare raiment, was Mr. Matthew Elgood, a performer of that particular line of dramatic business known in his own circle as "the first heavies," or, in less technical phrase, Mr. Elgood was the heavy man —the King in Hamlet, Iago, Friar Lawrence, the Robber Chief of melodrama—the relentless father of the ponderous top-booted and pig-tailed comedy. And Justina Elgood, his seventeen year old daughter, commonly called Judy? Was she Juliet or Desdemona, Ophelia or Imogen? No. Miss Elgood had not yet soared above the humblest drudgery. Her line was general utility, in which she worked with the unrequited patience of an East-end shirtmaker.

"Hasn't the Pro. supported you from the cradle?" growled Mr. Elgood between short, thoughtful puffs at his pipe.

"Had I ever a cradle, father?" the girl demanded, wonderingly. "If you were always moving about then as you are now, a cradle must have been a great inconvenience."

"I've a sort of recollection of seeing you in one, for all that," replied Mr. Elgood, shutting his eyes with a meditating air, as if he were casting his gaze back into the past,—"a clumsy edifice of straw, bulky and awkward of shape. It might have held properties pretty well—but I don't remember travelling with it. I dare say your mother borrowed the thing of her landlady. In the days of your infancy we were at Slowberry in Somersetshire, and the Slowberry people are uncommonly friendly. I make no doubt your mother borrowed it."

"I dare say, father. We're great people for borrowing!"

"Why not?" asked Mr. Elgood, lightly; "give and take, you know, Judy: that's a Christian sentiment."

"Yes, father, but we always take."

"Man is the slave of circumstances, my dear. 'Give to him that asketh thee, and from him that would borrow of thee turn not away.' That's the gospel, Justina. If I have been rather in the position of the borrower than the lender, that has been my misfortune, and not my fault. Had I been the possessor of ten thousand per annum, I would have been the last of men to refuse to take a box-ticket for a fellow-creature's benefit."

The girl gave a faint sigh, and began to arrange the bluebells and hawthorn into a nosegay somewhat listlessly, as if even her natural joy in these things were clouded by a settled gloom within her mind.

"You're in the first piece, aren't you, Judy?" inquired Matthew Elgood, after indulging himself with a snatch of slumber, his elbow deep in the buttercups, and his head rested on his hand.

"Yes, father," with a sigh, "the countess, you know."

"The countess in 'The Stranger,' a most profitable part. Don't put on that hat and feather you wore last time we played the piece. It made the gallery laugh. I wonder whether you'll ever be fit for the juvenile lead, Judy?" he went on meditatively. "Do you know, sometimes I am afraid you never will; you're so gawky and so listless. The gawkiness would be nothing—you'll get over that when you've done growing, I dare say—but your heart is not in your profession, Justina. There's the rub."

"My heart in it," echoed the girl, with a dreary laugh. "Why, I hate it, father; you must know that. Hasn't it kept me ignorant and shabby, and looked down upon all the days of my life, since I was two years old, and went on as the child in 'Pizarro?' Hasn't it kept me hanging about the wings till midnight, from year's end to year's end, when other children were snug in bed with a mother to look after them? Haven't I been told often enough that I've no talents, and no good looks to help me, and that I must be a drudge all my life?"

"No good looks! Well, I'm not so sure about that," said the father, thoughtfully. "Talent, I admit, you are deficient of, Judy; but your looks even now are by no means despicable, and will improve with time. You have a fine pair of eyes, and a complexion that lights up uncommonly well. I have seen leading ladies earning their three to four guineas a week with less personal advantages."

"I wish I could earn a good salary, father, for your sake; but I should never be fond of acting. I've seen too much of the theatre. If I'd been a young lady, now, shut up in a drawing-room all my life, and brought to the theatre for the first time to see 'Romeo and Juliet,' I could fancy myself wanting to play Juliet; but I've seen too much of the ladder Juliet stands on in the balcony scene, and the dirty-looking man that holds it steady for her, and the way she quarrels with

Mrs. Wappers the nurse, between the acts. I've read the play often, father, since you've told me to study Juliet, and I've tried to fancy her a real living woman in Verona, under a cloudless sky, as blue as these flowers—but I can't—I can only think of Miss Villeroy, in her whitey-brown satin, and Mrs. Wappers, in her old green and yellow brocade,—and the battered old garden scene—and the palace flats we use so often—and the scene-shifters in their dirty shirt-sleeves. All the poetry has been taken out of it for me, father."

"That's because yours is a commonplace mind, child," answered Mr. Elgood, with a superior air. "Look at me, now! If I feel as dull as ditch-water when I go on the stage, the first hearty round of applause kindles the poetic fire, and the second fans it into a blaze. The divine *afflatus*, Judy; that's what you want, the *afflatus!*"

"I suppose you mean applause, father. I know I don't get much of that."

"No, Justina, I mean the breath of the gods—the sacred wind which breathes from the nostrils of genius, which gives life and shape to the imaginings of the dramatic poet, which inspires a Kean,—and, occasionally, an Elgood. I suppose you didn't hear of their encoring my exit in Iago on Tuesday night?"

"Yes, father, I heard of it."

"Come, Judy, we must be going," said Mr. Elgood, raising himself from his luxurious repose among the buttercups, after looking at a battered silver watch; "it's past four, and we've a good two miles to walk before we get our teas."

"Oh, how I wish we could stay here just as long

as we like—and then go quietly home in the starlight to some cottage among those trees over there."

"Cottages among trees are proverbially damp, and the kind of existence you talk of—mooning about a meadow and going home to a cottage— would be intolerably dull for a man with any pretension to intellect."

"Oh, father, we might have books and music, and flowers, and birds, and animals, and a few friends, perhaps, who would like us and respect us—if we were not on the stage. I don't think we need be dull."

"The varied pages of this busy world comprise the only book I care to study, Justina. As for birds, flowers, and animals, I consider them alike messy and unprofitable. I never knew a man who had a pet dog come to much good. It's a sign of a weak mind."

They were both standing by this time looking across the verdant, undulating landscape to the valley where nestled the city of Eborsham. The roofs and pinnacles did not seem far off, but there was that intervening sea of meadow land about the navigation whereof these wanderers began to feel somewhat uncertain.

"Do you know your way home, Judy?"

The girl looked across the meadows doubtfully.

"I'm not quite sure, father, but I fancy we came across that field over there, where there's such a lot of sorrel."

"Fancy be hanged!" exclaimed Mr. Elgood, impatiently, "I've got to be on the stage at half-past seven o'clock, and you lead me astray in this confounded solitary place, to suit your childish whims, and don't know how to get me back. It would be a nice thing if I were to lose a week's salary through your tomfoolery."

"No fear of that, father. We shall find our way back somehow, depend upon it. Why, we can't go very far astray when we can see the cathedral towers."

"Yes, and we might wander about in sight of them from now till midnight without getting any nearer to 'em. You ought to have known better, Justina."

Justina hung her head, abashed by this stern reproof.

"I dare say somebody will come by presently, father, and we can ask——"

"Do you dare say? Then I don't dare say anything of the sort. Here we've been sitting in this blessed meadow full two hours without seeing a mortal, except a solitary ploughboy, who went across with a can of something half an hour ago—beer, most likely—I know the sight of it made me abominably thirsty—and according to the doctrine of averages there's no chance of another human being for the next hour. Never you ask me to come for a walk with you again, Justina, after being trapped in this manner."

"Look, father! there's some one," cried Justina.

"Some two," said Mr. Elgood. "Swells, by the cut of their jibs. Down for the races, I dare say."

Eborsham was a city which had its two brief seasons of glory every year. The "Eborsham Spring," and the "Eborsham Summer," were meetings famous in the sporting world; but the spring to the summer was as Omega to Alpha in the sidereal heavens—or, taking a more earthly standard of magnitude, while beds for the accommodation of visitors were freely offered at half a crown during the spring meeting, the poorest pallet on hire in Eborsham was worth half a guinea in the summer.

The strangers approached at a leisurely pace. Two men in the spring-time of their youth, clothed in grey. One tall, strong of limb, broad of chest, somewhat slovenly of attire; loose cravat, grey felt hat, stout, sportsmanlike boots, fishing-rod under his arm. The other shorter, slighter, smaller, dressed with a certain girlish prettiness and neatness that smacked of Eton.

Both were smoking as they came slowly strolling along the field path on the other side of the irregular hawthorn hedge. The younger and smaller held a paper cigarette between his girlish lips. The other smoked a black-muzzled clay, which would not have been out of keeping with the costume and bearing of an Irish navvy.

They came to a gap in the hedge, which brought them close to the strollers.

"Gentlemen, can you enlighten me as to the nearest way to Eborsham?" asked Mr. Elgood, with a grandiose air, which the prolonged exercise of his avocation had made second nature.

The elder of the strangers stared at him blankly, with that unseeing gaze of the deep thinker, and went on pulling at his blackened pipe. The younger smiled kindly, and made haste to answer, with a shy eagerness—just a little stammer in his speech at first—which was not unpleasing.

"I really am at a loss to direct you," he said. "We

are strangers here ourselves—only came to Eborsham last night."

"For the races, I opine?" interrupted Mr. Elgood.

"Not exactly for the races," replied the young man, doubtfully.

"You came for the races, Jim," said the taller stranger, looking down at his companion as from an altitude of wisdom and experience. "I came to see that you were not fleeced. There are no rogues like the rogues that haunt a race-course."

This with a dark glance at the actor.

"He looks the image of a tout," thought the tall stranger. His fancies had been up aloft in his own particular cloudland when the wayfarers accosted him, and he was slowly coming down to the level of work-a-day life. Only this instant had he become conscious of the girl's presence.

Justina stood in the shadow of her father's bulky figure, making herself as narrow as she possibly could. Her detractors in the theatre found fault with that narrowness of Justina's. She had been disadvantageously likened to gas-pipes, May-poles, and other unsubstantial objects, and was considered a mere profile of a girl, an outline sketch, only worth half the salary that might have been given to a plumper damsel.

"Good heavens, Elgood!" the manager had exclaimed once, when Justina played a page, "when will your daughter begin to have legs?"

The tall stranger's slow gaze had now descended upon Justina. To that bashful maiden, conscious of her gawkiness, the darkly bright eyes seemed awful as the front of Jove himself. She shrank behind her father, dazzled as if by a sunburst. There was such power in Maurice Clissold's face.

"We came here, anyhow, following the windings of yonder trout-stream," said Clissold, with a backward glance at the valley. "I haven't the faintest notion how we are to get back, except by turning our noses to the cathedral, and then following them religiously. We can hardly fail to get there, sooner or later, if we are true to our noses."

Justina began to laugh, as if it had been a green-room jokelet, and then checked herself, blushing vehemently. She felt it was taking a liberty to be amused by this tall stranger.

"Perhaps time is no object to you, sir?" said Mr. Elgood.

"Not the slightest. I don't think time ever has been any object to me, except when I was gated at Oxford," replied Clissold.

"To me, sir, it is vital. If I do not reach yon city before the clock strikes seven, the prospects of a struggling commonwealth are blighted."

"Father," remonstrated the girl plucking his sleeve, "what do these gentlemen know about commonwealths?"

"I have studied the subject but superficially in the pages of our friend Cicero," said Clissold, lightly. "Modern scholars call him Kikero, but your elder erudition might hardly accept the Kappa."

"The commonwealth to which I allude, sir, is a company of actors now performing on their own hook at the Theatre Royal, Eborsham. If I am not on the stage before eight o'clock to-night our chances in that town are gone. The provincial public, having paid its shillings and sixpences, will not brook disappointment. You will hardly credit the fact, perhaps, sir, but there are seven places taken in the dress-circle, paid in advance, sir, further secured by a donation to the box-keeper, for this evening's performance. Conceive the feelings of those seven dress circles, sir, if Matthew Elgood is conspicuous by his absence!"

"That must not be, sir," returned Maurice Clissold, gravely. "Pedestrian wanderings have somewhat developed my organ of locality; and if you like to trust yourself to my guidance I will do my best to navigate you in the desired direction. Is that young lady also required by the British public?"

"Yes," responded Elgood, indifferently, "she's in the first piece. But we might send a ballet-girl on for her part—if," as an after-thought, "we had any ballet."

"The numerical strength of your commonwealth is limited, I infer from your remark," observed Clissold, as the stroller stepped through the gap in the hedge, and joined those other strollers in the lane.

"Well, sir,—'lead on, I follow thee'—when a manager puts it to his company roundly that he must either make it a commonwealth or shut up shop altogether, the little people are generally the first to fall away."

"The little people!"

"Yes, sir, second walking gentleman, ditto lady, second chambermaid, general utility; second old man, proverbially duffing, and ballet. The little people lack that confidence in their own genius which sustains a man under the fluctuations of a commonwealth,

They want the *afflatus*, and when the ghost walks not——"

"The ghost?"

"In vulgar English—when there is no treasury, no reliable weekly stipend, the little people collapse. The second walking lady and chambermaid go home to their mothers; the second old man opens a sweetstuff shop. They fade and evanish from a profession they did nothing to adorn."

"What is a commonwealth?" asked the younger gentleman, interested by this glimpse of a strange world.

"In a theatrical sense," added Clissold.

"A theatrical commonwealth is a body without a head. There is no responsible lessee. The weekly funds are divided into so many shares, each share representing half a sovereign. The actor whose nominal salary is two pound ten takes five shares. The actor whose ordinary pay is fifteen shillings claims but a share and a half, and has his claim allowed. I have known the shares to rise to fourteen and ninepence halfpenny; I have seen them dwindle to one and sevenpence."

"Thanks for the explanation. Does prosperity attend you in Eborsham?"

"Sir, our receipts heretofore have been but middling. Our anchor of hope is the Spring Meeting, which begins, as you are doubtless aware, to-morrow."

"Do you remain here long?" asked Mr. Penwyn, the younger pedestrian.

"A fortnight at most. Our next engagement is Duffield, thence we proceed to Humberston, then

Slingerford, after which we separate to seek 'fresh woods and pastures new.'"

Mr. Penwyn looked at the vagabond wonderingly. The man spoke so lightly of his fortuitous life. James Penwyn, of Penwyn Manor, Cornwall, had been brought up like the Danish princess who discovered the presence of the pea under seven feather beds and seven mattresses. He had never been inconvenienced in his life; and this encounter with a fellow-creature, who anatomically resembled himself, and yet belonged to a world so wide apart from his world, at once interested and amused him. He pitied the stroller with a serio-comic pity, as he might have compassionated an octopus in an uncomfortable position.

Perhaps there was never in this world a better natured youth than this James Penwyn. He had not the knack of sending his thoughts far afield, never lost himself in a tangle of speculative fancies, like his dark-eyed, wide-browed friend and master, Maurice Clissold, but within its somewhat narrow limit his mind was clear as a crystal streamlet. His first thought in every relation of life was to do a kindness. He was a man whom sponges of every order, and college scouts, and cabmen, and tavern waiters adore; and for whom the wise and prudent apprehend a youth of waste and riot, and an after-life of ruin.

"I'll tell you what," said he with a friendly air. "We'll come to the theatre to-night and see you act —and the young lady," with a critical glance at Justina, who walked close beside her father, and did her best to extinguish herelf in the shadow of Mr. Elgood's bulky form. It was as much as James Penwyn could do to get a glimpse of the girl's face, which had a pale, tired look just now. "Humph!" thought James, "fine eyes; but not particularly pretty,—rather a washed-out look."

"Sir," said Mr. Elgood, "you will confer at once honour and substantial benefit upon us poor players. And if you like to take a peep at life behind the scenes, my position in the theatre warrants my admitting you to that esoteric region."

"I should like it of all things, and we can sup together afterwards. They've a decent cook at the inn where my friend and I are staying, though it's only a roadside tavern. You know it, perhaps—the 'Waterfowl,' half a mile out of the town. It's my friend's fancy that we should stop there."

"It's your friend's necessity that he should avoid costly hotels," said Maurice, lightly.

They had crossed a couple of meadows, where young lambs scuttled off at the sight of them, bleating vehemently, and now came to a green lane, a long grassy gully between tall hedges, where the earliest of the dog-roses were budding, creamy white, amidst tender green leaves. Mr. Penwyn took advantage of the change to slip behind Mr. Elgood and place himself beside Justina. Maurice looked after him darkly. A too general worship of the fair sex was one of James Penwyn's foibles.

No, decidedly she was not pretty, thought James, after a closer inspection of the pale young face, with its somewhat pensive mouth and greyish-blue eyes. She blushed a little as he looked at her, and the delicate rose tint became the oval cheek. All the lines of her face were too sharp, for want of that filling out and rounding of angles which is the ripening of beauty.

She was like a pale greenish-hued peach on a wall in early June, to which July and August will bring roundness, velvety texture, and richest bloom.

"I hope you are not very tired," said James, gently.

"Not very," answered Justina, with an involuntary sigh. "We had a long rehearsal this morning."

"Yes, there always must be long rehearsals while there are stupid people in a theatre," interjected Mr. Elgood, with a sharpness which made the remark sound personal.

"We are getting up a burlesque for the race nights, gentlemen," continued the actor,—"'Faust and Marguerite'—the last popular thing in London, and my daughter knows as much about burlesque business as an eating-house waiter knows of a holiday."

"Are you fond of acting?" asked James, confidentially, ignoring Mr. Elgood's remarks.

"I hate it," answered Justina, less shyly than she had spoken before. There was something friendly in the young man's voice and manner which invited confidence; and then he was so pleasant to look at, with his small clearly-cut features, light auburn moustache, crisp auburn hair cut close to the well-shaped head, garments of rough grey tweed, which looked more distinguished than any clothes Justina had ever seen before; thick cable chain and pendent locket—a large, dull gold locket, with a Gothic monogram in black enamel—tawny gloves upon the small hands,—altogether a very different person from the tall man in the shabby shooting coat, leather gaiters, and bulky boots, who walked on the other side of Mr. Elgood.

Justina was young enough to be impressed by externals.

"Hate it?" exclaimed Mr. Penwyn; "I thought actresses always adored the stage, and looked forward to acquiring the fame of an O'Neil or a Faucit."

"Do they?" said Justina; "those I know are like horses in a mill, and go the same round year after year. When I think that I may have to lead that kind of life till I die of old age, I almost feel that I should like to drown myself, if it wasn't wicked; but then I haven't any talent. I suppose it would all seem different if I were clever."

"Aren't you clever?" asked James, smiling at her simplicity. Although not pretty she was far from unpleasing. He was amused—interested even. But then he was always ready to interest himself in any tolerably attractive young woman.

Maurice Clissold fell away from the actor, and walked beside his friend, overlooking James and Justina from his superior height. There was plenty of space in the wide green lane for four to walk abreast.

"No," said Justina, confidentially, not wishing her father to hear ungrateful murmurs against the art he respected, "I believe I'm very stupid. If there is a point to be made I generally miss it—speak too fast, or too slow, or drop my voice at the end of a speech, or raise it too soon. Even in François I didn't get a round the other night. You know François?"

"Haven't the honour of his acquaintance."

"The page in 'Richelieu.' He has a grand speech. One is bound to get a tremendous round of applause;

but somehow I missed it. Father said he should like to have boxed my ears."

"He didn't do it, I hope."

"No, but it was almost as bad. He said it before everybody in the green-room."

"I understand—like a fellow saying something unpleasant of one at one's club."

They came to the end of the green lane at last. It opened upon a level sweep of land, across which they saw the city, all its roofs and walls steeped in the westering sunlight. The ground was marshy, and between low rush-grown banks gently flowed the Ebor, a narrow river that wound its sinuous course around the outskirts of Eborsham, without entering the city.

"I have not led you astray, you see, sir," said Maurice; "behold the cathedral. Yonder path by the water's edge will bring us to the lower end of the town."

"We have to thank you for extrication from a difficulty, sir," replied Mr. Elgood, with dignity. "You have brought us a shorter way than that which my daughter and I traversed when we came out this afternoon."

They followed the river path—a tow-path along which slow, clumsy horses were wont to drag the lingering chain of a heavily-laden barge. The dark green rushes shivered in the west wind—the slow river was gently rippled—the city had a look of unspeakable stillness—like a city in a picture.

Half way along the tow-path they encountered some stragglers—a man laden with oaken mats, who walked wide of his companions on the marshy ground outside the path—a boy running here and there at random, chasing the small yellow butterflies, and shouting at them in the ardour of the chase—an elderly woman of the gipsy race, carrying a string of light fancy baskets across her shoulder.

"That's the worst of a race-meeting," said James Penwyn, with reference to these nomads. "It brings together such a lot of rabble."

One of the rabble stopped and blocked his pathway. It was the elderly gipsy woman.

"Let me tell you your fortune, my pretty gentleman," she said, pouncing on Mr. Penwyn, as if she had discovered his superior wealth at a glance. "Cross the poor gipsy's hand with a bit of silver—half a crown won't hurt you—my pretty gentleman. You've riches in your face—you've never known what it is to want a sovereign, and never will. The world was made for such as you."

"Avaunt, harridan!" cried the tragedian, "and suffer us to proceed."

"What, you'd like to spoil my market, would you?" cried the sibyl, vindictively. "No one was ever a penny the richer for your generosity, and no one will be a penny the worse off when you're dead and gone, except yourself. Let me tell your fortune, pretty gentleman," she went on, laying a persuasive hand on James Penwyn's grey sleeve, and keeping up with the pedestrians as they strove to pass her. "There's plenty of pleasant things the old gipsy woman can tell you. You're a gentleman that likes a dark blue eye, and there's an eye that looks kindly upon you now, and though there's crosses for true lovers, all will come out happy in the end, if you'll listen to the old gipsy."

James laughed, and flung the prophetess a florin.

"Show me your hand, kind gentleman," she urged, after a string of thanks and benedictions, "your left hand. Yes, there's the mount of Venus, and not an ugly line across it, and you've a long thumb, my pretty gentleman, long between the first joint and the second—that means strength of will, for the thumb is Jupiter, and rules the house of life. Don't take your hand away, pretty gentleman. Let's see the line——"

"What's the matter, mother?" asked James, as the woman stopped in the middle of a sentence, still holding his hand and staring at the palm steadfastly with a scared look.

"What's that?" she asked, pointing to a short indented line across the palm.

"Why, what keen eyes you have, old lady! That's the mark of a hole I dug in my palm two years ago, cutting a tough bit of cavendish. My scout told me I was bound to have lockjaw, but I didn't realize his expectations. I suppose lockjaw doesn't run in our family."

"Right across the line of life," muttered the gipsy, still examining the seam left by the knife upon the pinkish, womanish palm.

"Does that mean anything bad—that I am to die young, for instance?"

"The scar of a knife can't overrule the planets," replied the sibyl, sententiously.

CHAPTER II.

Behind the Scenes.

James Penwyn and Maurice Clissold went to the Eborsham Theatre as soon as they had eaten their dinner and smoked a single cigar apiece, lounging by the open window in the gloaming, talking over their afternoon's adventure.

"What a fellow you are, Jim!" cried Maurice, with a half-contemptuous, half-compassionate air, as for the foolishness of a child. "To hear you go on about that scarecrow of a girl, one would suppose you had never seen a pretty woman in your life."

"I never saw prettier eyes," said James, "and she has a manner that a fellow might easily fall in love with—so simple, so childish, so confiding."

"Which means that she gazed with undisguised admiration upon the magnificent Squire Penwyn, of Penwyn Manor. A woman need only flatter you, Jim, for you to think her a Venus."

"That poor little thing didn't flatter me. She's a great deal too innocent."

"No, she only admired you innocently; opening those big blue eyes of hers to their widest in a gaze of rapture. Was it the locket, or the studs, or the moustache, I wonder, that struck her most?"

"Don't be a fool, Clissold. If we are to go to the theatre, we'd better not waste any more time. I want to see what kind of an actor our friend is."

"Student of humanity," jeered Maurice, "even a provincial player is not beneath your notice. Cuvier was profound upon spiders. Penwyn has a mind of a wider range."

"What is his name, by-the-bye?" mused James, thinking of Mr. Elgood. "We don't even know his name, and we've asked him to supper. That's rather awkward, isn't it?"

"Be sure he will come. No doubt he has already speculated on the possibility of borrowing five pounds from you."

Mr. Penwyn rang the bell and gave his orders with that easy air of a man unaccustomed to count the cost. The best supper the "Waterfowl" could provide, at half-past eleven.

They walked along the lonely country road into Eborsham. The "Waterfowl Inn" was upon one of the quietest, most obscure roads leading outside the city; not the great coach road to London, bordered for a mile beyond the town by snug villas, and bandboxical detached cottages—orderly homes of retired traders—but a by-road leading to a village or two, of no consequence save to the few humble folks who lived in them.

This road followed the wind of the river which traversed the lower end of Eborsham, and it was for its vicinity to the river, and a something picturesque in its aspect, that the two friends had chosen the "Waterfowl" as their resting place. There was a small garden behind the inn which sloped to the edge of the stream, and a rustic summerhouse where the young men smoked their pipes after dinner.

Between the "Waterfowl" and Eborsham the landscape was low and flat; on one side a narrow strip of marshy ground between road and river, with a scrubby brush here and there marking the boundary, on the other a tall neglected hedgerow at the top of a steep bank, divided from the road by a wide weedy ditch.

The two friends entered Eborsham through a Gothic archway called Lowgate. The old town had been a strongly fortified city, famous for its walls, and there were several of these stone gateways. The theatre stood in the angle of a small square, almost overshadowed by the mighty towers of the cathedral, as if the stage had gone to the church for sanctuary and protection from the intolerance of bigots.

Here Mr. Penwyn and Mr. Clissold placed themselves among the select few of the dress-circle, a cool and airy range of seats, whose sparsely scattered occupants listened with rapt attention to the gloomy prosings of "The Stranger." James Penwyn was not ravished by that Germanic drama. Even Mrs. Haller bored him. She dropped her h's, and expressed the emotions of grief and remorse by spasmodic chokings and catchings of her breath. But Mr. Penwyn lighted up a little when the Countess appeared, for the Countess had the large melancholy blue eyes of the girl he had met in the meadow.

Miss Elgood did not look her best on the stage. Tall, slim, and willow-waisted, sharp of elbow and angular of shoulder, dressed in cheap finery, soiled satin, tarnished silver lace, murky marabouts, badly painted with two dabs of rouge that were painfully visible upon the pure pale of her young cheeks. Artistically, Justina was a failure, and feeling herself a failure suffered from an inability to dispose of her arms, and a lurking conviction that the audience regarded her with loathing.

Mr. Clissold exchanged his front seat for a place on the hindmost bench before "The Stranger" was halfway through his troubles, and here, secure in the shade, slept comfortably. James Penwyn endured two acts and a half, and then, remembering Mr. Elgood's offer to show him life behind the scenes, slipped quietly out of the dress-circle, and asked the box-keeper how he was to get to the side scenes.

That official, sweetened by a liberal donation, unlocked a little door behind the proscenium box, a door sacred to the manager, and let Mr. Penwyn through into the mystic world of behind the scenes. He would hardly have done such a thing under a responsible lessee, but in a commonwealth morals become relaxed.

The mystic world looked dark and dusty, and smelt of gas and dirt, to the unaccustomed senses of Mr. Penwyn.

The voices on the stage sounded loud and harsh now that they were so near his ear. There was hardly room for him to move between the side scenes and the wall—indeed, it was only by screwing himself against this whitewashed wall that he made his way in the direction which a scene-shifter had indicated as the way to the green-room.

Mr. Penwyn's experience of life had never before led him behind the scenes. He had a vague idea that a green-room was a dazzling saloon, lighted by crystal chandeliers, lined with mirrors, furnished with divans of ruby velvet, an idealized copy of a club-house smoking-room. He found himself in a small dingy chamber, carpetless, curtainless, uncleanly, provided with narrow baize-covered benches, and embellished with one cloudy looking-glass, on either side whereof flared an unscreened gas jet.

Here over the narrow wooden mantelshelf hung castes of pieces in preparation, "Jack Sheppard," "Delicate Ground," "Courier of Lyons," "Box and Cox," a wide range of dramatic art, and calls for next day's rehearsal. Here, in divers attitudes of weariness, lounged various members of the dramatic commonwealth; among them Mr. Elgood, in the frogged coat, crimson worsted pantaloons and Hessian boots of the Baron; and Justina, seated disconsolately, with her limp satin trailing over the narrow bench beside her, studying her part in the piece for to-morrow night.

"My dear sir," exclaimed Matthew Elgood, shaking hands with enthusiasm, "this is kind! Dempson,"—this to a gentleman in mufti, small, sallow, close-cropped, and smelling of stale tobacco—"this is my pioneer of to-day. Mr. Dempson, Mr.?—stay, we did not exchange cards."

"Penwyn," said James, smiling.

Mr. Elgood stared at the speaker curiously, as if he hardly believed his own ears, as if this name of Penwyn had some strange significance for him.

"Penwyn," he repeated, "that's a Cornish name isn't it?"

"By Tre, Pol, and Pen you may know the Cornish men. There is nothing more Cornish; I was born and brought up near London, but my race belongs to the Cornish soil. We were indigenous at Penwyn, I believe, the founders and earliest inhabitants of the settlement. Do you know Cornwall?"

"Not intimately. Merely as a traveller."

"Were you ever at Penwyn?"

"I don't think so, I have no recollection."

"Well, it's a place you might easily forget, not a promising locality for the exercise of your art. But you seemed struck by my name just now, as if you had heard it before."

"I think I must have heard it somewhere, but I can't recall the occasion. Let that pass." And with a majestic wave of the hand Mr. Elgood performed the ceremony of introduction.

"Mr. Dempson, Mr. Penwyn. Mr. Penwyn, Mr. Dempson. Mr. Dempson is our sometime manager, now a brother professional. He has resigned the round and top of sovereignty, and the carking cares of Saturday's treasury."

Mr. Dempson assented to this statement with a plaintive sigh.

"A harassing profession, the drama, Mr. Penwyn," he said. "The many-headed is a monster of huge ingratitudes."

James bowed assent.

"The provincial stage is in its decline, sir. Time was when this very theatre could be kept open for ten consecutive months in every year, to the profit of the manager, and when the good old comedies and the Shaksperian drama were acted week after week to an intelligent and approving audience. Now-a-days a man must rack his brains in order to cater for a frivolous and insatiable public, which has been taught to consider a house on fire, or a railway smash, the end and aim of dramatic composition. I speak from bitter experience. My grandfather was manager of the Eborsham

A Strange World. I.

circuit, and retired with a competency. My father inherited the competency, and lost it in the Eborsham circuit. I have been cradled in the profession, and have failed as manager, with credit to my head and heart, as my friends have been good enough to observe, some three or four times, and now hang on to dramatic art, 'quite out of fashion, like a rusty nail in monumental armour.' That's what I call the decline of the drama, Mr. Penwyn."

James assented, and was not sorry that Mr. Dempson, having "vented his woe," went off to dress for the after-piece.

"What a melancholy person!" said James.

"An excellent low comedian," replied Mr. Elgood. "You'll hear the people screaming at him in the 'Spitalfields Weaver' by and by. His business with the tea and bread and butter is the finest thing I ever saw, not second to Wright's. Indeed," added Mr. Elgood, as an after-thought, "I believe it is Wright's business."

"Then it can hardly claim the merit of originality."

"Genius, Mr. Penwyn, finds its material where it can."

"Baron," screamed a small boy, putting his head in at the door.

"My scene!" exclaimed Mr. Elgood, and vanished.

James seated himself on the narrow bench beside Justina.

"I have been in the boxes to see you act," he said, in that gentle winning voice which had made him a favourite among women. To Justina it sounded fresh as a voice from another world. No one in her world spoke like that, in tones so deferential, with accents so pure.

"I am very sorry for it," said Justina.

"Sorry! but why?"

"Because you must hate me. The audience always do hate me. I feel it in their looks—feel it freezing me directly I go on the stage. 'Oh, there *she* is again!' they say to themselves. 'Can't they manage to get through the piece without sending *her* on?'"

"What a curious notion! I thought actresses were conceited people."

"Yes, when they are favourites."

"I don't know about the rest of the audience, Miss Elgood," said James, almost tenderly, "but I know I did not hate you,—my feelings leaned too much the other way."

Justina blushed through those two dabs of rouge —compliments were so new to her, and a compliment from this elegant stranger was worth all the loud praises of the vulgar herd. She hardly envied Miss Villeroy—the leading lady—whose chokings and sobbings in Mrs. Haller had been applauded to the echo, while the poor countess in her draggle-tailed sky-blue satin had walked on and off unnoticed.

"So this is the way you enjoy the legitimate drama, Mr. Penwyn," said a sonorous voice—the full rich baritone of Maurice Clissold—and, looking up, James and Justina beheld that gentleman watching them from the doorway.

"I left *you* asleep," replied James, abashed by his friend's advent.

"Yes, sneaked off, and left me to grope my way to this abominable den as best I could. I beg your pardon, Miss Elgood, but it really is a den."

"You can't hate it worse than I do," said Justina, "or so badly—I have to sit here every night."

"Poor child! It's a strange life—and a hard one. Seen from the outside there seems a not unpleasant Bohemian flavour about it—but when one comes behind the scenes the Bohemian flavour appears to be mainly dirt. I've inhaled enough dust and escaped gas within the last ten minutes to last me comfortably for my lifetime. And you breathe this atmosphere for four or five hours every night! Poor child!"

James sighed. His benevolent heart longed to rescue the girl from such a life—a girl with pensive violet eyes, fringed by darkest lashes—soft brown hair, so luxuriant that it made a crown of plaits upon the well-shaped head,—altogether a girl whom benevolence would fain benefit.

"Come, Jim," said Clissold, who had a knack of reading his friend's thoughts, "you've seen enough of behind the scenes."

"No, I haven't," answered James, sturdily, as the countess ran off to act her part in the close of the play. He was wont to be plastic as wax in the hands of his guide, philosopher, and friend, but to-night there glowed a spark of rebellion in his soul. "I am going to stop to see Mr. Elgood, and to ask him to bring his daughter to supper."

"Bring his daughter! To visit two young men at a roadside inn?"

"*Honi soit—*," said James. "Can a girl be safer anywhere than with her father?"

"Look here, Penwyn," said Clissold, earnestly, "I've made it the business of my life for the last two years to keep you in the straight path. I won't have you kicking over the traces for any blue-eyed chit in the universe. Remember what I promised your poor mother, Jim."

"That you'd act the part of an elder brother—supply the balance of good sense wanting to my shallow brains. That's all very well, Maurice. I always respected my poor mother's ideas even when they took the shape of prejudices. But a man must enjoy his life."

"Yes, but he is bound to enjoy life with the least possible injury to other people."

"Whom am I going to injure?" demanded Mr. Penwyn, with an impatient shrug, as he moved towards the wings.

"You are putting foolish ideas into that poor child's head."

"What nonsense! Simply because I am civil to her. I mean to ask her to supper, whether you like it or not."

"I hope her father will have the sense to refuse."

"If you come to that, I'll invite the whole company!" cried the spoiled child of fortune.

The curtain came down at this moment, and Mr. Elgood returned to the green-room, unbuckling his sword-belt as he came along.

"I waited to remind you of your promise to sup with us to-night, Mr. Elgood," said James.

"My dear sir, it is not an engagement to be forgotten. I shall be there."

"Will half-past eleven be too early?"

"No; 'The Stranger' has played quick to-night, and the after-piece is short. I shall be there."

"Miss Elgood will accompany you, I hope?"

"Thanks, no. The proprieties would be outraged

by her appearance at a bachelor's table. The only lady present."

"We could easily remedy that, if any other lady of the company would honour us."

"Upon my word you are very kind; and I know the child would consider it a treat. If you put the question in such a friendly manner I feel sure that Mr. and Mrs. Dempson would be delighted to join us."

"Pray bring them. Is Mrs. Dempson also dramatic?"

"You have seen her to-night in one of her greatest parts—Mrs. Haller."

"I thought the lady was a Miss Villeroy."

"Her professional name, merely. Joe Dempson and Miss Villeroy have been united in the sacred bonds of matrimony for some years."

"I shall be charmed to make the lady's acquaintance. You know your way to the 'Waterfowl?'"

"It is familiar to me as the path of my infancy."

"And you'll be sure to bring Miss Elgood?"

"Judy shall come without fail."

"Judy?"

"The pet name chosen by affection. She was christened Justina. Pardon me if I leave you hastily, I play in the next piece."

Mr. Elgood hurried away. James Penwyn glanced at his friend with the glance of triumph.

"Out of leading-strings, you see, Maurice," he said.

Maurice Clissold shrugged his shoulders and turned away with a sigh. James, more touched by silence than reproof, put his arm through his friend's with a gay laugh, and they went out of the green-room and out of the theatre together, arm-in-arm, like brothers who loved each other.

CHAPTER III.

"Éveillons le plaisir, son aurore est la nuit."

THE supper at the "Waterfowl" was a success. Every one, except perhaps Clissold, was in the humour to be pleased with everything, and even Clissold could not find it in his heart to make himself vehemently disagreeable amidst mirth so harmless, gaiety so childishly simple. To an actor, supper after the play is just the one crowning delight of life—that glimpse of paradise upon earth which we all get in some shape or other. A supper at a comfortable hostelry like the "Waterfowl," where the landlord knew how to do things in good style for a customer who could pay the piper, was certainly not to be despised. In this northern district there was a liberal plenty, a bounteous wealth of provision hardly known elsewhere. Tea at Eborsham meant dinner and breakfast rolled into one. Supper at Eborsham meant aldermanic barn-door fowls, and a mighty home-cured ham, weighing five-and-twenty pounds, or so—lobsters nestling among crisp green lettuces—pigeon pie—cheese-cakes—tarts —and, lest these lighter trifles should fail to satisfy appetite, a lordly cold sirloin by way of *corps de reserve*, to come in at a critical juncture, like Blucher at Waterloo.

Mr. Dempson made himself the life of the party. The small melancholy man who had bewailed the decline of the drama, vanished altogether at sight of that plenteously-furnished table, and in his place appeared a jester of the first water. So James Penwyn thought at any rate, as he laughed—with youth's gay silver-clear laughter—at the low comedian's jokes. Even Miss Villeroy was sprightly, though she had a worn look about the eyes, as if she had aged herself prematurely with the woes of Mrs. Haller, and other heroines of tragedy. Justina sat next to James Penwyn, and was supremely happy, though only an hour ago she had shed tears of girlish shame at the idea of coming to a supper party in her threadbare brown merino gown—last winter's gown—which she was obliged to wear in the warm glad spring for want of fitter raiment. No one thought of her shabby gown, however, when the pale young face brightened and flushed with unwonted pleasure, and the large thoughtful eyes took a new light, and darkened to a deeper grey.

James Penwyn did his uttermost to make her happy and at ease, and succeeded only too well. There is no impression so swift and so vivid as that which the first admirer makes upon a girl of seventeen. The tender words, the subdued tones, the smiles, the praises, have such a freshness. The adulation of a Cæsar in after years would hardly seem so sweet as first flatteries of commonplace youth to the girl on the threshold of womanhood.

Mr. Elgood saw what was going on, but was by no means alarmed by the aspect of affairs. He felt himself quite able to take care of Justina, even if Mr. Penwyn had been a hardened libertine instead of a kind-hearted youth fresh from the university. He had no desire to stifle admiration which might mean very little, but which would most likely result in liberal patronage for his own benefit, and a trifling present or two for Justina, a ring, or a bracelet, or a box of gloves.

"I don't want to stand in Justina's light," mused Mr. Elgood, as he leaned back in his chair and sipped his last glass of champagne, when the pleasures of the table had given way to an agreeable sense of repletion.

"What did that gipsy woman mean by the line of life, and the planets?" asked Justina. She had lost all sense of shyness by this time, and she and James were talking to each other in lowered voices, as much alone as if the rest of the party had been pictures on the wall. Maurice marked them as he sat a little way apart from the others, smoking his black-muzzled pipe.

"Pshaw, only the professional jargon. What does she know of the planets?"

"But she stared at your hand in such a curious way, and looked so awful that she frightened me. Do tell me what she meant."

James laughed, and laid his left hand in Justina's, palm upwards. "Look there," he said; "you see that line, a curved channel that goes from below the first finger to the base of the thumb—that is to say, it should go to the base of the thumb, but in my hand it doesn't. See where the line disappears, midway, just by that seam left by my pocket-knife. You can see no line beyond that scar, *ergo* the line never travelled further than that point."

Justina closely scrutinized the strong unwrinkled palm.

"What does that mean?" she asked; "I don't understand even now."

"It means a short life and a merry one."

The rare bloom faded from Justina's cheek.

"You don't believe in that?" she said, anxiously.

"No more than I believe in gipsies, or spirit-rappers, or the cave of Trophonius," answered James, gaily. "What a silly child you are to look so scared!"

Justina gave a little sigh, and then tried to smile. Even this first dawn of a girlish fancy, airy as a butterfly's passion for a rose, brought new anxieties along with it. The gipsy's cant was an evil omen that disturbed her like a shapeless fear. Women resemble those mediæval roysterers of whom the old chronicler wrote. They take their pleasure sadly.

The moon was at the full. There she sailed, a silver targe, above the distant hill-tops. James looked up at her, looked into that profound world above, which draws the fancies of youth with irresistible power. The room opened on the garden by two long windows, and the one nearest to Mr. Penwyn's end of the table stood open.

"Let us get away from the smoke," he said, vexed to see Clissold's eye upon him, fixed and gloomy. The room was tolerably full of tobacco-smoke by this time, and Mr. Elgood was urging Mr. Dempson to favour the company with his famous song, "The Ship's Carpen*teer*."

"Come into the garden, Maud," said James, gaily, flinging a look of defiance at his monitor.

Justina blushed, hesitated, and obeyed him. They went out into the moonlit night together, and strolled side by side across the rustic garden, a slope of grass on which the most ancient of apple-trees, and pear-trees, big enough to have been mistaken for small elms, cast their crooked shadows. It was more orchard than garden, a homely, useful place altogether. Pot-herbs grew among the rose-bushes on the border by the boundary hedge, and on one side of the inn there was a patch of ground that grew cabbages and broad-beans; but all the rest was grass and apple-trees.

At the end of that grassy slope ran the river, silver-shining under the moon. Eborsham, seen across the level landscape, looked a glorified city in that calm and mellow light. The boy and girl walked silently down to the river's brim and looked at the distant hills and woods, scattered cottages with lowly thatched roofs and antique chimney-stacks, here and there the white walls of a mansion silvered by the moon, and, dominating all in sublime and gloomy grandeur, the mighty towers of the cathedral, God's temple, rising, like fortalice and sanctuary, above all human habitations, as of old the Acropolis.

Justina gazed and was silent. It was one of those rare moments of exaltation which poets tell us are worth a lifetime of sluggish feeling. The girl felt as if she had never lived till now.

"Pretty, isn't it?" remarked James, very much in the tone of Brummel, who after watching a splendid sunset was pleased to observe, "How well he does it!"

"It is too beautiful," said Justina.

"Why too beautiful?"

"I don't know. It hurts me somehow, like actual pain!"

"You are like Byron's Lara,—

'But a night like this,
A night of beauty, mocked such breast as his.'

I hope it is not a case of bad conscience with you, as it was with him?"

"No, it is not my conscience. The worst I have ever done has been to grumble at the profession; and though father says it is wicked, the thought of my wickedness has never troubled me. But to me there's something awful in the beauty of night and stillness, a solemnity that chills me. I feel as if there were some trouble hanging over me, some great sorrow. Don't you?"

"Not the least in the world. I think moonlight awfully jolly. Would you much mind my lighting a cigar? You'll hardly feel the effects of the smoke out here."

"I never feel it anywhere," answered Justina, frankly. "Father hardly ever leaves off smoking."

There was a weeping willow at the edge of the garden, a willow whose lower branches dipped into the river, and just beside the willow a bench where these two seated themselves, in the full glory of the moon. A much better place than the dusky summerhouse, which might peradventure be a harbour for frogs, snails, or spiders. They sat by the river's brim, and talked—talked as easily as if they had a thousand ideas in common, these two, who had never met until to-day, and whose lives lay so far apart.

They had youth and hope in common, and that bond was enough to unite them.

James asked Justina a good many questions about stage life, and was surprised to find the illusions of his boyhood vanish before stern truth.

"I thought it was such a jolly life, and the easiest in the world," he said. "I've often fancied I should like to be an actor. I think I could do it pretty well. I can imitate Buckstone, and Charles Mathews."

"Pray don't think of it," exclaimed Justina. "You'd be tired to death in a year."

"I dare say I should. I'm not much of a fellow for sticking to anything. I got 'ploughed' a year ago at Oxford, and now I've been trying to read with Clissold walking through England and Wales, and putting up at all the quietest places we can find. Clissold is a first-rate coach, and it won't be his fault if I don't get my degree next time. How do you like him?"

"I don't know. I haven't thought about him," answered the girl, simply. This younger and fairer stranger had made her oblivious of Maurice Clissold, with his tall, strong frame, dark, penetrating eyes, and broad brow. Too manly a man altogether to be admired by a girl of seventeen.

"He is as good a fellow as ever breathed; a little bitter, perhaps; but most wholesome things are bitter," said James. "He has his crotchets. One is that I am to be a model master of Penwyn by and by, go into Parliament, marry an heiress, set up as a fine old English gentleman, in fact. Rather a wearisome *métier*, I should think. The worst of it is, he keeps it continually before my mind's eye, is always reminding me of how much I owe to Penwyn Manor and my race, and won't let me get much enjoyment out of youth's brief holiday. He's a good fellow, but I might love him better if I didn't respect him so much. He was a great favourite of my poor mother's. A romantic story, by the way. She was engaged to Maurice's father some years before she married mine. He was a captain in the East India

Company's service, and fell fighting the niggers at Goojerat. Years afterwards, when my father was dead and gone, Clissold and I met at Eton. My mother burst into tears when she heard my schoolfellow's name, and asked me to bring him to see her. Of course I obeyed, and from that time to the day of her death my mother had a second son in Maurice. I think she loved him as well as she loved me."

"And you were never jealous?"

"No, I was too fond of both of them for that. And then my dear mother was all love, all tenderness. I could afford to share her affection with my adopted brother. And now tell me something about your own life."

"There is so little to tell," answered the girl, drearily. "Ever since I can remember we have lived the same kind of life—sometimes in one town, sometimes in another. When father could afford the money he used to send me to a day school, so I've been a little educated somehow, only I dare say I'm very ignorant, because my education used to stop sometimes, and by the time it began again I had forgotten a good deal."

"Poor child," murmured James, compassionately. "Is your mother still living?"

"She died seven years ago. She had had so much trouble, it wore her out at last." And Justina paid her dead mother the tribute of a hidden tear.

"I say, Jim, do you know that it is half-past two o'clock, and that Mr. Elgood is waiting for his daughter?" asked the voice of common sense in the tones of Maurice Clissold.

The two children started up from the bench by

the willow, scared by the sudden question. There stood Mr. Clissold, tall and straight, and severe-looking.

"I heard the cathedral clock a few minutes ago, and I am quite aware of the time. If Mr. Elgood wants his daughter he can come for her himself," replied James.

Mr. Penwyn was resolved to make a stand against his mentor, and he felt that now was the time for action.

Mr. Elgood and Mr. Dempson came strolling out into the garden, cigars in their mouths. Penwyn's choicest brand had been largely sacrificed at the altar of hospitality.

"Judy, have you forgotten the time?" asked the heavy father, with accents that had a *legato* sound— one syllable gliding gently into another,—a tone that was all sweetness and affection, though indistinct.

"Yes, father," answered the girl, innocently. "It's so beautiful out here."

"Beautiful," echoed the father, thickly. "'Look how the floor of heaven is thick inlaid with—what's its names—of bright gold.' Come, Jessica—Judy— put on your bonnet and shawl. Mrs. Dempson has been fast asleep for the last half-hour. 'But look! The morn, in russet mantle clad, walks o'er the dew of yon high eastern hill,' which reminds me that we have nearly a mile to walk before we get home."

"I'll go with you," said James. "I want to arrange about to-morrow. We must make up a jolly party for the races. I'll get a roomy carriage that will hold all of us."

"I haven't seen a race in anything like comfort for the last fifteen years," responded Mr. Elgood.

"We'll make a day of it. Clissold and I will come to the theatre in the evening."

"Make your own engagements if you please, James, and allow me to make mine," said Mr. Clissold. "I shall not go to the races to-morrow—or if I do, it will be by myself, and on foot; and I shall not go to the theatre in the evening."

"Please yourself," answered James, offended.

They were all ready by this time. Mrs. Dempson had been awakened, and shaken out of the delusion that she had fallen asleep on the sofa in her own lodgings, and somewhat harshly reminded that she had a mile or so to walk before she could obtain complete repose. Mr. Dempson had finished his cigar, and accepted another as solace during the homeward walk. Justina had put on her shabby little bonnet and mantle. Every one was ready.

The players took their leave of Maurice Clissold, who was but coldly civil. James Penwyn went out with them, and gave his arm to Justina, as if it were the most natural thing in the world. These two walked on in front, the other three straggling after them—walked arm in arm along the lonely footpath. The low murmur of the river sounded near—the stream showed silvery now and again between a break in the screen of alders.

They talked as they had talked in the garden—about each other—their thoughts—and fancies—hopes—dreams—imaginings.

Oh youth! oh glamour! Strange world in which for the first bright years we live as in a dream! Sweet dawn of life, when nothing in this world seems so real as the hopes that are never to know fruition!

CHAPTER IV.

"Love's a mighty lord."

SIR NUGENT BELLINGHAM was one of those men who are born and reared amidst pecuniary difficulties, and whose existence is spent upon the verge of ruin. Yet it seems a tolerably comfortable kind of life notwithstanding, and men of Sir Nugent's type hardly realize the meaning of the word deprivation. Sir Nugent had never known what it was to be out of debt. The Bellingham estate was mortgaged up to the hilt when he inherited it. Indeed, to be thus encumbered was the normal condition of all Bellingham property.

Of course Sir Nugent had from time to time possessed money. He hardly could have drifted on so long without some amount of specie, even in such an easy-going world as that patrician sphere in which he revolved. He had inherited a modest fortune from his mother, with which he had paid his creditors something handsome on account all round, and made them his bondslaves for all time to come, since they cherished the hope of something more in the future. Sir Nugent had received legacies from an aunt and uncle or two, and these afforded further sops for his Cerberus, and enabled the baronet's dainty little household to sail gaily down the stream of time for some years.

When the amelioration of manners brought bankruptcy within the reach of any gentleman, Sir Nugent

Bellingham availed himself of the new code, and became insolvent in an easy, gentleman-like fashion. And what with one little help and another, the *bijou* house in May Fair, where Sir Nugent lived with his two motherless girls, was always kept up in the same good style. The same dinners—small and *soigné*—the same lively receptions after the little dinners. The best music, the newest books, the choicest hothouse flowers, were always to be found at No. 12, Cavendish Row, May Fair. There were only a dozen houses in Cavendish Row, and Sir Nugent Bellingham's was at the corner, squeezed into an angle made by the lofty wall of Lord Loamshire's garden—one of those dismal, awe-inspiring London gardens, grey and dull and blossomless, which look like a burial-ground without any graves. Seen from the street, No. 12 looked a mere doll's house, but the larger rooms were behind, abutting upon Lord Loamshire's garden. It was an irregular old house, full of corners, but, furnished after the peculiar tastes of Miss Bellingham, was one of the most charming houses in London. No upholsterer had been allowed to work his will—Madge Bellingham had chosen every item. The chairs and tables, and sofas and cabinets, were the cheapest that could be had, for they were all of unstained light woods, made after designs from Miss Bellingham's own pencil. The cabinets were mere frames for glass doors, behind which appeared the Bellingham collection of bric-a-brac, upon numerous shelves covered with dark-green silk. Madge's own clever hands had covered the deal shelves; and the bronzes, the Venetian glass, the Sèvres, Copenhagen, Berlin, Vienna, and Dresden porcelains looked all the better for so simple a setting.

There were no draperies but chintz, the cheapest that could be bought, but always fresh. The looking-glasses had no frame save a natural garland of ivy. The floors were beeswaxed only, a Persian carpet here and there offering accommodation for the luxurious. The one costly object in the two drawing-rooms, after that bric-a-brac upon which the Bellingham race had squandered a small fortune, was the piano, a Broadwood grand, in a case made by a modern workman out of veritable Louis Seize marqueterie. The old ormolu mountings, goat's head, festoons, and masques, had been religiously preserved, and the piano was a triumph of art. It occupied the centre of the back drawing-room, the largest room in the house, and when Madge Bellingham sat before it, girl and piano made a cabinet picture of the highest school.

"People know we are out at elbows," Madge said to her father when they began housekeeping in Cavendish Row. "If we have expensive furniture every one will be sure we haven't paid for it; but if you let me carry out my ideas, the bills will be so light that you can pay them at once."

"I can give the fellows something on account, at any rate," replied Sir Nugent.

Lady Bellingham's death, which occurred soon after the birth of Viola, the second daughter, had left Sir Nugent free to lead the life of a bachelor, for the most part in other people's houses, while his girls were in his sister's nursery or at school. When they grew to womanhood—and a very lovely womanhood, for good looks were hereditary in the Bellingham family—Sir Nugent found it incumbent upon him to provide them with a home; so he took the house in Cavendish

Row, and brought home the Bellingham bric-a-brac, which had been left him by the aforesaid aunts and uncles, and lodged at the Pantechnicon pending his settlement in life. He began housekeeping at five-and-forty years of age, and gave his little dinners at home henceforward, instead of at one or other of his clubs, and cherished high hopes of seeing his daughters splendidly established by and by.

"I think you have seen enough of what it is to be tormented by a set of harpies to teach you the value of money, Madge," said Sir Nugent one morning, pointing to a small heap of letters which he had just now opened and dismissed with a glance. The harpies in question were his creditors, who expressed an unwarrantable eagerness for something more "on account."

"With your knowledge of life you are not likely to marry a pauper," pursued Sir Nugent, dipping into a Strasburg pie.

"No, papa, not with my knowledge of life," answered Madge, with ever so slight an upward curl of the firm lip. Miss Bellingham fondly loved her father, but it is possible that respect may have been somewhat lessened by her experience of that financial scramble in which his life was spent.

Two or three evenings before the night which made James Penwyn acquainted with life behind the scenes of a small provincial theatre, Sir Nugent Bellingham gave one of his snug little dinners—a dinner of eight —the guests of choicest brands, like the wines. Lady Cheshunt, one of the most exalted matrons in the great world, kept the Miss Bellinghams in countenance. Madge was her pet *protegée* whose praises she was never tired of sounding among the chosen ones of the earth. Mr. Albert Noyce, a distinguished wit and *littérateur*, supplied the salt of the banquet. He was a small, mild-looking man, with a pretty, unoffending wife, and dined out perpetually during the London season. Mr. Shinebar, the famous barrister, made a fourth. Lord George Bulrose, a West of England man, a *gourmet*, and, in so far as after-dinner talk went, a mighty hunter, was the fifth; and Sir Nugent and his two daughters completed the circle.

After dinner there was to be an evening party, and before the small hours of the morning a great many famous people would have dropped in at the corner house in Cavendish Row.

The ladies had retired, leaving Sir Nugent and his chosen friends to talk about law, and horses, and the last new burlesque actress, as they drew closer in to the dainty round table, where the glass sparkled and the deep-hued blossoms brightened under the cluster of wax lights in the central chandelier.

Viola and Lady Cheshunt went upstairs arm-in-arm, the girl nestling affectionately against the substantial shoulder of the portly matron. Mrs. Noyce tripped lightly after these two, and Madge followed, alone, with a grave brow, and that lofty air which so well became Sir Nugent Bellingham's elder daughter.

Rarely were sisters less alike than these two. Viola was a blonde, complexion alabaster, hair the colour of raw silk—plenteous flaxen hair which the girl wound into a crown of pale gold upon the top of her small head; eyes of turquoise blue; figure a thought too slim, but the perfection of grace in every movement and attitude; foot and hand absolutely faultless: altogether a girl to be put under a glass case.

"I should admire the younger Miss Bellingham more if she were a little less like Sèvres china," one of the magnates of society had observed.

Madge was a brunette—hair almost black, and with a natural ripple—complexion a rich olive, eyes darkest hazel — features the true Bellingham type, clearly cut as a profile on an old Roman medal—figure tall and commanding, a woman born to rule, one would say, judging by externals—a woman with the stuff in her to make a general, Sir Nugent was wont to boast. But although she was of a loftier mould than the generality of women, there was no hardness about Madge Bellingham. In love or in anger she was alike strong. For hate she was too noble.

The rooms were deliciously cool, the light somewhat subdued, the windows open to the warm spring night. There were flowers enough in the small front drawing-room to make it an indoor garden.

The dowager seated herself upon the most comfortable sofa in this room, a capacious, square-backed sofa, in a dusky corner, fenced off and sheltered by a well-filled *jardinière*.

"Come here, Madge," she cried, with good-natured imperiousness, "I want to talk to you.—Viola, child, go and amuse yourself with Mrs. Noyce. Show her your photograph album, or *parlez chiffons*. I want Madge all to myself."

Madge obeyed without a word, and squeezed herself into the corner of the sofa, which Lady Cheshunt and Lady Cheshunt's dress almost filled.

"How big you are growing, child! there's hardly room enough for you!" remarked the matron. "And now tell me the truth, Madge; what is the matter with you to-night?"

"I don't think there is anything the matter more than usual, Lady Cheshunt."

"I know better than that. You were dull and *distraite* all dinner-time. True, there was no one to talk to but two married men, and that old twaddler, Bulrose; but a young lady should be always equally agreeable—that is one of the fundamental principles of good breeding."

"If I seemed a little out of spirits you can hardly wonder. Papa's sadly involved state is enough to make me uneasy."

"My dear, your papa has been involved ever since my first season—when my waist was only eighteen inches, and Madame Devy made my gowns. He is no worse off now than he was then, and he will go on being hopelessly involved till the end of the chapter. I don't see why you should be unhappy about it. He will be able to give you and Viola a tolerable home till you marry and make better homes for yourselves, which it is actually incumbent upon you to do."

This was said with a touch of severity. Madge sighed, and the slender foot in the satin shoe tapped the ground with a nervous, impatient movement.

"Madge, I hope there is no truth in what I hear about you and Mr. Penwyn."

A deep tell-tale glow burned in Miss Bellingham's cheek. She fanned herself vehemently.

"I cannot imagine what you have heard, Lady Cheshunt."

"I have heard your name coupled with Mr. Penwyn's—the poor Mr. Penwyn."

"I only know one Mr. Penwyn."

"So much the worse for you, my dear. You know the wrong one. There is a cousin of that young man's who has a fine estate in Cornwall—the Penwyn estate. You must have heard of that."

"Yes, I have heard Mr. Penwyn speak of his cousin's property."

"Of course. Poor penniless young man; very natural that he should talk of it. Don't suppose that I have no feeling for him. He is next heir to the property, but no doubt the other young man, James Penwyn's son, will marry and have a herd of children. I knew James Penwyn, this young man's father, years ago. There were three brothers—George, the eldest, who was in the army, and was killed in a skirmish with some wild Indians in Canada—very sad story; James, who was in the church, and had a living somewhere near London; and Balfour, in the law, I believe, whose son you know."

"Yes," sighed Madge.

She had heard the family history from Churchill Penwyn, but the dowager liked to hear herself talk, and did not like to be interrupted.

"Now, if by any chance the present James Penwyn, who is little more than a lad, were to die unmarried, Churchill Penwyn could come into the property under his grandfather's will, which left the estate to the eldest surviving son and his children after him. George died unmarried. James left an only son. Churchill is therefore heir presumptive. But it's a very remote contingency, my love, and it would be madness for you to give it a thought—with your chances."

Madge shrugged her shoulders despondently.

"I don't think my chances are particularly brilliant, Lady Cheshunt."

"Nonsense, Madge! Everybody talks of the beautiful Bellinghams. And you refused a splendid offer only the other day—that Mr. Cardingham, the great manufacturer."

"Who had only seen me four times when he had the impudence to ask me to marry him! He was old and ugly, too."

"When the end is a good establishment one must not look at the means too closely. Poor dear Cheshunt was many years my senior, and no beauty, even in his wig. You must take a more serious view of things, my dear Madge. It will not do for you and your sister to hang fire. The handsomer girls are, the more vital it is for them to go off quickly. A plain little unobtrusive thing may creep through half a dozen seasons and surprise everybody by making a good match at last. But a beauty who doesn't marry soon is apt to get talked about. Malicious people put it down to too much flirtation. And then, my love, consider your milliner's bills; what will they be at the end of a few seasons?"

"Not very much, Lady Cheshunt. I cut out all my own dresses and Viola's too, and our maid runs them together. Viola and I help sometimes, when we can steal an hour from society. I couldn't bear to wear anything that wasn't paid for."

"Upon my word you are an exemplary girl, Madge," exclaimed Lady Cheshunt, astounded by such Roman virtue. "What a wife you will make!"

"Yes, I think I might make a tolerable wife, for a poor man."

"Don't speak of such a thing. You were born for wealth and power. You are bound to make a great marriage—if not for your own sake, for Viola's. See what a poor helpless child she is—sadly wanting in moral stamina. If you had a good establishment she would have a haven of refuge. But if you were to marry badly what will become of her? She would never be able to manage your papa."

Madge sighed again, and this time deeply. Love for her sister was Madge Bellingham's weakest point. She positively adored the fair fragile girl who had been given into her childish arms eighteen years ago, on that bitter day which made her an orphan. There was only four years' difference between the ages of the sisters, yet Madge's affection was always maternal in its protecting thoughtfulness. To marry well would be to secure a home for Viola. Sir Nugent was but a feeble staff to lean upon.

"I have no objection to marrying well whenever a fair opportunity arises, Lady Cheshunt," she said, firmly; "but I will never marry a man whom I cannot respect and like."

"Of course not, my poor pet," murmured the widow, soothingly; "but, fortunately, there are so many men in the world one can like and respect. It is that foolish sentimental feeling called love which will only fit one person. In the meantime, Madge, take my advice, and don't let people talk about you and Mr. Penwyn."

"I don't know why they should talk about us."

"Yes, you do, Madge—in your heart of hearts. You know that you have sat together in corners, and that you have a knack of blushing when he comes into the room. It won't do, Madge, it won't do. That young fellow has nothing except what he can earn himself. I know his mother had a struggle to bring him up, and if he hadn't been an only son could hardly have brought him up at all. He was a Blue-coat boy, I believe, or something equally dreadful. It is not to be thought of, Madge."

"I do not think of it, Lady Cheshunt," replied Miss Bellingham, resolutely, "and I wish you would not worry yourself and me about imaginary dangers."

"Your visitors are beginning to come; go and receive them, and leave me in my corner. Mr. Penwyn is to be here, I've no doubt."

"I don't know. He knows that Saturday is our night."

"Mr. Churchill Penwyn!" announced a footman at the door of the larger room.

"I thought so," said Lady Cheshunt, "and the first to arrive, too. That looks suspicious."

CHAPTER V.

"Il ne faut pas pousser au bout les malheureux."

CHURCHILL PENWYN was one of those men who are sure to obtain a certain amount of notice in whatsoever circle they appear — a man upon whom the stamp of good blood, or good breeding, had been set in a distinct and palpable manner — a man who had no need for self-assertion.

It would have been difficult for any one to state in what the distinction lay. He was not particularly good-looking. Intellect, rather than regularity of feature, was the leading characteristic of his countenance. Already, though he was still on the sunward side of his thirtieth birthday, the dark brown hair grew thinly upon the broad high brow, showing signs of premature baldness. His features were sharply cut, but by no means faultless, the mouth somewhat sunken, the lips thin. His light grey eyes had a keen, cold lustre; only those who saw Churchill Penwyn in some rare moment of softer feeling knew that those severe orbs could be beautiful. Mr. Penwyn was a barrister, still in the uphill stage of his career. He got an occasional brief, went on circuit assiduously, and did a little in the literature of politics — a hard, dry kind of literature, but fairly remunerative — when he got it to do. He had contributed hard-headed statistical papers to the *Edinburgh* and the *Westminster*, and knew a good deal about the condition of the operative classes. He had lectured in some of the northern manufacturing towns, and knew the black country by heart. People talked of him as a young man who was sure to make his mark by and by; but by and by might be a long way off. He would be fifty years of age, perhaps, before he had worked his way to the front.

Churchill Penwyn went a great deal into society, when it is considered how hard and how honestly he worked; but the houses in which he was to be found were always houses affected by the best people. He never wasted himself among second-rate circles. He was an excellent art critic; knew enough about music to talk of it cleverly, though he had hardly the faculty of distinguishing one tune from another; waltzed like a Viennese; rode like a centaur; spoke three Continental languages perfectly. It was his theory that no man should presume to enter society who could not do everything that society could require him to do. Society was worth very little in itself, according to Churchill Penwyn, but a man owed it to himself to be admired and respected by society.

"I see a good many men who go into the world to stare about them through eye-glasses," said Churchill. "If I couldn't do anything more than that I should spend my evenings in my own den."

Churchill Penwyn went into the gay world with a definite aim—some of the people he met must needs be useful to him sooner or later.

Ohne Hast, ohne Rast—without haste, without rest —was his motto. He had it engraved on his signet ring, instead of the Penwyn crest. He was never in a hurry. While striving for success he had the air of a man who had already succeeded. He occupied a third floor in the Temple, and lived like an anchorite, but his tailor and bootmaker were among the best in London, and he was a member of the Travellers' and the Garrick. He was to be seen sometimes lunching at his club, and occasionally entertained a friend at luncheon, but he rarely dined there, and was never seen to drink anything more costly than a pint of La Rose, or Medoc. No man had ever mastered the art of economy more thoroughly than Churchill Penwyn, and yet he had never laid himself open to the charge of meanness.

Miss Bellingham received him with a bright look of welcome, despite the dowager's warning, and their hands met, with a gentle pressure on Churchill's part. Viola was discreetly occupied in showing Mrs. Noyce a new photograph, and only gave the visitor a bow and a smile. So he had a fair excuse for seating himself next Madge, on the divan by the fireplace, where there was just room for those two.

"I did not think you would come to-night," said Madge, opening and shutting her large black fan, with a slightly nervous movement.

"Why not?"

"I saw your name in the paper, at Halifax, or somewhere, hundreds of miles away."

"I was at Halifax the day before yesterday, but I would not miss my Saturday evening here. You see I have come a quarter of an hour in advance of your people, so that I might have you to myself for a few minutes."

"It is so good of you," faltered Madge, "and you know I am always glad."

"I should be wretched if I did not know it."

This was going further than Mr. Penwyn's usual limits. The man was the very soul of prudence. No sweet words, no tender promises, had ever passed between these two, and yet they knew themselves beloved. Madge knew it to her sorrow, for she was fain to admit the wisdom of the dowager's warning. It would never do for her to marry Churchill Penwyn.

Happily for her, up to this time Churchill had never asked her to be his wife.

"He is too wise," she said to herself, with the faintest touch of bitterness. "Too much a man of the world."

But that this man of the world loved her she was very sure.

For just ten minutes they sat side by side, talking of indifferent things, but only as people talk who are not quite indifferent to each other. And then more visitors were announced. Sir Nugent and his friends came upstairs; the rooms began to fill. Musical people arrived. A German with long rough hair, bony wrists, and an eye-glass, seated himself at the piano, and began a performance of so strictly classical a character that he had the enjoyment of it all to himself, for nobody else listened. Minor chords chased one another backwards and forwards about the middle of the piano as if they were hunting for the melody and couldn't find it. Little runs and arpeggio passages went under and over each other, and wriggled in and out and up and down in a distracted way, still searching for the subject, and finally gave up the quest in utter despair, appropriately expressed by vague grumblings in the bass, which slowly faded into silence. Whereupon every one became enthusiastic in their admiration.

After this a young lady in pink sang an airy little *chanson*, with elaborate variations—using her bright soprano voice as freely as if she had been Philomel, trilling her vespers in the dusky woods of June. And then Madge Bellingham sat down to the piano, and played as few young ladies play—as if her glad young soul were in the music.

It was only an Hungarian march that she played. There were no musical fireworks—no difficulties conquered; none of those passages which make the listeners exclaim, "Poor girl! how she must have practised!" It was but a national melody—simple and spirit-stirring—played as if the soul of a patriot were guiding those supple fingers. The graceful figure was bent a little over the key-board—the dark eyes followed the swift flight of the hands over the keys. She seemed to caress the notes as she struck them—to play with the melody. Pride, love, hope, rage, every passion expressed itself by turns as she followed that wild strange music through the mazes of its variations, never losing the subject. It sounded like the war-cry of a free people. Even Churchill Penwyn, who in a general way cared so little for music, listened entranced to this. He could hardly have recalled the air half an hour later, but for the moment he was enchanted. He stood a little way from the instrument, watching the player, watching the beautiful head, with its dark rippling hair wound into a Greek knot at the back, the perfect throat, with its classic necklet of old Wedgwood medallions set in plainest gold; the drooping lashes as the downcast eyes followed the flying touch. To hear Madge play was delightful, but to see her was still better. And this man's love had all the strength of a passion repressed. He had held himself in check so long, and every time he saw her he found her more and more adorable.

The evening wore on. People came in and out. Madge played the hostess divinely, always supported by Lady Cheshunt, who sat in the smaller drawing-room as in a temple, and had all the best people brought to her. Some came to Cavendish Row on their way somewhere else, and were careful to let their acquaintance know that they were "due" at some very grand entertainment, and made rather a favour of coming to Sir Nugent. The last of the guests went about half an hour after midnight, and among the last Churchill Penwyn.

"May I bring you that book after church to-morrow?" he asked. The book was a comedy of Augier's lately produced at the Français, which he had been telling her about.

Madge looked embarrassed. She had a particular wish to avoid a *tête-à-tête* with Mr. Penwyn, and Sunday was an awkward day. Sir Nugent would be at Hurlingham, most likely, and Viola was such a foolish little thing, almost as bad as nobody.

"If you like," she answered. "But why take the trouble to call on purpose? You might bring it next Saturday, if you come to us."

"I shall bring it you to-morrow," he said, as they shook hands.

That tiresome Viola was in a hopeless state of headache and prostration next morning, so Madge had

A Strange World. I.

to go to church alone. Coming out of the pretty little Anglican temple she found herself face to face with Churchill Penwyn. He had evidently been lying in wait for her.

"I was so afraid I might not find you at home," he said, half apologetically, "so I thought I might as well walk this way. I knew this was your church. I've brought you the play we were talking about."

"You're very kind, but I hope you don't think I read French comedies on Sundays?"

"Of course not; only Sunday is my leisure day, and I thought you would not shut your door upon me even on Sunday."

The church was only five minutes' walk from Cavendish Row. When Sir Nugent's door was opened Mr. Penwyn followed Miss Bellingham into the house as a matter of course. She had no help for it but to go quietly upstairs to her fate. She almost knew what was coming. There had been something in his manner last night that told her it was very near.

"Prudence, courage," she whispered to herself, and then, "Viola!" The last word was a kind of charm.

The rooms looked bright and gay in the noontide sunlight, tempered by Spanish blinds. The flowers, the feminine prettiness scattered about, struck Churchill's eye, they gave such a look of home.

"If I could afford to give her as good a home as this!" he thought.

He shut the door carefully behind him, and glanced round the room to make sure they were alone, and went close to Madge as she stood by one of the small tables, fidgeting with the clasp of her prayer-book.

"I think you know why I came to-day," he said.

"You have told me about three times,—to bring me '*La Quarantaine.*'"

"I have come to tell you a secret I have kept more than a year. Have you never guessed it, Madge? Have I been clever enough to hide the truth altogether? I love you, dearest. I, penniless Churchill Penwyn, dare to adore one of the belles of the season. I, who cannot for years to come offer you a house in May Fair. I, who at most can venture to begin married life in a Bloomsbury lodging, supported by the fruits of my pen. It sounds like madness, doesn't it?"

"It is madness," she answered, looking full at him with her truthful eyes.

The answer surprised and humiliated him. He fancied she loved him—would be ready to face poverty for his sake. She was so young, and would hardly have acquired the wisdom of her world yet awhile.

"I beg your pardon," he said, a curious change coming over his face, a sudden coldness that made those definite features look as if they had been cut out of stone. "I have been deceiving myself all along, it seems. I did not think I was quite indifferent to you."

The eyelids drooped over the dark eyes for a moment, and were then lifted suddenly, and the eyes met Churchill's. That one look told all. She loved him.

"I have been learning to know the world while other girls are allowed to dream," she said. "I know what the burden of debt means. Poverty brings debt as a natural sequence. If you were a woodcutter and we could live in a hovel and pay our way, there would be nothing appalling in marriage. But our world will not let us live like that. We must play at being fine ladies and gentlemen while our hearts are breaking, and our creditors being ruined. Ever so long ago I made up my mind that I must marry a rich man. If I have ever seemed otherwise to you than a woman of the world, bent upon worldly success, I humbly beg you to forgive me."

"Madge," cried Churchill, passionately, "I will forgive anything if you will only be frank. Were my luck to turn speedily, through some unlooked-for professional success, for instance, would you have me then?"

"If I stood alone in the world, if I had not my sister to consider, I would marry you to-morrow. Yes, though you were a beggar," she answered, grandly.

He clasped her to his breast and kissed those proud lips. The first lover's kiss that had ever rested there.

"I will be rich for your sake, distinguished for your sake," he said impetuously, "if wealth and fame are within the reach of man's effort."

CHAPTER VI.

"There is no life on earth but being in love."

THE first faint streak of day parted the eastern clouds when James Penwyn got back to the "Waterfowl," but late as it was, and though a long day's various fatigues might have invited him to repose, Maurice Clissold had waited up for his friend. He was walking up and down the inn parlour, where empty bottles and glasses, cigar ashes, and a broken clay pipe or two bestrewed the table, and gave a rakish look to the room. The windows stood wide open to the pale cold dawn, and the air was chill.

"Not gone to bed yet, Maurice?" exclaimed James, surprised, and perhaps somewhat embarrassed by this unexpected encounter.

"I was in no humour for sleep. I never can sleep when I have anything on my mind. I waited up to ask you a question, Jim."

Something like defiance sparkled in Mr. Penwyn's eyes as he planted himself upon the arm of the substantial old sofa, and lighted a final cigar.

"Don't restrain your eloquence," he said, "I should hardly have considered four o'clock in the morning a time for conversation, but if you think so, I'm at your service."

"I want to know, in plain words, what you mean by this, James?"

"By what?"

"Your conduct to that girl."

"I shouldn't think anything so simple needed explanation. I meet a strolling player and his daughter. The strolling player is something of a character; the daughter—well, not pretty, perhaps, though she has lovely eyes, but interesting. I offer them the small attention of a supper, and, seeing that my friend the player is a trifle the worse for the champagne consumed, humanity urges me to escort the young lady to her own door, lest her father should lead her into one of the ditches which beset the way. I believe that is the sum-total of my offences."

"It sounds simple enough, Jim," answered the other, gravely, but not unkindly, "and I dare say no harm will come of it if you let things stop exactly where they are. But I watched you and that poor child to-night—she is little more than a child, at best —and I saw that you were doing your utmost, unconsciously, perhaps, to turn her silly head. I saw you together in the moonlight afterwards."

"If there was anything sentimental, you must blame the moon, not me," said James, lightly.

"And now you talk of spending to-morrow with these people, and taking them to the races."

"And I mean to do it. There's a freshness about them that amuses me. I've been getting rather tired of nature and Greek—though, of course, we've had an uncommonly jolly time of it together, dear old boy,—and I find a relief in a glimpse of real life. When you turn mentor, you make yourself intensely disagreeable. Do you suppose that I harbour one wicked intention about this girl?"

"No, James, I don't suppose you do. If I thought

you were a deliberate sinner I should leave you to go your own road, and only try to save the girl. But I know what misery has been wrought in this world by gentlemanly trifling, and what still deeper wretchedness has been brought about by unequal marriages."

"Do you suppose I think of marrying Mr. Elgood's daughter, because I say a few civil words to her?" cried James, forgetting how much earnestness there had been in those civil words only an hour ago.

"If you have no such thought you have no right to cultivate an acquaintance that can only end in unhappiness to her, if not to yourself."

James answered with a sneer, to which Clissold replied somewhat warmly, and there were angry words between the two young men before they parted in the corridor outside their bedrooms. The people of the house, already thinking about morning, heard the raised voices and angry tones—heard and remembered.

It was ten o'clock when James Penwyn went down to breakfast next morning. The sun was shining in at the open windows—all traces of last night's revelry were removed—the room was in the nicest order—the table spread for breakfast, with spotless linen and shining tea service, but only set for one. James plucked impatiently at the bell-rope. It irked him not to see his friend's face on the other side of the board. He had come downstairs prepared to make peace on the easiest terms; ready even to own himself to blame.

"Has Mr. Clissold breakfasted?" he asked the girl who answered his summons.

"No, sir. He wouldn't stop for breakfast; he went

out soon after seven this morning, with his fishing-rod. And he left a note, please, sir."

There it was among the shells and shepherdesses on the mantelpiece. A little pencil scrawl twisted into a cocked hat:—

"Dear Jim,

"Since it seems that my counsel irritates and annoys you, I take myself off for a day's fly fishing. You must please yourself about the races. Only remember, that it is easy for a man to drift upon quicksands from which he can hardly extricate himself without the loss of honour or of happiness. The sum-total of a man's life depends very much upon what he does with the first years of his manhood. I shall be back before night.

"Yours always, "M. C."

James Penwyn read and re-read the brief epistle, musing over it frowningly. It was rather tiresome to have a friend who took such a serious view of trifles. Towards what quicksand was he drifting? Was it a dishonourable thing to admire beautiful eyes, to wish to do some kindness to a friendless girl, *en passant?* As to the races, he could not dream of disappointing the people he had invited. Was he to treat them cavalierly because they were poor? He rang the bell again and ordered the largest landau or barouche which the "Waterfowl" could obtain for him, with a pair of good horses.

"And get me up a picnic basket," he said, "and plenty of champagne."

At two and twenty, with the revenues of Penwyn

Manor at his command, a man would hardly do things shabbily.

He had arranged everything with his guests. The Dempsons and the Elgoods lodged in the same house, an ancient dwelling not far from the archway at the lower end of the city. Mr. Penwyn was to call for them in a carriage at twelve o'clock, and they were to drive straight to the racecourse.

James breakfasted slowly, and with little appetite. He missed the companion whose talk had been wont to enliven all their meals. He thought it unkind of Maurice to leave him—was at once angry with his friend, and with himself for his contemptuous speeches of last night. He left his breakfast unfinished at last, and went out into the garden, and down by the narrow river, which had a different look by day. It was beautiful still—the winding stream with its sedgy banks, and far-off background of low hills, and the grave old city in the middle distance—but it lacked the magic of night—the mystic charms of moonbeam and shadow.

The scene—even without the moonlight—put him painfully in mind of last night, when Justina and he had sat side by side on the bench by yonder willow.

"Why shouldn't I marry her if I love her?" he said to himself; "I am my own master. Who will ask Squire Penwyn for his wife's pedigree? It isn't as if she were vulgar or ignorant. She speaks like a lady, and she seems to know as much as most of the girls I have met."

He strolled up and down by the river, smoking and musing until the carriage was ready. It was a capacious vehicle, of the good old Baker Street Repository build, a vehicle which looked as if it had been a family travelling carriage about the period of the Bourbon Restoration, and had done the tour of Europe, and been battered and bruised a good deal between the Alps and the Danube. There was a vast amount of leather in its composition, and more iron than sticklers for absolute elegance would desire, whereby it jingled considerably in its progress. But it was roomy, and, for a racecourse, that was the main point.

James drove to the dingy old street where the players lodged, an old-fashioned street, with queer old houses, more picturesque than clean. The players' lodgings were above a small shop in the chandlery line, and as there was no private door, James had to enter the realms of Dutch cheese, kippered herrings, and dip candles—pendent from the low ceiling like stalactites—in quest of his new acquaintance.

The ladies were ready, but Mr. Elgood was still in his shirt-sleeves, and his countenance had a warm and shiny look, as if but that moment washed. Justina came running down the stairs and into the shop, where James welcomed her warmly. She was quite a transformed and glorified Justina—decked in borrowed raiment, which Mrs. Dempson had good-naturedly supplied for the occasion. "There is no knowing what may come of to-day's outing," the leading lady had remarked significantly. "Mr. Penwyn is young and foolish, and seems actually taken with Justina—and it would be such a blessing if she could marry well, poor child, seeing that she has not a spark of talent for the profession."

Justina wore a clean muslin dress, which hardly

reached her ankles, a black silk jacket, and a blue crape bonnet, not too fresh, but quite respectable—a bonnet which had been pinned up in paper and carefully kept since last summer.

"I shall trim it up with a feather or two and wear it for light comedy by and by," said Mrs. Dempson, as she pulled the bonnet into shape upon Justina's head.

The girl looked so happy that she was almost beautiful. There was a soft bloom upon her cheek, a tender depth in the dark blue eyes, a joyous, smiling look that charmed James Penwyn, who liked people to be happy and enjoy themselves when he was in a humour for festivity.

"How good of you to be ready!" cried James, taking her out to the carriage, "and how bright, and fresh, and gay you look!" Justina blushed, conscious of her borrowed bonnet. "I've got a nice old rattle-trap to take us to the racecourse."

"Oh, beautiful!" exclaimed Justina, gazing at the patriarchal tub with respectful admiration.

"Are the others ready?"

"Father's just putting on his coat, and the Dempsons are coming downstairs."

The Dempsons appeared as she spoke. Mrs. Dempson superb in black moire antique and the pinkest of pink bonnets, and a white lace shawl, which had been washed a good many times, and had rather too much darning in proportion to the pattern, but, as Mrs. Dempson remarked, "always looked graceful." It was her bridal veil as Pauline Deschappelles. She wore it as Juliet—and as Desdemona before the senate.

"Now, then," cried James, as Mr. Elgood appeared, still struggling with his coat. The carriage was packed without further delay. Mrs. Dempson and Justina in the seat of honour, Mr. Penwyn and Mr. Dempson opposite them, Mr. Elgood on the box. He had declared his preference for that seat.

Off they went, oh! so gaily, Justina thought, the landlady gazing at them from her shop door, and quite a cluster of small children cheering their departure. "As if it had been a wedding," Mrs. Dempson said archly.

Away they went through the quaint old city which wore its holiday look to-day. Crowds were pouring in from the station; coffee-houses and eating-houses had set forth a Rabelaisian abundance in their shining windows; taverns were decorated with flags and greenery; flies, driven by excited coachmen with ribbons on their whips, shot up and down the streets. All was life and brightness; and Justina, who had rarely ridden in a carriage, felt that just in this one brief hour she could understand how duchesses and such people must feel.

CHAPTER VII.

"Let the world slip; we shall ne'er be younger."

They left the town behind them and rattled along the wide high road for half a mile or so, before they turned off to the race-ground. Perhaps the Eborsham course is one of the prettiest in England. An oval basin of richest greensward set among low wooded hills. A waterpool shining here and there in the valley, where the placid kine browse in pensive solitude, save during the race week, when the placid kine are wisely withdrawn from the dangerous neighbourhood of tramps and gipsies, and the wild excitement of the turf.

The grand stand—a permanent building of white freestone—looked very grand to Justina's eyes, as the family ark blundered and jingled into a place exactly opposite: one of the best places on that privileged piece of ground, for which James paid three shining sovereigns. Temporary stands of woodwork bordered the course, crowded with warm humanity. Justina wondered where so many people came from, and how it was so few of them came to the theatre, and sighed to think that the drama has never taken a grip upon the public mind as a thoroughly national amusement. See how the people congregated to-day, tier above tier on yonder fragile stages, pressed together with scarce breathing-room; and yet there would be room to spare in the little theatre to-night, Justina feared, despite immense attractions and an unparalleled combination of talent, as advertised in the playbills.

But after this one sigh for the neglected drama, Justina abandoned herself to the delight of the hour, and was supremely content. James told her all about the horses; how that one had done great things at Newmarket, how the other was winner of the Chester Cup. He showed her the colours, explained everything, and the race assumed a new interest. Mr. Dempson left the carriage to stretch his legs a bit, he said, and see who was on the course; but in reality because he was of a roving disposition and soon tired of repose. Mr. Elgood devoted himself exclusively to Mrs. Dempson, "Villeroy," as he called her, being more accustomed to her professional *alias* than the name she rendered illustrious in domestic life. So James and Justina were left to themselves, and behaved very much as if they had been plighted lovers ever so long, quite unconsciously upon Justina's part, for she knew little of real lovers and their ways.

Presently there was a sudden stir, a dispersement of pedestrians from the racecourse, as a policeman or two galloped up and down, and the clerk of the course, in his scarlet coat and buckskins, cantered briskly over the grass; then a dog driven past with hootings and ignominy; then more ringing of bells, the preliminary canter, and then the race.

A few minutes of breathless attention, a thundering rush past all the carriages and the eager a-tiptoe spectators, and white jacket with red spots had pulled off the first stakes.

"Did you see it?" asked James, turning to the girl's bright face, glowing with excitement.

"Oh! it was beautiful. I don't wonder at people coming to races now. I feel as if I had never been quite alive before. Just that one moment when the horses were tearing past. It was wonderful."

"A very fair race," said James, with a patronizing air, "but there were some wretched screws among them. You'll see a better set by and by, for the cup. Iphianassa, the Oak's winner, is first favourite. The bookmen call her Free-and-Easy, for short. And now we'll have a bottle of cham."

"Not a bad move," said Mr. Elgood, approvingly. "That kind of thing makes a fellow dryish."

He made himself very useful in helping to open the baskets; there were two hampers, one for wine and the other for comestibles, the "Waterfowl" having done things handsomely. Mr. Elgood took one of the golden-necked bottles out of the rush case, found the glasses, the nippers, and opened the bottle as neatly as a waiter. He had the lion's share of the wine for his trouble.

James and Justina had only one glass between them. They could very easily have had two, but they liked this mutual goblet, and sipped the bright wine gaily, Justina taking about as much as Titania might have consumed from a chalice made of a harebell.

The champagne bottle was hardly open when a gipsy appeared at the carriage door, as if attracted by the popping of the cork, an elderly gipsy, with an orange silk handkerchief tied across her black hair, amongst which a few silver threads were visible. She was the identical gipsy woman who had stopped James

Penwyn and his companions, yesterday afternoon, by the river.

"Give the poor old gipsy woman a little drop of wine, kind gentleman," she asked, insinuatingly.

Justina drew back shuddering, drew nearer her companion, till her slight form pressed against his shoulder, and he could feel that she trembled.

"Why, what's the matter, you timid bird?" he whispered tenderly, drawing his arm round her by an instinctive movement. They were standing up in the carriage as they had stood to see the race, Mrs. Dempson with her face towards the box, whence Mr. Elgood was pointing out features of interest on the course.

"It's the same woman," exclaimed Justina, in a half-whisper.

"What woman, my pet?"

It had come to this already, and Justina at this particular moment was too absorbed to remonstrate.

"The woman who told you about the mark on your hand."

"Is it really? I didn't notice," answered James, smiling at her concern. The gipsy had gone to the next carriage, whose occupants were in the act of discussing a bottle of sherry and a packet of appetising sandwiches. Thin and daintily trimmed sandwiches, made to provoke rather than appease appetite.

"Upon my word I didn't notice," repeated James. "All gipsies are alike to my eye, the same tawny skins, the same shiny black hair. But why should you be frightened at her, pretty one? She prophesied no evil about me."

"No, but she looked at you so curiously; and then

a line across the line of life—that must mean something dreadful."

"My dearest, do you think any reasonable being believes in lines of life or any such bosh? Gipsies must have some kind of jargon, or they would get no dupes. But I think you and I are too wise to believe in their nonsense. We'll give the harridan a tumbler of fiz, and I'll warrant she'll prophesy smooth things. Hi! mistress, this way."

The gipsy, having paid unfruitful homage to the carriage of sandwich consumers, came quickly at James Penwyn's bidding.

"Let me drink your health, pretty gentleman," she pleaded, "and the health of the young lady that loves you best, and I know of one that loves you well, and a beautiful young lady, and is well belóved by you. You've courted a many, young gentleman, in your time, the old gipsy knows, for you've a wicked eye and a wanton 'art, but the most fickle must fix at last, and may you never rove no more, for you've fixed upon one as can be constant to you. Thank you, sir, and here's health and happiness to you and the young lady, and a short courtship and a long fambly; and give the poor gipsy a mossel of somethink to eat, like a dear young lady," appealing to the blushing Justina, "for fear the wine should turn acid upon my inside."

The picnic basket had to be opened in order to meet this judicious demand, and this being done, the Sibyl was gratified with a handsome wedge of veal pie. This partly despatched and partly pocketed, she made the familiar request for a piece of silver to cross the young lady's palm, which charm being performed she could tell things that would please her. James complied, and Justina surrendered her hand, most unwillingly, to the gipsy's brown claw.

The Sibyl told the usual story—happy wooing, prosperous wedded life—all things were to go smoothly for the blue-eyed lady and the blue-eyed gentleman.

"But beware of a dark man," said the witch, who felt it necessary to introduce some shadow in her picture, "beware of a dark-complexioned man. I won't say as he's spades; better call him clubs, perhaps. Be on your guard against a club man, my sweet young lady and gentleman, for he bears a jealous heart towards you both, and he stands to do you harm, if he has the power."

"That will do," said James, "we've had enough for our money, thank you, old lady; you can move on to the next carriage."

"Don't be offended with the poor gipsy, your honour. She's truth-spoken and plain-spoken, and she sees deeper into things than some folks would give her credit for."

And thus, after an affectionate farewell, the prophetess pursued her way. Other prophetesses followed in her wake, all begging for food and wine, and James lavished more champagne in this direction than Mr. Elgood approved, but even his good nature wore out at last, and he grew tired of these copper-skinned mendicants, some with babies in arms, for whom they begged a little drop of champagne or the claw of a lobster.

The races went on. The great race was at hand.

"Now, then, Justina, we must have something on," said James. "You don't mind me calling you Justina, do you?"

"I don't mind," the girl answered simply, "if father doesn't."

"Well, you see, I can't ask him now, but I will by and by. We can let the question stand over, and I may call you Justina meanwhile, mayn't I, Justina?" he asked softly.

"If you like," she answered almost in a whisper. They stood so near together that there was no need for either of them to speak loud, even amidst the noise of the racecourse.

"Look here, now, Justina. I'll bet you a dozen gloves, even money, that Free-and-Easy doesn't win. That's giving you a great advantage, for they are laying three to two on the favourite."

"I don't think I can bet," said Justina, embarrassed. "If I were to lose I could not pay you."

"Ladies never pay debts. Come, if Iphianassa wins you shall have a dozen pairs of the prettiest gloves I can buy, straw-coloured, pink, pearl-grey—which is your favourite colour?"

"I like any kind of gloves," answered the girl, remembering two wretched pairs which had been to the cleaner's so often that their insides were all over numbers, like a multiplication table.

Now came the start, breathlessness, attention strained almost to agony, a hoarse clamour yonder in and about the ring, one big man, wearing a white hat with a black hat-band, offering frantically to bet ten to one against anything, bar one; then a shout as of universal victory, for Free-and-Easy has shot suddenly to the front, after having been tenderly nursed during the first half-mile or so; and now she comes along gallantly, with a great lead, and her backers tremble, and now cold dews break out upon the foreheads of those eager backers, for another horse, almost an unknown animal, creeps up to Iphianassa, gallops shoulder to shoulder, with the Oaks winner, passes her, and wins by a neck, while a suppressed groan from the many losers mingles with the hurrahs of that miserable outside public which never stakes more than half a sovereign, and is ready to cheer any horse. Only among the bookmen is there real rejoicing, for they have been betting against the favourite.

"You've lost your gloves, Justina. Never mind, we'll have another venture on the next race. It's a selling stake; and we can go and see the auction afterwards—such fun. And now for the basket.—Make yourself useful, Elgood.—Mrs. Dempson, you must be famishing."

Mrs. Dempson, upon being pressed, owned to feeling a little faint. A lady of Mrs. Dempson's calibre never confesses to being hungry; with her, want of food only produces a genteel faintness.

The basket was emptied—lobster, chicken, pie, set out upon a tablecloth, laid on the front seat of the carriage. Then the scrambling meal began—the ladies seated with plates in their laps, the gentlemen standing. Again James and Justina shared the same glass of champagne, while Mr. Elgood obligingly held on by the bottle, and filled his own glass by instalments, so that it was never empty, and never full. Mr. Dempson was moderate, but jovial; Mrs. Dempson protested vehemently every time her glass was replenished, but contrived to drink the wine, out of politeness.

James was the gayest of Amphitryons. He kept

on declaring that he had never enjoyed himself so much—never had such a jolly day.

"I am sorry your friend is not with us," remarked Mr. Elgood, with his mouth full of lobster. "He has lost a treat."

"His loss is our gain," observed Mr. Dempson. "There'd have been less champagne for the rest of us if he'd been here."

"My friend is an ass," said James, carelessly. His errant fancy, so easily caught, was quite enchained by this time. He had been growing fonder of Justina all day, and, with the growth of his boyish passion, his anger against Maurice increased. He had almost made up his mind to do the very thing which Clissold had stigmatised as madness. He had almost made up his mind to marry the actor's daughter. He was in love with her, and how else should his love end? He came of too good a stock, had too good a heart, to contemplate a dishonourable ending. It only remained for him to discover if he really loved her—if this fancy that had but dawned upon him yesterday were indeed the beginning of his fate, or that considerable part of a man's destiny which is involved in his marriage. He had been very little in the society of women since his mother's death. His brief, harmless flirtations had been chiefly with damsels of the barmaid class; and, after these meretricious charmers, Justina, with her wild-rose tinted cheeks and innocent blue eyes, seemed youth and purity personified.

Justina looked shyly up at her admirer, happier than words could have told. Little had she ever tasted of pleasure's maddening cup before to-day. The flavour of the wine was not stranger to her lips than the flavour of joy to her soul. For her, girlhood had meant hard work and deprivation. Since she had been young enough to play hop-scotch on the doorstep with a neighbour's children, and think it happiness, she had hardly known what it was to be glad. To-day life brimmed over with enchantment—a carriage, a picnic, races, all the glad, gay world smiling at her. She looked at James with a grateful smile when he asked her if she was enjoying herself.

"How can I help enjoying myself?" she said. "I never had such a day in my life. It will all be over to-night, and to-morrow the world will look just as it does when one awakens from a wonderful dream. I have had dreams just like to-day," she added, simply.

"Might we not lengthen the dream, find some enjoyment for to-morrow?" asked James. "We might even come to the races again, if you like."

"We couldn't come. There will be a long rehearsal to-morrow. We play the new burlesque to-morrow night. And I thought you were going away to-morrow. Your friend said so."

"My friend would have been wiser had he spoken for himself, and not for me. I shall stay till the races are over; longer perhaps. How long do you stay?"

"Till next Saturday week, unless the business should get too bad."

"Then I think I shall stay till next Saturday week. I can read a Greek play at Eborsham as well as anywhere else, and I don't see why I should be hurried from place to place to please Clissold," added the young man, rebelliously.

There had been no hurrying from place to place

hitherto. They had done a good deal of Wales, and the English lakes, by easy stages, stopping at quiet inns, and reading hard in the intervals of their pedestrianism, and James had been completely happy with the bosom friend of his youth. It was only since yesterday that the bosom friend had been transformed into a tyrant. Clissold had warned and reproved before to-day; he had spoken with the voice of wisdom when James seemed going a little too far in some village flirtation; and James had listened meekly enough. But this time James Penwyn's soul rejected counsel. He was angry with his friend for not thinking it the most natural thing in the world that he, Squire Penwyn, of Penwyn, should fall head over ears in love with a country actor's daughter.

"I may come behind the scenes to-night, mayn't I, Justina?" asked James by and by, when the last race was over, and he and Justina had seen the winner disposed of to the highest bidder, and the patriarchal tub was rolling swiftly, oh, too swiftly, back to the town; back to common life, and the old dull world.

"You must ask father, or Mr. Dempson," Justina answered meekly. "Sometimes they make a fuss about any one coming into the green-room, but I don't suppose they would about you. It would be very ungrateful if they did."

James asked the question of Mr. Elgood, and was answered heartily. He was to consider the Eborsham green-room an adjunct to his hotel, and the Eborsham Theatre as open to him as his club, without question of payment at the doors.

"Your name shall be left with the money-taker," the heavy father said, somewhat thickly.

Mr. Dempson laughed.

"Our friend is a trifle screwed," he said, "but I dare say he'll get through Sir Oliver pretty well."

The play was the "School for Scandal," a genteel entertainment in honour of the patrons of the races.

The roomy travelling carriage was blundering through one of the narrower streets near the cathedral, when James Penwyn stood up suddenly and looked behind him.

"What's the matter?" asked Mr. Dempson.

"Nothing. I thought I saw a fellow I know, that's all. He's just gone into that public-house—the quiet-looking little place at the corner. I fancied I saw him on the course, but I don't see how it could be the man," added James, dubiously. "What should bring him down here? It isn't in his line?"

CHAPTER VIII.

"Have the high gods anything left to give?"

Mr. Penwyn set down his guests at the chandler's door, and drove home to the "Waterfowl" in solitary state, the chariot in which he sat seeming a great deal too big for one medium-sized young man.

His ample meal on the course made dinner an impossibility, so he ordered a cup of coffee to be taken to him in the garden, and went out to smoke a cigar, on his favourite bench by the willow. The "Waterfowl" was too far off the beaten tracks for any of the race people to come there, so James had the garden all to himself, even this evening.

The sun was setting beyond the bend of the river, just where the shining water seemed to lose itself in a rushy basin. The ruddy light shone on the windows of the town till they looked like fiery eyes gleaming through the grey evening mist; while, above the level landscape and the low, irregular town, rose the dusky bulk of the cathedral, dwarfing the distant hills, and standing darkly out against that changeful sky.

James Penwyn was in a meditative mood, and contemplated the landscape dreamily as he smoked an excellent cigar with Epicurean slowness, letting pleasure last as long as it would. Not that his soul was interpenetrated by the subtle beauties of the scene. He only thought that it was rather jolly, that solemn stillness after the riot of the racecourse—that lonely landscape after the movement of the crowd.

Only last night had Justina and he stood side by side in the moonlight—only last night had their hands met for the first time, and yet she seemed a part of his life, indispensable to his happiness.

"Is it love?" he asked himself, "first love? I didn't think it was in me to be such a spoon."

He was at the age when that idea of "spooniness" is to the last degree humiliating. He had prided himself upon his manliness—thought that he had exhausted the well-spring of sentiment in those passing flirtations, the transitory loves of an undergraduate. He had talked big about marrying by and by for money and position—to add new lustre to the house of Penwyn —to carry some heiress's arms on his shield, upon an escutcheon of pretence.

Was it really love?—love for a foolish girl of seventeen, with sky-blue eyes, and a look of adoration when she raised them, ever so fearfully, to his face? Justina had a pensiveness that charmed him more than other women's gaiety, and till now sprightliness had been his highest quality in woman—a girl who would light his cigar for him, and take three or four puffs, daintily, before she handed him the weed—a girl who was quick at retort, and could "chaff" him. This girl essayed not repartee—this girl was fresh, and simple as Wordsworth's ideal woman. And he loved her. For the first time in his glad young life his heart throbbed with the love that is so near akin to pain.

"I'll marry her," he said to himself. "She shall be mistress of Penwyn Manor."

The sun went down and left the landscape gloomy. James Penwyn rose from the bench with a faint shiver.

"These early summer evenings are chilly," he thought, as he walked back to the house. He felt lonely somehow, in spite of his fair new hope. It was so strange to him not to have Clissold at his side—to reprove, or warn. But, at worst, the voice was a friendly one. The silence of this garden; the dusky gloom on yonder river; the solemn gloom of the cathedral, chilled him.

The great clock boomed eight, and reminded him that the play had begun half an hour. It would be a relief to find himself in the lighted playhouse among those rollicking actors.

He went down to the theatre, and made his way straight to the green-room. There was a good house—a great house, Mr. Elgood told James—and the commonwealth's shares were already above par. Everybody was in high spirits, and most people's breath was slightly flavoured with beer.

"We have been turning away money at the gallery door," said Mr. Dempson, who was dressed for Moses, "I should think to the tune of seventeen shillings. This is the right sort of thing, sir. It reminds me of my poor old governor's time; when the drama was respected in the land, and all the gentry within a twenty-mile radius used to come to his benefit."

Justina was the Maria of the piece, dressed in an ancient white satin—or rather an ancient satin which had once been white, but which, by long service and frequent cleaning, had mellowed to a pleasing canary colour. She had some airy puffings of muslin about her, and wore a black sash in memory of her departed parents, and her plenteous brown hair fell over her neck and shoulders in innocent ringlets.

Justina had never looked prettier than she looked to-night. She even had a round of applause when she made her curtsey to Sir Peter. The actors told her that she was growing a deuced fine girl, after all, and that one of these days she would learn how to act. Was it the new joy in her soul that embellished and exalted her?

James thought her lovely, as he stood at the wing and talked to her. Miss Villeroy, who was esteemed a beauty by her friends, seemed, to this uninitiated youth, a painted sepulchre; for she had whitened her complexion to match her powdered wig, and accentuated her eyebrows and eyelids with Indian ink, and picked out her lips with a rose pink saucer, and encarnadined her cheek-bones; by which artistic efforts she had attained that kind of beauty to which distance lends enchantment, but which, seen too near, is apt to repel. Miss Villeroy had the house with her, however. She had the audience altogether with her as Lady Teazle, and, being a virtuous matron, cared not to court James Penwyn's admiration. Indeed, she was very glad to see that the foolish young man was taken with poor Judy, Mrs. Dempson told her husband; for poor dear Judy wasn't everybody's money, and about the worst actress the footlights ever shone upon.

Mr. Elgood being in high spirits, and feeling himself flush of money—his share in to-night's receipts could hardly be less than fifteen shillings—was moved to an act of hospitality.

"I'll tell you what I'll do, Mr. Penwyn," he said, "the treating shan't be all on your side, though you're a rich young swell and we are poor beggars of actors. Come home with us to-night, after the last piece, and I'll give you a lobster. Judy knows how to make a salad, and if you can drink bitter you shall have enough to swim in."

Mr. Penwyn expressed his ability to drink bitter beer, which he infinitely preferred to champagne. But what would he not have drunk for the pleasure of being in Justina's society?

"It's a poor place to ask you to come to," said Mr. Elgood. "Dempson and I go shares in the sitting-room, and we don't keep it altogether as tidy as we might, the womenkind say, but I'll take care the lobster's a good one, for I'll go out and pick it myself. I don't play in the last piece, luckily."

The afterpiece was "A Roland for an Oliver," in which Justina enacted a walking lady who had very little to do. So there was plenty of time for James to talk to her as she stood at the wing, where they were quite alone, and had nobody to overhear them except a passing scene-shifter now and then.

This seemed to James Penwyn the happiest night he had ever spent in his life, though he was inhaling dust and escaped gas all the time. It seemed a night that flew by on golden wings. He thought he must have been dreaming when the curtain fell, and the lights went out, and people told him it was midnight.

He waited amidst darkness and chaos while Justina ran away to change her stage dress for the garments of common life. She was not long absent, and they went out together, arm-in-arm. It was only a little way from the theatre to the actor's lodgings, so James persuaded her to walk round by the cathedral, just to see how it looked in the moonlight.

"Your father said half-past twelve for supper, you know," he pleaded, "and it's only just the quarter."

The big bell chimed at the instant, in confirmation of this statement, and Justina, who could not for her life have said no, assented hesitatingly.

The cathedral had a colossal grandeur seen from so near, every finial and waterspout clearly defined in the moonlight. Justina looked up at it with reverent eyes.

"Isn't it grand!" she whispered. "One could fancy that God inhabits it. If I were an ignorant creature from some savage land, and nobody told me it was a church, I think I should know that it was God's house."

"Should you?" said James, lightly. "I think I should as soon take it for a corn exchange or a wild beast show."

"Oh!"

"You see I have no instinctive sense of the fitness of things. You would just suit Clissold. He has all those queer fancies. I've seen him stand and talk to himself like a lunatic sometimes, among the lakes and mountains; what you call the artistic faculty, I suppose."

They walked round the cathedral-square arm-in-arm, Justina charmed to silence by the solemn splendour of the scene. All was quiet at this end of the city. Up at the subscription rooms there might be riot and confusion; but here, in this ancient square, among these old gabled houses, almost coeval with the cathedral, silence reigned supreme.

"Justina," James began presently, "you told me yesterday that you didn't care about being an actress."

"I told you that I hated it," answered the girl, candidly. "I suppose I should like it better if I were a favourite, like Villeroy."

"I prefer your acting to Miss Villeroy's ever so much. You do it rather too quietly, perhaps, but that's better than yelling as she does."

"I'm glad you like me best," said Justina, softly. "But then you're not the British public. Yes, I hate theatres. I should like to live in a little cottage, deep, deep, deep down in the country, where there were woods and fields, and a shining blue river. I could keep chickens, and live upon the money I got by the new-laid eggs."

"Don't you think it would be better to have a nice large house, with gardens and orchards, and a park, in a wild, hilly country beside the Atlantic Ocean?"

"What should I do with a big house, and how should I earn money to pay for it?" she asked, laughing.

"Suppose some one else were to find the money, some one who has plenty, and only wants the girl he loves to share it with him? Justina, you and I met yesterday for the first time, but you are the only girl I ever loved, and I love you with all my heart. It may seem sudden, but it's as true as that I live and speak to you to-night."

"Sudden!" echoed Justina. "It seems like a dream; but you mustn't speak of it any more. I won't believe a word you say. I won't listen to a word. It can't be true. Let's go home immediately. Hark! there's the half-hour. Take me home, please, Mr. Penwyn."

"Not till you have answered me one question."

"No, no!"

"Yes, Justina. I must be answered. I have made up my mind, and I want to know yours. Do you think you care for me, just a little?"

"I won't answer. It is all more foolish than a dream."

"It is the sweetest dream that ever was dreamed by me. Obstinate lips! Cannot I make them speak? No? Then the eyes shall tell me what I want to know. Look up, Justina. Just one little look—and then we'll go home."

The heavy lids were lifted, slowly, shyly, and the young lover looked into the depths of those dark eyes. A girl's first, purest love, that love which is so near religion, shone there like a star.

James Penwyn needed no other answer.

"You shall never act again unless you like, darling," he said. "I'll speak to your father to-night, and we'll be married as soon as the business can be done. When you leave Eborsham it shall be as mistress of Penwyn Manor. There is not a soul belonging to me who has the faintest right to question what I do. And it is my duty to marry young. The Penwyn race has been sorely dwindling of late. If I were to die unmarried, my estate would go to my cousin, a fellow I don't care two straws about."

Perhaps this was said more to himself than to Justina. She understood nothing about estates and heirships, she to whom property was an unknown quantity. She only knew that life seemed changed to a delicious dream. The hard, work-a-day world, which had not been too kind to her, had melted away, and left her in paradise. Her hand trembled beneath the touch of her lover as he clasped it close upon his arm.

They walked slowly through the silent shadowy street, so narrow that the moonlight hardly reached it, and went in by the shop door, which had been left ajar, in a friendly way, for their reception.

"What a time you've been, Judy!" cried Mr. Elgood, standing before the table, stirring a bowl of green stuff, with various cruets at his elbow. "I've had to make the salad myself.—Sit down and make yourself at home, Penwyn.—Dempson, draw the cork of that bitter. The right thing now-a-days is to pour it into a jug. When I was a young man we couldn't have too much froth."

Mrs. Dempson had smartened her usual toilet with a bow or two, and a black lace veil, which she wore gracefully festooned about her head, to conceal the curl-papers in which she had indued her tresses for to-morrow evening's performance. She would be too tired to curl her hair by the time they got rid of this foolish young man.

The supper was even gayer than the luncheon on the racecourse. There was a large dish of cold corned beef, ready sliced, from the cook's shop; a cucumber, a couple of lobsters, and a bowl of salad, crisp and oily, upon which Mr. Elgood prided himself.

"There are not many things that this child can do," he remarked, "but he flatters himself he can dress a salad."

The ale, being infinitely better of its kind than the champagne provided by the "Waterfowl," proved more exhilarating. James Penwyn's spirits rose to their highest point. He invited everybody to Penwyn Manor; promised Miss Villeroy a season's hunting; Mr. Dempson any amount of sport. They would all go down to Cornwall together, and have a jolly time of it. Not a word did he say about his intended marriage—even though elated by beer, he felt a restraining delicacy which kept him silent on this one subject.

Justina was the quietest of the party. She sat by her father's side, looking her prettiest, with eyes that joy had glorified, and a delicate bloom upon her cheeks. She neither ate nor drank, but listened to her lover's careless rattle, and felt more and more that life was like a dream. How handsome he was; how good; how brave; how brilliant! Her simplicity accepted the young man's undergraduate jocosity for wit of the purest water. She laughed her gay young laugh at his jokes.

"If you could laugh like that on the stage, Judy, you'd make as good a comedy actress as Mrs. Jordan," said her father.

"As if any one could laugh naturally to a cue," cried Justina.

They sat late, almost as late as they had sat on the previous night, and when James rose at last to take his leave—urged thereto by the unquiet slumbers of Villeroy, who had fallen asleep in an uncomfortable position on the rickety old sofa, and whose snores were too loud to be agreeable—Mr. Elgood had arrived at that condition of mind in which life wears its rosiest hue. He was anxious to see his guest home, but this favour James declined.

"It's an—comm'ly bad ro'," urged the heavy father. "Y'd berrer let me see y' 'ome—cut thro' ro';" which James interpreted to mean "a cut-throat road." "Don' like y' t' go 'lone."

Justina watched her father with a troubled look. It was hard that he should show himself thus degraded just now, when, but for this, life would be all sweetness. James smiled at her reassuringly, undisturbed by the thought that such a man might be an undesirable father-in-law.

He pushed his entertainer back into his seat.

"Talk about seeing me home," he said, laughing, "why, it isn't half an hour's walk. Good night, Mr. Dempson. I'm afraid I've kept your wife up too late, after her exertions in Lady Teazle.—Will you open the door for me, Justina?"

Justina went down the narrow crooked staircase with him—one of those staircases of the good old times, better suited to a belfry tower than a dwelling-house. They went into the dark little shop together, and just at the door, amidst odours of Irish butter and Dutch cheese, Scotch herrings and Spanish onions, James took his betrothed in his arms and kissed her, fondly, proudly, as if he had won a princess for his helpmeet.

"Remember, darling, you are to be my wife. If I had a hundred relations to bully me they wouldn't make me change my mind. But I've no one to call me to account, and you are the girl of my choice. I haven't been able to speak to your father to-night, but I'll talk to him to-morrow morning, and settle everything. Good night, and God bless you, my own dear love!"

One more kiss, and he was gone. She stood on the door-step watching him as he walked up the narrow street. The moon was gone, and only a few stars shone dimly between the drifting clouds. The night-wind came coldly up from the water side yonder and made her shiver. A man crossed the street and walked briskly past her, going in the same direction as James Penwyn. She noticed, absently enough, that he wore a heavy overcoat and muffler, for defence against that chill night air, no doubt, but more clothing than people generally wear in the early days of June.

CHAPTER IX.

"Other sins only speak; murder shrieks out."

VERY radiant were Justina's dreams during the brief hours that remained to her for slumber after that Bohemian supper party—dreams of her sweet new life, in which all things were bright and strange. She was with her lover in a garden—the dream-garden which those sleepers know who have seen but little of earthly gardens—a garden where there were marble terraces and statues, and fountains, and a placid lake lying in a valley of bloom; a vision made up of faint memories of pictures she had seen, or poems she had read. They were together and happy in the noonday sunshine. And then the dream changed. They were together in the moonlight again—not outside the cathedral, but in the long solemn nave. She could see the distant altar gleaming faintly in the silver light, while a solemn strain of music, like the muffled chanting of a choir, rolled along the echoing arches overhead. Then the silvery light faded, the music changed to a harsh dirge-like cry, and she woke to hear the raindrops pattering against her little dormer window—Justina's room was the worst of the three bedchambers, and in the garret story,—and a shrill-voiced hawker bawling watercresses along the street.

She had the feeling of having overslept herself, and not being provided with a watch had no power to ascertain the fact, but was fain to dress as quickly as she could, trusting to the cathedral clock to inform her of the hour. To be late for rehearsal involved a good deal of snubbing from the higher powers, even in a commonwealth. The stage manager retained his authority, and knew how to make himself disagreeable.

Life seemed all reality again this morning as Justina plaited her hair before the shabby little mirror, and looked out at the dull grey sky, the wet sloppy streets, the general aspect of poverty and damp which pervaded the prospect. She had need to ask herself if yesterday and the night before had not been all dreaming. She the chosen bride of a rich young squire—she the mistress of Penwyn Manor! It was surely too fond a fancy. She, whose shabby weather-stained under garments—the green stuff gown of two winters ago converted into a petticoat last year, and worn threadbare—the corset which a nursemaid might have despised—lay yonder on the dilapidated rush-bottomed chair, like the dull reality of Cinderella's rags, after the fairy ball dress had melted into air.

She hurried on her clothes, more ashamed of their shabbiness than she had ever felt yet, and ran down to the sitting-room, which smelt of stale lobster and tobacco, the windows not having been opened on account of the rain. Breakfast was laid. A sloppy cup and saucer, the dorsal bone of a haddock on a greasy plate indicated that some one had breakfasted. The cathedral clock chimed eleven. Justina's rehearsal only began at half-past. She had time to take her breakfast comfortably, if she liked.

Her first act was to open the window, and let in the air, and the rain—anything was better than stale lobster. Then she looked into the teapot, and wondered who had breakfasted, and if her father were up. Then she poured out a cup of tea, and sipped it slowly, wondering if James Penwyn would come to the theatre while she was rehearsing. He had asked her the hour of the rehearsal. She thought she would see him there, most likely; and the dream would begin again.

A jug of wild flowers stood on the table by the window—the flowers she had gathered two days ago, before she had seen *him.*

They were a little faded—wild flowers droop so early—but in no wise dead; and yet a passion had been born and attained its majority since those field flowers were plucked.

Could she believe in it? could she trust in it? Her heart sank at the thought that her lover was trifling with her—that there was nothing but foolishness in this first love dream.

Her father had not yet left his room. Justina saw his one presentable pair of boots waiting for him outside his door, as she went by on her way downstairs.

She found Mr. and Mrs. Dempson at rehearsal, both with a faded and washed-out appearance, as if the excitement of the previous day had taken all the colour out of them.

The rehearsal went forward in a straggling way. That good house of last night seemed to have demoralized the commonwealth, or perhaps the scene of dissipation going on out of doors, the races and holiday-makers, and bustle of the down, may have had a disturbing influence. The stage manager lost his temper, and said business was business, and he didn't want the burlesque to be a "munge"—a word borrowed from some unknown tongue, which evidently made an impression upon the actors.

Justina had been in the theatre for a little more than an hour, when Mr. Elgood burst suddenly into the green-room, pale as a sheet of letter-paper, and wearing his hat anyhow.

"Has anybody heard of it?" he asked, looking round at the assembly. Mrs. Dempson was sitting in a corner covering a satin shoe. Justina stood by the window studying her part in the burlesque. Mr. Dempson, with three or four kindred spirits, was smoking on some stone steps just outside the green-room. Everybody looked round at this sudden appeal, wondering at the actor's scared expression of countenance.

"Why, what's up, mate?" asked Mr. Dempson. "Is the cathedral on fire? Bear up under the affliction; I dare say it's insured."

"Nobody has heard, then?"

"Heard what?"

"Of the murder."

"What murder? Who's murdered?" cried every one at once, except Justina. Her thoughts were slower than the rest, perhaps. She stood looking at her father, fixed as marble.

"That poor young fellow, that good-hearted young fellow who stood treat yesterday. Did you ever know such a blackguard thing, Demps? Shot from behind a hedge, on the road between Lowgate and the 'Waterfowl.' Only found this morning between five and six, by some labourers going to their work.

Dead and cold; shot through the heart. He's lying at the 'Lowgate Arms,' just inside the archway, and there's to be a coroner's inquest at two o'clock this afternoon."

"Great Heaven, how awful!" cried Dempson. "What was the motive? Robbery, I suppose."

"So it was thought at first, for his pockets were empty, turned inside out. But the police searched the ditch for the weapon, which they didn't find, but found his watch and purse and pocket-book, half an hour ago, buried in the mud, as if they had been rammed down with a stick. So there must have been revenge at the bottom of the business, unless it was that the fellows who did it—I dare say there was more than one—took the alarm, and hid the plunder, with the intention of fishing it up again on the quiet afterwards."

"It looks more like that," said Mr. Dempson. "The haymakers are beginning to be about—a bad lot. Any scoundrel can use a scythe. Don't cry, old woman;" this to his wife, who was sobbing hysterically over the satin shoe. "He was a nice young fellow, and we're all very sorry for him; but crying won't bring him back."

"Such a happy day as we had with him!" sobbed the leading lady. "I never enjoyed myself so much, and to think that he should be m—m—murdered. It's too dreadful."

Nobody noticed Justina, till the thin straight figure suddenly swayed, like a slender sapling in a high wind, when Matthew Elgood darted forward and caught her in his arms, just as she was falling. Her face lay on his shoulder white and set.

"I'm blessed if she hasn't fainted!" cried her father. "Poor Judy! I forgot that he was rather sweet upon her."

"You didn't ought to have blurted it out like that," exclaimed Mrs. Dempson, more sympathetic than grammatical. "Run and get a glass of water, Dempson. Don't you fuss with her," to the father. "I'll bring her to, and take her home, and get her to lie down a bit. She shan't go on with the rehearsal, whatever Pyecroft says." Pyecroft was the stage manager. "She'll be all right at night."

Justina, after having water splashed over her poor pale face, recovered consciousness, stared with a blank awful look at her father and the rest, and then went home to her lodgings meekly, leaning on Mrs. Dempson's arm. A bleak awakening from her dream.

Yes, it was all true. The gay, light-hearted lad, the prosperous lord of Penwyn Manor, had been taken away from the fair fresh world, from the life which for his unsated spirit meant happiness. Slain by a secret assassin's hand he lay in the darkened clubroom of the "Lowgate Arms," awaiting the inquest.

The Eborsham police were hard at work, but not alone. The case was felt to be an important one. A gentleman of property was not to be murdered with impunity. Had the victim been some agricultural labourer, slain in a drunken fray, some turnpike-man murdered for plunder, the Eborsham constabulary would have felt itself able to cope with the difficulties of the case. But this was a darker business, a crime which was likely to be heard of throughout the length and breadth of the land, and the Eborsham constable felt that the eyes of Europe were upon him. He knew that his own men were slow and blundering, and, doubtful of their power to get at the bottom of the mystery, telegraphed to Spinnersbury for a couple of skilled detectives, who came swift as an express train could carry them.

"Business is business!" said the Eborsham constable. "Whatever reward may be offered by and by—there's a hundred already, by our own magistrates—we work together, as between man and man, and share it honourably."

"That's understood," replied the gentlemen from Spinnersbury, the chief centre of that northern district. And affairs being thus established on an agreeable footing, the skilled detectives went to work.

The watch and purse had been found by the local police before the arrival of these Spinnersbury men. The purse was empty, so it still remained an open question whether plunder had not been the motive. The man who took the money might have been afraid to take the watch, as a compromising bit of property likely to bring him into trouble. Higlett, one of the Spinnersbury men, went straight to the "Waterfowl," to hunt up the surroundings of the dead man. Smelt, his companion, remained in Eborsham, where he made a round of the low-class public-houses, with a view of discovering what doubtful characters had been hanging about the town during the last day or two. A race meeting is an occasion when doubtful characters are apt to be abundant; yet it seemed a curious thing that Mr. Penwyn, whom nobody supposed to be a winner of money, should have been waylaid on his return from the town—rather than one of those numerous gentlemen who had gone home from the Rooms that night with full pockets and wine-bemused heads.

Mr. Higlett found the "Waterfowl" people as communicative as he could desire. They had done nothing but talk about the murder all the morning with a ghoulish gusto, and could talk of nothing else. From them Mr. Higlett heard a good deal that set his sapient mind working in what he considered a happy direction.

"Smelt may do all he can in the town," he thought, "I'm not sorry I came here."

The landlady, who was dolefully loquacious, took Mr. Higlett aside, having ascertained that he was a detective officer from Spinnersbury, and informed him that there were circumstances about the case she didn't like—not that she wished to throw out anything against anybody, and it would weigh heavy on her mind if she suspected them that were innocent, still, thought was free, and she had her thoughts.

Pressed home by the detective, she went a little further, and said she didn't like the look of things about Mr. Clissold.

"Who is Mr. Clissold?" asked Higlett.

"Mr. Penwyn's friend. They came here together three days ago, and seemed as comfortable as possible together, like brothers, and they went out fishing together the day before yesterday, and then in the evening they brought home some of the play-actors to supper, the best of everything; and going up to bed they had high words. Me and my good man heard them, for the loud talking wakened us, and it was all along of some girl. And they were both very much excited, and Mr. Penwyn banged his door that violent as to shake the house, being an old house, as you may see."

"A girl!" said Mr. Higlett, "that sometimes means mischief. But there's not much in a few high words between two young gentlemen after supper, even if it's about a girl. They were all right and friendly again next morning, I suppose?"

"I dare say they would have been," replied the hostess, "only Mr. Clissold went out early next morning with his fishing-rod, leaving a bit of a note for Mr. Penwyn, and didn't come back till twelve o'clock to-day."

"Curious," said Mr. Higlett.

"That's what struck me. Mr. Penwyn expected him back yesterday evening, and left word to say where he'd gone, if his friend came in. Of course, Mr. Clissold was awfully shocked when he came in to-day and heard of the murder. I don't think I ever saw a man turn so white. But it did strike me as strange that he should be out all night, just that very night."

"Did he tell you where he had been?"

"No. He went out of the house again directly with the police. He was going to telegraph to Mr. Penwyn's lawyer, and some of his relations I think."

"Ready to make himself useful," muttered Mr. Higlett. "I should like to have a look round these gentlemen's rooms."

Being duly armed with authority, this privilege was allowed Mr. Higlett. He examined bedchambers and sitting-room, looked at the few and simple belongings of the travellers, who were naturally not encumbered with much luggage. Finding little to employ him here, Mr. Higlett took a snack of lunch in the public parlour, heard the gossip of the loungers at the bar through the half-open door, meditated, smoked a pipe, and went out into the high road.

He met Smelt, who seemed dispirited.

"Nothing turned up?" asked Higlett.

"Less than half nothing. How's yourself?"

"Well, I think I'm on the right lay. But it's rather dark at present."

They went back to the inn together, conferring in half-whispers. A quarter of an hour later, Maurice Clissold returned from his mission. He looked pale and wearied, and hardly saw the two men whom he passed in the porch. He had scarcely entered the house when these two men came close up to him, one on each side.

"I arrest you on suspicion of being concerned in the murder of James Penwyn," said Higlett.

"And bear in mind that anything you say now will be used against you by and by," remarked Smelt.

CHAPTER X.

"Nothing comes amiss, so money comes withal."

THE inquest was held at two o'clock, and adjourned. Few facts were elicited beyond those which had been in everybody's mouth that morning, when Matthew Elgood heard of the murder at the bar of that tavern where he took his noontide dram—the three penn'orth of gin and bitters which revivified him after last night's orgies.

James Penwyn had been shot through the heart by a hidden assassin. It seemed tolerably clear that the murderer had taken aim from behind the ragged bushes which divided the low-lying land by the river from the road just at this point. There were footprints on the marshy turf—not the prints of a clodhopper's bulky boots. The line of footsteps indicated that the murderer had entered the field by a gate a hundred yards nearer the city, and had afterwards gone across the grass to the towpath. Here, on harder ground, the footsteps ceased altogether. They were the impressions of a gentleman's sole—or so thought the detectives, who were anxious to find a correspondence between these footprints and the boots of Maurice Clissold. Here, however, they were somewhat at fault. Maurice's stout shooting boot made a wider and longer print on the sward.

"He may have worn a smaller boot last night," said Smelt. "But they say up at the inn that he has only two pairs, one off, one on, both the same make. I looked at those he's wearing, and they are just as big as these."

This was a slight check to the chain, which had run out pretty freely till now. True that there seemed little or no motive for the crime; but the one fact of the quarrel was something to go upon; and the curious absence of Maurice Clissold on that particular night was a circumstance that would have to be accounted for.

Who could tell how serious that quarrel might have been?—perhaps the last outbreak of a long-smouldering flame; perhaps a dispute involving deepest interests. Further evidence would come out by degrees. At any rate, they had got their man.

Maurice was present at the inquest, very calm and quiet. He made no statement whatever, by the advice of the local solicitor, Mr. Brent, whose aid he had not rejected. He would have been more agitated, perhaps, by the fact of his friend's untimely death, but for this monstrous accusation. That made him iron.

The inquest was adjourned, the facts being so few, and Mr. Clissold was taken to Eborsham Castle, a mediæval fortress, which our modern civilization had converted into the county jail.

Here he was comfortable enough, so far as surroundings went; for he was a young man of adventurous mind, and tastes so simple that a hard bed and a carpetless room were no afflictions to him.

Mr. Brent, the solicitor, visited him in his confinement, and discussed the facts of the case.

"It's hard upon you, both ways," said the lawyer;

"hard to lose your friend, and still harder to find yourself exposed to this monstrous suspicion."

"I don't care two straws for the suspicion," answered Maurice, "but I do care very much for the loss of my friend. He was one of the best fellows that ever lived—so bright, so brimming over with freshness and vitality. If I had not seen him lying in that tavern, stark and cold, I couldn't bring myself to believe in his death. It's hard to believe in it, even with the memory of that poor murdered clay fresh in my mind. Poor James! I loved him like a younger brother!"

"You have no knowledge of any circumstances in his life that can help us to find the murderer?" asked Mr. Brent.

"I know of nothing. He had picked up some people I didn't care about his being intimate with, strolling players, who are acting at the theatre in this place. But my worst fear was that he might be trapped into some promise of marriage. I can hardly fancy these people concerned in a crime."

"No. They are for the most part harmless vagabonds," replied the lawyer. "Do you know where Mr. Penwyn spent last night?"

"With these people, no doubt—a man called Elgood, and his daughter. The man ought to be called as a witness, I should think."

"Unquestionably. We'll have him before the coroner next Saturday, and we'll keep an eye upon him meanwhile."

The inquest had been adjourned for three days, to give time for new facts to be elicited.

"Your friend had no enemies, you say?"

"Not one," answered Clissold. "He was one of those men who never make an enemy. He hadn't the strength of mind to refuse a favour to the veriest blackguard. It was my knowledge of his character that made me anxious about this Elgood's acquaintance. I saw that he was fascinated by the girl, and feared he might be lured into some false position. That was the sole cause of our dispute the other night."

"Why did you leave him?"

"Because I saw that my interference irritated him, and was likely to arouse a lurking obstinacy which I knew to be in his nature. He was such a spoiled child of fortune that I fancied if I left him alone to take his own way his passion would cool. Opposition fired him."

"There is only one awkward circumstance in the whole case—as regards yourself, I mean."

"What is that?" asked Clissold.

"Your objection to state where you spent last night."

"I should be sorry if I were driven to so poor a defence as an *alibi.*"

"I don't think there's any fear of that. The evidence against you amounts to so little. But why not simplify matters by accounting for your time up to your return to-day? You only came back to Eborsham by the twelve o'clock train from Spinnersbury, you say?"

"I came by that train."

"Do you think any of the porters or ticket collectors would remember seeing you?"

"Not likely. The train was crowded with people

coming to the races. It was as much as I could do to get a seat. I had to scramble into a third-class compartment as the train began to move."

"But why not refer to some one at Spinnersbury, to prove your absence from Eborsham last night?"

"When my neck is in danger I may do that. In the meantime you may as well let the matter drop. I have my own reasons for not saying where I was last night, unless I am very hard pushed."

Mr. Brent was obliged to be satisfied. The case against his client was of the weakest as yet; but it was curious that this young man should so resolutely refuse to give a straightforward account of himself. Mr. Brent had felt positive of his client's innocence up to this point; but this refusal disturbed him. He went home with an uncomfortable feeling that there was something wrong somewhere.

Messrs. Higlett and Smelt were not idle during the interval. Higlett lodged at the "Waterfowl," and heard all the gossip of the house, where the one absorbing topic was the murder of James Penwyn.

Among other details the Spinnersbury detective heard Mrs. Marport, the landlady, speak of a certain letter which the morning's post brought Mr. Clissold the day he went away. It came by the first delivery, which was before eight o'clock. Jane, the housemaid, took it up to Mr. Clissold's room with his boots and shaving water.

"I never set eyes upon such a letter," said Mrs. Marport. "It seemed to have been all round the world for sport, as the saying is. It had been to some address in London, and to Wales, and to Cumberland, and was all over post-marks. I suppose it must have been something rather particular to have been sent after him so."

"A bill, I dare say—or a lawyer's letter, perhaps."

"Oh no, it wasn't. It was a lady's handwriting. I took particular notice of that."

"Any cress or mornagarm," asked Higlett.

"No, there was nothing on the envelope; but the paper was as thick as parchment. Whoever wrote that letter was quite the lady."

"Ah," said Higlett, "Mr. Clissold's sweetheart, very likely."

"That's what I've been thinking, and that it was that letter, perhaps, that took him off so suddenly, and that he really may have been far away from Eborsham on the night of the murder."

"If he was, he'll be able to prove it," replied Mr. Higlett, who was not inclined to entertain the idea of Mr. Clissold's innocence. To earn his share of the reward he must find the murderer, and it mattered very little to Higlett where he found him.

* * * * * *

In the afternoon of the day succeeding the inquest, two persons of some importance to the case arrived at Eborsham. They came by the same train, and had travelled together from London. One was Churchill Penwyn, the inheritor of the Penwyn estate. The other was Mr. Pergament, the family solicitor, chief partner in the firm of Pergament and Pergament, New Square, Lincoln's Inn.

Churchill Penwyn and the solicitor met at King's Cross station, five minutes before the starting of the ten o'clock express for Eborsham. They were very well acquainted with each other; Churchill's meagre portion, inherited under the will of old Mrs. Penwyn, his grandmother, who had been an heiress in a small way, having passed through Mr. Pergament's hands. Nicholas Penwyn's will, which disposed of Penwyn Manor for two generations, had been drawn up by Mr. Pergament's father, and all business connected with the Penwyn estate had been transacted in Mr. Pergament's office for the last hundred years. Pergaments had been born and died during the century, but the office was the same as in the time of Penruddock Penwyn, who, inheriting a farm of a hundred and fifty acres or so, had made a fortune in the East Indies, and extended the estate by various important additions to its present dimensions. For before the days of Penruddock the race of Penwyn had declined in splendour, though it was always known and acknowledged that the Penwyns were one of the oldest families in Cornwall.

Of course Mr. Pergament, knowing Nicholas Penwyn's will by heart, was perfectly aware of the alteration which this awful event of the murder made in Churchill's circumstances. Churchill had been a cadet of the house heretofore, though his cousin James's senior by nearly ten years—a person of no importance whatever. Mr. Pergament had treated him with a free and easy friendliness—was always ready to do him a good turn—sent him a brief now and then, and so on. To-day Mr. Pergament was deferential. The old friendliness was toned down to a subdued respect. It seemed as if Mr. Pergament's eye, respectfully raised to Churchill's broad pale brow, in imagination beheld above it the round and top of sovereignty, the lordship of Penwyn Manor.

"Very distressing event," murmured the lawyer, as they seated themselves opposite each other in the first-class carriage. This was a comfortable train to travel by, not arriving at Eborsham till three. The race traffic had been cleared off by a special, at an earlier hour.

"Very," returned Churchill, gravely. "Of course I cannot be expected to be acutely grieved by an event which raises me from a working man's career to affluence, especially as I knew so little of my cousin; but I was profoundly shocked at the circumstances of his death. A commonplace, vulgar murder for gain, I apprehend, committed by some rustic ruffian. I doubt if that class of man thinks much more of murder than of sparrow-shooting."

"I hope they'll get him, whoever he is," said the lawyer.

"If the acuteness of the police can be stimulated by the hope of reward, that motive shall not be wanting;" returned Churchill. "I shall offer a couple of hundred pounds for the conviction of the murderer."

"Very proper," murmured Mr. Pergament, approvingly. "No, you had seen very little of poor James, I apprehend," he went on, in a conversational tone.

"I doubt if he and I met half a dozen times. I saw him once at Eton, soon after my father's death, when I was spending a day or two at a shooting-box near Bracknell, and walked over to have a look at the college. He was a little curly-headed chap, playing cricket, and I remember tipping him, ill as I could afford the half-sovereign. One can't see a schoolboy without tipping him. I daresay the young rascal ran off and spent my hard-earned shillings on strawberry ices and pound-cake as soon as my back was turned. I saw him a few years afterwards in his mother's house, somewhere near Baker Street. She asked me to a dinner party, and as she made rather a point of it, I went. A slowish business—as women's dinners generally are—all the delicacies that were just going out of season, and some elderly ladies to adorn the board. I asked James to breakfast at my club—put him up for the Garrick—and I think that's about the last time I ever saw him."

"Poor lad," sighed the family solicitor. "Such a promising young fellow. But I doubt if he would have kept the property together. There was very little of his grandfather, old Squire Penwyn, about him. A wonderful man that, vigorous in body and mind to the last year of his life. I spent a week at Penwyn about seventeen years ago, just before your poor uncle was killed by those abominable red-skins in Canada. I can see the Squire before me now, a hale old country gentleman, always dressed in a Lincoln-green coat, with basket buttons, Bedford cords, and vinegar tops—hunted three times a week every season, after he was seventy years of age—the Assheton Smith stamp of man. The rising generation will never ripen into that kind of thing, Mr. Penwyn. The stuff isn't in 'em."

"I never saw much of my grandfather," said Churchill, in his grave quiet voice, which expressed so little emotion, save when deepest passion warmed his spirit to eloquence. "My father's marriage offended him, as I dare say you heard at the time."

Mr. Pergament nodded assent.

"Prejudice, prejudice," he murmured, blandly.

"Elderly gentlemen who live on their estates are prone to that sort of thing."

"He did my mother the honour to call her a shop-keeper's daughter—her father was a brewer at Exeter, in a very fair way of business—upon which my father, who had some self-respect, and a great deal of respect for his wife, told the Squire that he should take care not to intrude the shopkeeper's daughter upon his notice. 'If I hadn't made my will,' said my grandfather, 'it might be the worse for you. But I have made my will, as you all know. I made it six years ago, and I don't mean to budge from it. When I do a thing it's done. When I say a thing it's said. I never undo or unsay. The estate will be kept together, for the next half-century I think, come what may.'"

"Just like him," said Mr. Pergament, chuckling, "The man to the life. How well you hit him off."

"I've heard my father repeat that speech a good many times," answered Churchill.

"Then you never saw the old Squire?"

"Once only. I was a day boy at Westminster, and one afternoon when I was playing ball in the quadrangle, a curious-looking elderly gentleman, with a drab overcoat, and a broad-brimmed white hat, breeches and topboots, a bunch of seals at his fob, and a gold-headed hunting-crop in his hand, came into the court and looked about him. He looked like a figure out of a sporting print. Yet he looked a gentleman all the same. 'Can anybody tell me where to find a boy called Penwyn?' he inquired. I ran forward. 'What, you're Churchill Penwyn, are you, youngster?' he asked, with his hands upon my shoulders, looking at me straight from under his bushy grey eyebrows. 'Yes, you're a genuine Penwyn, none of the brewer here. It's a pity your father was a younger son. You wouldn't have made a bad Squire. I dare say you've heard of your grandfather?' 'Yes, sir, very often,' I said; 'are you he?' 'I am; I'm up in London for a week, and I took it into my head I should like to have a look at you. It isn't likely the estate will ever come to you, but if, by any chance, it should come your way, I hope you'll think of the old Squire sometimes, when he lies under the sod, and try and keep things together, in my way.' He tipped me a five-pound note, shook hands, and walked out of the quad., and that's the only time I ever saw Nicholas Penwyn."

"Curious," said Mr. Pergament.

"By the way, talking of estates, what is Penwyn worth? My inheritance seemed so remote a contingency that I have never taken the trouble to ask the question."

"The estate is a fine one," replied the lawyer, joining the tips of his fat fingers, and speaking with unction, as of a favourite and familiar subject, "but land in Cornwall, as you are doubtless aware, is not the most remunerative investment. The farm lands of Penwyn produce on an average a bare three per cent. on their value, that is to say, about three pounds an acre. There are eleven hundred acres of farm land, and thus we have three thousand three hundred pounds. But," continued the lawyer, swelling with importance, "the more remunerative portion of the estate consists of mines, which after lying idle for more than a quarter of a century, were re-opened at the latter end of the Squire's life, and are now being worked by a company who pay a royalty upon their profits, which royalty in the aggregate amounts to something between two and four thousand a year, and is likely to increase, as they have lately opened a new tin mine, and come upon a promising lode."

"My grandfather risked nothing in the working of these mines, I suppose?"

"No," exclaimed the lawyer, with tremendous emphasis. "Squire Penwyn was much too wise for that. He let other people take the risks, and only stood in for the profits."

They talked about the estate for some little time after this, and then Churchill threw himself back into his corner, opened a newspaper and appeared to read—appeared only, for his eyes were fixed upon one particular bit of the column before him in that steady gaze which betokens deepest thought. In sooth he had enough to think of. The revolution which James Penwyn's death had wrought in his fate was a change to set most men thinking. From a struggling man just beginning to make a little way in an arduous profession, he found himself all at once worth something like seven thousand a year, master of an estate which would bring with it the respect of his fellow-men, position and power—the means of climbing higher than any Penwyn had yet risen on the ladder of life.

"I shall not bury myself alive in a stupid old manor-house," he thought, "like my grandfather. And yet it will be rather a pleasant thing playing at being a country squire."

Most of all he thought of her who was to share

his fortunes—the new bright life they could lead together—of her beauty, which had an imperial grandeur that needed a splendid setting—of her power to charm, which would be an influence to help his aggrandizement. He fancied himself member for Penwyn, making his mark in the House, as he had already begun to make it at the Bar. Literature and statecraft should combine to help him on. He saw himself far away, in the fair prosperous future, leader of his party. He thought that when he first crossed the threshold of the Senate House as a member, he should say to himself, almost involuntarily, "Some day I shall enter this door as Prime Minister."

He was not a man whose desires were bounded by the idea of a handsome house and gardens, a good stable, wine-cellar, and cook. He asked Fortune for something more than these. If not for his own sake, for his betrothed, he would wish to be something more than a prosperous country gentleman. Madge would expect him to be famous. Madge would be disappointed if he failed to make his mark in the world. He fell to calculating how long it would have been in the common course of things, plodding on at literature and his profession, before he could have won a position to justify his marrying Madge Bellingham. Far away to the extreme point in perspective stretched the distance.

He gave a short bitter sigh of very weariness. "It would have been ten or fifteen years before I could have given her as good a home as her father's," he said to himself. "Why fatigue one's brain by such profitless speculations? She would never have been my wife. She is a girl who must have made a great marriage. She might be true as steel, but everybody else would have been against me. Her father and her sister would have worried her almost to death, and some morning while I was marching bravely on towards the distant goal I should have received a letter, tear-blotted, remorseful, telling me that she had yielded to the persuasions of her father, and had consented to marry the millionaire stockbroker, or the wealthy lordling, as the case might be."

"Who is this Mr. Clissold?" Churchill asked by and by, throwing aside his unread paper, and emerging from that brown study in which he had been absorbed for the last hour or so.

"A college friend of poor James's, his senior by some few years. They had been reading together in the north. You must have met Clissold in Axminster Square, I should think, when you dined with your aunt. He and James were inseparable."

"I have some recollection of a tall, dark-browed youth, who seemed one of the family."

"That was young Clissold, no doubt."

"Civil of him to telegraph to me," said Churchill, and there the subject dropped. The two gentlemen yawned a little. Churchill looked out of the window, and relapsed into thoughtfulness, and so the time went on, and the journey came to an end.

Churchill and the lawyer drove straight to the police station, to inquire if the murderer had been found. There they heard what had befallen Maurice Clissold.

"Absurd!" exclaimed the solicitor. "No possible motive."

The official in charge shook his head sagely.

"There appears to have been a quarrel," he said, in his slow ponderous way, "between the two young gents, the night previous. High words was over-'eard at the hinn, and on the night of the murder Mr. Cliss'll was absent, which he is unwilling to account for his time."

Mr. Pergament looked at Churchill, as much as to say, "This is serious."

"Young men do not murder each other on account of a few high words," said Mr. Penwyn. "I dare say Mr. Clissold will give a satisfactory account of himself when the proper time comes. No one in their right senses could suspect a gentleman of such a crime—a common robbery, with violence, on the high road. In the race week, too, when a place is always running over with ruffians of every kind."

"I beg your pardon, sir," said the superintendent, "but that's the curious part of the case. The footsteps of the murderer have been traced. Mr. Penwyn was shot at from behind a hedge, you see, and the print of the sole looks like the print of a gentleman's boot—narrow, and a small heel; nothing of the clodhopper about it. The ground's a bit of marshy clay just there, and the impression was uncommonly clear."

Churchill Penwyn looked at the man thoughtfully for a moment, with that penetrating glance of his which was wont to survey an adverse witness in order to see what might be made of him — the glance of a man familiar with the study of his fellow-men.

"There are vagabonds enough in the world who wear decently made boots," he said, "especially your racing vagabonds."

He made all necessary inquiries about the inquest,

and then adjourned to one of the chief hotels, crowded with racing men, though not to suffocation, as at the Summer Meeting.

"You'll watch the case in the interests of the family, of course," he said to Mr. Pergament. "I should like you to do what you can for this Mr. Clissold, too. There can be no ground for his arrest."

"I should suppose not—he and James were such friends."

"And then the empty purse shows that the murder was done for gain. My cousin may have won money, or have been supposed to have won, on the race-course, and may have been watched and followed by some prowling ruffian—tout, or tramp, or gipsy."

"It's odd that Mr. Clissold refused to account for his time last night."

"Yes, that is curious; but I feel pretty sure the explanation will come when he's pressed."

And then the gentlemen dined together comfortably.

A little later on, Mr. Pergament got up to go out.

"There are the last melancholy details to be arranged," he said; "have you any wish on that point, as his nearest relation?"

"Only that his own wishes should be respected."

"His father and mother are buried at Kensal Green. I dare say he would rather be there than at Penwyn."

"One would suppose so."

"Then I'll go and see about the removal, and so on," said Mr. Pergament, taking up his hat. "By the way—perhaps, before it is too late, you would like to see your cousin?"

Churchill gave a little start, almost a shudder.

"No," he said, "I never went in for that kind of thing."

CHAPTER XI.

"What, then, you knew not this red work indeed?"

JUSTINA lived through the day and acted at night pretty much as she had been accustomed to act; but she saw her audience dimly through a heavy, blinding cloud, and the glare of the footlights seemed to her hideous as the fires of Pandemonium. People spoke to her in the dressing-room where she dragged on her shabby finery, and dabbed a little rouge on her pale, wan face, and she answered them somehow, mechanically. She had lived that kind of life among the same people so long that the mere business of existence went on without any effort of her own. She felt like a clock that had been wound and must go its appointed time. She sat in a corner of the green-room, looking straight before her, and thought how her bright new world had melted away; and no one took any particular notice of her.

Mrs. Dempson had been kind and compassionate, and, after Justina's fainting fit, had dabbed her forehead with vinegar and water, and sat with her arm round the girl's waist, consoling her and reasoning with her, reminding her that they had only known poor Mr. Penwyn a day and a half, and that it was against nature to lament him as if he had been a near relation or an old friend. Who, in sober middle age, when the sordid cares of every-day life are paramount; who, when youth's morning is past, can comprehend the young heart's passionate mystery—the love which, like some bright tropical flower, buds and blooms in a single day—the love which is more than half fancy—the love of a lover of no common clay, but the fair incarnation of girlhood's poetic dream—love wherein the senses have no more part than the phosphor lights of a rank marsh in the clear splendour of the stars?

Justina kept the secret of her brief dream. She thought Mrs. Dempson, and even her father, would have laughed her to scorn had she told them that the generous young stranger had asked her to be his wife. She held her peace, and shut herself in her garret chamber, and flung her weary head face downward on the flock pillow, and thought of her murdered lover—thought of the bright, handsome face fixed in death's marble stillness, and cursed the wretch who had slain him.

Mr. Elgood and his daughter were both subpœnaed for the adjourned inquest. The actor, who rather rejoiced in the opportunity of exhibiting his powers in a new arena, and seeing his name in the papers, appeared in grand form on the morning of the examination. He had brushed his coat, sported a clean white waistcoat and a smart blue necktie, wore a pair of somewhat ancient buff leather gloves, and carried the cane which he was wont to flourish as the exasperated father of old-fashioned comedy.

Justina entered the room pale as a sheet, and sat by her father's side, with her large dark eyes fixed on the coroner, as if from his lips could issue the secret of her lover's doom. She had the most imperfect idea of the nature of an inquest, and the coroner's power.

The jury were seated round the coroner at the upper end of the room. Mr. Pergament, the solicitor, stood at the end of the table ready to put any questions he might desire to have answered by the witnesses.

On the right of the coroner, a little way from the jury, sat Maurice Clissold, with a constable at his side. Nearly opposite him, and next to the lawyer, stood the new master of Penwyn Manor, ready to prompt a question if he saw his solicitor at fault. Churchill and Mr. Pergament had gone into the case thoroughly together, with the Spinnersbury detectives and the local constabulary, and had their facts pretty well in hand.

The jury answered to their names, and the inquiry began, Mr. Pergament interrogating, the coroner taking notes of the evidence. Mr. Elgood was one of the first witnesses sworn.

"I believe you were in the company of the deceased on the night, or rather morning, of the murder?" said the coroner.

"Yes, he supped at my lodging on that night."

"Alone with you?"

"No. Mr. Dempson and his wife, and my daughter were of the party."

"At what hour did Mr. Penwyn leave you?"

The actor's countenance assumed a look of perplexity.

"It was half-past twelve before we sat down to supper," he said, "but I can't exactly say how long we sat afterwards. We smoked a few cigars, and, to be candid, were somewhat convivial. I haven't any clear idea as to the time; my daughter may know."

"Why your daughter, and not you?"

"She let him out through the shop when he went away. Our apartments are respectable but humble, over a chandler's."

"And your daughter was more temperate than you, and may have some idea as to the time? We'll ask her the question presently. Do you know if Mr. Penwyn had any considerable sum of money about him at the time he left you?"

"I don't know. He had entertained us handsomely at the 'Waterfowl' on the previous night, and he stood a carriage and any quantity of champagne to the races that day, but I did not see him pay away any money except for the standing-place for his carriage."

"Did you see him receive any money on the racecourse?"

"No."

"Was he with you all day?"

"From twelve o'clock till half-past six in the evening."

"And in that time you had no knowledge of his winning or receiving any sum of money?"

"No."

"Do you know of his being associated with disreputable people of any kind—betting men, for instance?"

"I know next to nothing of his associations. There was an old gipsy woman who pretended to tell his fortune by the river side the day before the races, when he and the rest of us happened to be walking together.

He gave her money then, and he gave her money on the race day, when she was hanging about the carriage, begging for drink."

Churchill Penwyn, who had been looking at the ground, in a listening attitude hitherto, raised his eyes at this juncture, half in interrogation, half in surprise.

"Is that all you know about the deceased?" continued Mr. Pergament.

"About all. I had only enjoyed his acquaintance six-and-thirty hours at the time of the murder."

"You can sit down," said Mr. Pergament.

"Justina Elgood," cried the summoning officer, and Justina stood up in the crowded room, pale to the lips, but unfaltering.

Again Churchill Penwyn raised those thoughtful eyes of his, and looked at the girl's pallid face.

"Not a common type of girl," he said to himself.

CHAPTER XII.

"Brave spirits are a balsam to themselves."

MAURICE CLISSOLD also looked at the girl as she stood up at the end of the table in the little bit of clear space left for the witnesses. A shaft of sunshine slanted from the skylight. The room was built out from the house, and lighted from the top, an apartment usually devoted to Masonic meetings and public dinners. In that clear radiance the girl's face was wondrously spiritualized. Easy to fancy that some being not quite of this common earth stood there, and that from those pale lips the awful truth would speak as if by the voice of revelation.

So Maurice Clissold thought as he looked at her. Never till this moment had she appeared to him beautiful; and now it was no common beauty which he beheld in her, but a strange and spiritual charm impossible of definition.

"You were the last person who saw Mr. Penwyn alive, except his murderer?" said Mr. Pergament, interrogatively, after the usual formula had been gone through.

"I opened the shop door for him when he went out, after supper."

"At what o'clock?"

"Half-past two."

"Was he perfectly sober at that time?"

"Oh yes," with an indignant look.

"Was he going back to the 'Waterfowl' alone?"

"Quite alone."

"Did he say anything particular to you just at last?—anything that it might be important for us to know?"

A faint colour flushed the pale face at the question.

"Nothing."

"Is that all you can tell us?"

"There is only one thing more," the girl answered, calmly. "I stood at the door a few minutes to watch Mr. Penwyn walking up the street, and just as he turned the corner a man passed on the opposite side of the way in the same direction."

"Towards Lowgate?"

"Yes."

"What kind of a man?"

"He was rather tall, and wore an overcoat, and a thick scarf around his neck, as if it had been winter."

"Did you see his face?"

"No."

"Or notice anything else about him—anything besides the overcoat and the muffler?"

"Nothing."

"You say he was tall. Was he as tall as that gentleman, do you suppose?—Stand up for a moment, if you please, Mr. Clissold."

Clissold stood up. He was above the average height of tall men, well over six feet.

"No, he was not so tall as that."

"Are you sure of that? A man would look taller in this room than in the street. Do you allow for that difference?" inquired Mr. Pergament.

"I do not believe that the man I saw that night

was so tall as Mr. Clissold, nor so broad across the shoulders."

"That will do."

The chief constable next gave evidence as to the finding of the body, the watch buried in the ditch, the empty purse. Then came the landlady of the "Waterfowl," with an account of the high words between the two gentlemen, and Mr. Clissold's abrupt departure on the following morning. The Spinnersbury detectives followed, and described Mr. Clissold's arrest, the tracing of footsteps behind the hedge and down to the towpath, and how they had compared Mr. Clissold's boot with the footprints without being able to arrive at any positive conclusion.

"It might very easily be the print of the same foot in a different boot," said Higlett. "It isn't so much the difference between the size of the feet as the shape and cut of the boot. The man must have been tall, the length of his stride shows that."

There was no further evidence. The coroner addressed the jury.

After a few minutes' consultation they returned their verdict,—"That the deceased had been murdered by some person or persons unknown."

Thus Maurice Clissold found himself a free man again, but with the uncomfortable feeling of having been, for a few days, supposed the murderer of his bosom friend. It seemed to him that a stigma would attach to his name henceforward. He would be spoken of as the man who had been suspected, and who was in all probability guilty, but who had been let slip because the chain of evidence was not quite strong enough to hang him.

"I suppose if I had been tried in Scotland the verdict would have been 'Non Proven,'" he thought.

One only means of self-justification remained open to him, viz., to find the real murderer. He fancied that Higlett and Smelt looked at him with unfriendly eyes. They were aggravated by the loss of the reward. They would turn their attention in a new direction, no doubt, but considerable time had been lost while they were on a wrong scent.

Maurice Clissold could not quite make up his mind about those Bohemians of the Eborsham Theatre; whether this vagabond heavy father might not know something more than he cared to reveal about James Penwyn's fate. He had given his evidence with a sufficiently straightforward air, and the girl was above doubt. Truth was stamped on the pale sorrowful face,—truth, and a silent grief. Could that grief have its root in some fatal secret? Did she know her father guilty of this crime, and shield him with heroic falsehoods, only less sublime than truth?

She stood by her father's side, a little way apart from the crowd, as she had stood throughout the inquiry, intently watchful.

While Maurice lingered, debating whether he should follow up the strolling players, Churchill Penwyn came straight across the room towards him, before the undispersed assembly.

"I congratulate you on your release, Mr. Clissold," he said, offering his hand with a friendly air, "and permit me to assure you that I, for one, have been fully assured of your innocence throughout this melancholy business."

"I thank you for doing me justice, Mr. Penwyn.

I was very fond of your cousin. I liked him as well as if he had been my brother, and if the question had been put to me whether harm should come to him or me, I believe I should have chosen the evil lot for myself. His mother was a second mother to me, God bless her. She asked me to take care of him a few hours before her death, and I felt from that time as if I were responsible for his future. He was little more than a boy when his poor mother died. He was little more than a boy the last time I saw him alive, the night we had our first quarrel."

"What was the quarrel about?"

Mr. Clissold shrugged his shoulders, and glanced round the room, which was clearing by degrees, but not yet empty.

"It's too long a story to enter upon here," he said.

"Come and dine with me at the 'Castle,' at eight o'clock, and tell me all about it," said Churchill.

"You're very good. No. I can't manage that. I have something to do."

"What is that?"

"To begin a business that may take a long time to finish."

"May I ask the nature of that business?"

"I want to find James Penwyn's murderer."

Churchill shrugged his shoulders and smiled—a half compassionate smile.

"My dear sir," he said, "do you think that the murderer is ever found in such a case as this—given a delay of three days and nights—ample time for him to ship himself for any port in the known world? A low, clodhopping assassin, no doubt, in no way distinguishable from other clodhoppers. Find him! did you say? I can conceive no endeavour more hopeless. It is the fashion to rail at our police because they find it a little difficult to put their hands upon every delinquent who may be wanted, but it is hardly the simplest business in the world, to pick the right man out of ten or fifteen millions."

Maurice Clissold heard him with a troubled look and short impatient sigh.

"I dare say you are right," he said, "but I shall do my best to unravel the mystery, even if I am doomed to fail."

He asked some questions about his friend's funeral. It was to be at three o'clock on the following day, and Churchill was going back to London by an early train in order to attend as chief mourner.

"I shall be there," said Maurice Clissold, and they parted with a friendly hand-shake.

Clissold was touched by Mr. Penwyn's friendliness. That stigma of *non proven* had not affected Churchill's opinion at any rate.

He followed Matthew Elgood and his daughter into the street, and joined them as they walked slowly homeward, the girl's face half hidden by her veil.

"I want to have a talk with you, Mr. Elgood, if you've no objection," said Maurice. "Unless you consider me tainted by the suspicion that has hung over me for the last three days, and object to hold any intercourse with me."

"No, sir, I suspect no man," answered the actor, with dignity. "Although you were pleased to object to your lamented friend's inclination for my society I bear no malice, and I do you the justice to believe you had no part in his untimely end."

"I thank you, Mr. Elgood, for your confidence. Since I have been in that abominable gaol I feel as if there were some odour of felony hanging about me. With regard to the objections of which you speak, I can assure you that they were founded upon no personal dislike, but upon prudential reasons, which I need not enlarge upon."

"Enough, Mr. Clissold, it boots not now! If you will follow to our humble abode, and share the meal our modest means provide, I will enlighten you upon this theme, so far as my scant knowledge serve withal," said the actor, unconsciously lapsing into blank verse.

Maurice accepted the invitation. He had a curious desire to see more of that girl, whose pale face had assumed a kind of sublimity just now in the crowded court. Could she really have cared for his murdered friend? She, who had but known him two days? Or was there some dark secret which moved her thus deeply? The man seemed frank and open enough. Hard to believe that villainy lurked beneath the Bohemian's rough kindliness.

They went straight to the lodging in the narrow street leading down to the river. Here all seemed comfortable enough. The evening meal, half tea, half dinner, was ready laid when Mr. Elgood and his visitor went in, and Mr. and Mrs. Dempson were waiting with some impatience for their refreshment. They looked somewhat surprised at the appearance of Clissold, and Mrs. Dempson returned his greeting with a certain stiffness. "It isn't the pleasantest thing in the world to sit down to table with a suspected murderer," she remarked afterwards, to which Justina replied, with a sudden flash of anger, "Do you suppose I would sit in the same room with him if I thought him guilty?"

The low comedian took things more easily than his wife.

"Well, Mat," he said, "I thought you were never coming. I've been down at the 'Arms,' and heard the inquest. Glad to see you at liberty again, Mr. Clissold. A most preposterous business, your arrest. I heard all the evidence. I think those Spinnersbury detectives ought to get it hot. I dare say the press will slang 'em pretty tolerably. Well done, Judy!" he went on, with a friendly slap on Justina's shoulder, "you spoke up like a good one. If you spoke as well as that on the stage, you'd soon be fit for the juvenile lead!"

Justina spoke no word, but took her place quietly at the table, where Mrs. Dempson was pouring out the tea, while Mr. Elgood dispensed a juicy rump-steak.

"I went to the butcher's for it myself," he said. "There's nothing like personal influence in these things. They wouldn't dare give me a slice off some superannuated cow. They know when they've got to deal with a judge. 'That's beef,' said the butcher, as he slapped his knife across the loin, and beef it is. Do you like it with the gravy in it, Mr. Clissold?"

There was a dish of steaming potatoes, and a bowl of lettuces, which greenstuff Mrs. Dempson champed as industriously as if she had been a blood relation of Nebuchadnezzar's.

Never had Maurice Clissold seen any one so silent

or so self-sustained as this pale, thin, shadowy-looking girl, whom her friends called Judy. She interested him strangely, and he did sorry justice to Mr. Elgood's ideal steak, while watching her. She herself hardly eat anything; but the others were too deeply absorbed in their own meal to be concerned about her. She sat by her father, and drank a little tea, sat motionless for the most part, with her dark thoughtful eyes looking far away, looking into some world that was not for the rest.

So soon as the pangs of hunger were appeased, and the pleasures of the table in some measure exhausted, Mr. Elgood became loquacious again. He gave a detailed description of that last day on the racecourse—the supper—all that James Penwyn had said or done within his knowledge. And then came a discussion as to who could have done the deed.

"He was in the theatre all the evening, you say," said Maurice. "Is it possible that any of the scene-shifters, or workmen of any kind, may have observed him—seen him open a well-filled purse, perhaps—and followed him after he left this house? It was one of his foolish habits to carry too much money about him—from twenty to fifty pounds, for instance. He used to say it was a bore to sit down and write a cheque for every trifle he wanted. And of course, in our travels, ready money was a necessity. Could it have been one of your people, do you think?"

"No, sir," replied Mr. Elgood. "The stage has contributed nothing to the records of crime. From the highest genius who has ever adorned the drama to the lowest functionary employed in the working of its machinery, there has been no such thing as a felon."

"I am glad to hear you say so, Mr. Elgood; yet it is clear to me that this crime must have been committed by some one who watched and followed my poor friend—some one who knew enough of him to know that he had money about him."

"I grant you, sir," replied the actor.

It was now time for these Thespians to repair to the theatre, all but Justina, who, for a wonder, was not in the first piece. Maurice took notice of this fact, and after walking to the theatre with Mr. Elgood, went back to that gentleman's lodgings to have a few words alone with his daughter.

He passed through the shop unchallenged, visitors for the lodgers being accustomed to pass in and out in a free and easy manner. He went quietly upstairs. The sitting-room door stood ajar. He pushed it open, and went in.

CHAPTER XIII.

"My love, my love, and no love for me."

Justina was leaning before an old easy chair, her face buried in the faded chintz cushion, sobbing vehemently—curiously changed from the silent, impassible being Maurice had taken leave of ten minutes earlier. The sight of her sorrow touched him. Whatever it meant, this was real grief at any rate.

"Forgive me for this intrusion, Miss Elgood," he said, gently, remaining near the door lest he should startle her by his abrupt approach. "I am very anxious to talk to you alone, and ventured to return."

She started up, hastily wiping away her tears.

"I am sorry to see you in such deep grief," he said. "You must have a tender heart to feel my poor friend's sad fate so acutely."

The pallid face crimsoned, as if this had been a reproof.

"I have no right to be so sorry, I dare say," faltered Justina, "but he was very kind to me—kinder than any one ever was before,—and it is hard that he should be taken away so cruelly, just when life seemed to be all new and different because of his goodness."

"Poor child. You must have a grateful nature."

"I am grateful to *him.*"

"I can understand that just at first you may feel his death as if it were a personal loss, but that cannot last long. You had known him so short a time.

Granted that he admired you, and paid you pretty compliments and attentions which may be new to one so young. If he had lived to bid you good-bye tomorrow, and pass on his way, you would hardly have remembered him a week."

"I should have remembered him all my life," said Justina, firmly.

"He had made a deep impression upon your mind or your fancy, then, in those two days."

"He loved me," the girl answered, with a little burst of passion, "and I gave him back love for love with all my heart, with all my strength, as they tell us we ought to love God. Why do you come here to torment me about him? You cannot bring him back to life. God will not. I would spend all my life upon my knees if he could be raised up again, like Lazarus! I meant never to have spoken of this. I have kept it even from my father. He told me that he loved me, and that I was to be his wife, and that all our lives to come were to be spent together. Think what it is to have been so happy and to have lost all."

"Poor child," repeated Clissold, laying his hand gently, as priest or father might have laid it, on the soft brown hair, thrust back in a tangled mass from the hot brow. "Poor children, children both. It would have been a foolish marriage at best, my dear girl, if he had lived, and kept in the same mind. Unequal marriages bring remorse and misery for the most part. James Penwyn was not a hard-working wayfarer like me, who may choose my wife at any turn on the world's high road. He was the owner of a good old estate, and the happiness of his future depended on his making a suitable marriage. His wife must have been somebody before she was his wife. She must have had her own race to refer to, something to boast of on her own side, so that when their children grew up they should be able to give a satisfactory account of their maternal uncles and aunts. I dare say you think me worldly-minded, poor child; but I am only worldly-wise. If it were a question of personal merit you might have made the best of wives."

The girl heard this long speech with an absent air, her tearful eyes fixed on vacancy, her restless hands clasped tightly, as if she would fain have restrained her grief by that muscular grip.

"I don't know whether it was wise or foolish," she said, "but I know we loved each other."

"I loved him too, Justina," said Maurice, using her Christian name involuntarily—she was not the kind of person to be called Miss Elgood—"as well as one man can love another. I take his death quietly enough, you see, but I would give ten years of my life to find his murderer."

"I would give all my life," said Justina, with a look that made him think she would verily have done it.

"You know nothing more than you told at the inquest this afternoon?—nothing that could throw any light upon his death?"

"Nothing. You ought to know much more about it than I."

"How so?"

"You know all that went before that time—his circumstances—his associates. I have lain awake thinking of this thing from night till morning, until I believe that every idea that could be thought about it has come into my head. There must have been some motive for his murder."

"The motive seems obvious enough,—highway robbery."

"Yet his watch was found in the ditch."

"His murderer may naturally have feared to take anything likely to lead to detection. His money was taken."

"Yes. It may have been for that. Yet it seems strange that he should have been chosen out of so many—that he should have been the only victim—murdered for the sake of a few pounds."

"Unhappily, sordid as the motive is, that is a common kind of murder," replied Maurice.

"But might not some one have a stronger motive than that?"

"I can imagine none. James never in his life made an enemy."

"Are you quite sure of that?"

"As sure as I can be of anything about a young man whom I knew as well as if he had been my brother," replied Maurice, wondering at the girl's calm clear tone. At this moment she seemed older than her years—his equal, or more than his equal in shrewdness and judgment.

"Is there any one who would be a gainer by his death?" she asked.

"Naturally. The next heir to the Penwyn estate is a very considerable gainer. For him James Penwyn's death means the difference between a hard-working life like mine and a splendid future."

"Could he have anything to do with the crime?"

"He! Churchill Penwyn? Well, no; it would be about as hard to suspect him as it was to suspect me. Churchill Penwyn is a gentleman, and, I conclude, a man of honour. His conduct towards me to-day showed him a man of kind feeling."

"No. I suppose gentlemen do not commit such crimes," mused Justina. "And we shall never know who killed him. That seems hardest of all. That bright young life taken, and the wretch who took it left to go free."

Tears filled her eyes as she turned away from Clissold, ashamed of her grief; tears which should have been shed in secret, but which she could not keep back when she thought of her young lover's doom.

Clissold tried too soothe her, assured her of his friendship—his help should she ever need it.

"I shall always be interested in you," he said. "I shall think of you as my poor lad's first and last love. He had had his foolish, boyish flirtations before; but I have reason to know that he never asked any other woman to be his wife; and he was too staunch and true to make such an offer unless he meant it."

Justina gave him a grateful look. It was the first time he had seen her face light up with anything like pleasure that day.

"You do believe that he loved me, then?" she exclaimed, eagerly. "It was not all my own foolish dream. He was not"—the next words came slowly, as if it hurt her to speak them—"amusing himself at my expense."

"I have no doubt of his truth. I never knew him

tell a lie. I do not say that his fancy would have lasted—it may have been too ardent, too sudden, to stand wear and tear. But be assured for the moment he was true—would have wrecked his life, perhaps, to keep true to the love of a day."

This time the girl looked at him angrily.

"Why do you tell me he must have changed if God had spared him?" she added. "Why do you find it so hard to imagine that he might have gone on loving me? Am I so degraded a creature in your eyes?"

"I am quite ready to believe that you are a very noble girl," answered Maurice, "worthy a better lover than my poor friend. But you are Miss Elgood, of the Theatre Royal, Eborsham, and he was Squire Penwyn, of Penwyn. Time would not have changed those two facts, and might have altered his way of looking at them."

"Don't tell me that he would have changed," she cried, passionately. "Let me think that I have lost all—love, happiness, home, wealth, all that any woman ever hoped to win. It cannot add to my grief for him. It would not take away from my love for him even to know that he was fickle, and would have grown tired of me. Those two days were the only happy days of my life. They will dwell in my mind for ever, a changeless memory. I shall never see the sunshine without thinking how it shone once upon us two on Eborsham racecourse. I shall never see the moonlight without remembering how we two sat side by side watching the willow branches dipping into the river."

"A childish love," thought Maurice; "a young

heart's first fancy! a fabric that would wear out in six months or so."

"Happy days will come again," he said, gently. "You will go on acting, and succeed in your profession. You are just the kind of girl to whom genius will come in a flash—like inspiration. You will succeed and be famous by and by, and look back with a sad, pitying smile at James Penwyn's love, and say to yourself with a half-regretful sigh, 'That was youth!' You will be loved some day by a man who will prove to you that true love is not the growth of a few summer hours."

"I should like to be famous some day," the girl answered, proudly, "just to show you that I might have been worthy of your friend's love."

"I fear I have offended you by my plain speaking, Miss Elgood," returned Maurice, "but if ever you need a friend, and will honour me with your confidence, you shall not find me unworthy of your trust. I have not a very important position in the world; but I am a gentleman by birth and education, and not wanting in some of those commonplace qualities which help a man on the road of life; such as patience and perseverance, industry and strength of purpose. I have chosen literature as my profession; for that calling gives me the privilege I should be least inclined to forego, liberty. My income is happily just large enough to make me independent of earning, so that I can afford to write as the birds sing—without cutting my coat according to any other man's cloth. If ever you and your father are in London, Miss Elgood, and inclined to test my sincerity, you may find me at this address."

He gave Justina his card—

> MR. MAURICE CLISSOLD,
> Hogarth Place,
> Bloomsbury.

"Not a fashionable locality, by any means," he said, "but central, and near the British Museum where I generally spend my mornings when I am in London."

Justina took the card listlessly enough, not as if she had any intention of taxing Mr. Clissold's friendship in the future. He saw how far her thoughts were from him, and from all common things. She rose with a startled look as the cathedral clock chimed the three-quarters after seven.

"I shall be late for the piece," she exclaimed with alarm; "I forget everything."

"It is my fault for detaining you," said Maurice, concerned to see her look of distress. "Let me walk to the theatre with you."

"But I've some things to carry," she answered, hurriedly rolling up some finery which had bestrewed a side table—veil, shoes, ribbons, feathers, a dilapidated fan.

"I am not afraid of carrying a parcel."

They went out together, Justina breathless, and hurried to the stage door.

Maurice penetrated some dark passages, and stumbled up some break-neck stairs, in his anxiety to learn if his companion were really late. The band was grinding away at an overture. The second piece had not begun.

"Is it all right?" asked Maurice, just as the light figure that had sped on before him was disappearing behind a dusky door.

"Yes," cried Justina, "I don't go on till the second scene. I shall have just time to dress."

So Mr. Clissold groped his way to the outer air, relieved in mind.

It was a still summer evening, and this part of the city had a quiet, forgotten air, as of a spot from which busy life had drifted away. The theatre did not create any circle of animation and bustle in these degenerate days, and seen from the outside might have been mistaken for a chapel. There were a few small boys hanging about near the stage door as Mr. Clissold emerged, and these, he perceived, looked at him with interest and spoke to one another about him. He was evidently known, even to these street boys, as the man who had been suspected of his friend's murder.

He walked round to the quiet little square in front of the theatre, lighted his pipe, and took a turn up and down the empty pavement, meditating what he should do with himself for the rest of the evening.

Last night he had slept placidly enough in the mediæval jail, worn out with saddest thoughts. To-night there was nothing for him to do but go back to the "Waterfowl," where the rooms would seem haunted —put his few belongings together, and get ready for going back to London. His holiday was over, and how sad the end!

He had been very fond of James Penwyn. Only

now, when they two were parted for ever, did he know how strong that attachment had been.

The bright young face, the fresh, gay voice, all gone!

"I am not quick at making friendships," thought Maurice. "I feel as if his death had left me alone in the world."

His life had been unusually lonely, save for this one strong friendship. He had lost his father in childhood, and his mother a few years later. Happily Captain Clissold, although a younger son, had inherited a small estate in Devonshire, from his mother. This gave his orphan son four hundred a year—an income which permitted his education at Eton and Oxford, and which made him thoroughly independent as a young man, to whom the idea of matrimony and its obligations seemed far off.

His uncle, Sir Henry Clissold, was a gentleman of some standing in the political world, a county member, a man who was chairman of innumerable committees, and never had a leisure moment. This gentleman's ideas of the fitness of things were outraged by his nephew's refusal to adopt any profession.

"I could have pushed you forward in almost any career you had chosen," he said, indignantly. "I have friends I can command in all the professions; or if you had cared to go to India, you might have been a judge in the Sudder before you were five-and-thirty."

"Thanks, my dear uncle, I shouldn't care about being broiled alive, or having to learn from twenty to thirty dialects before I could understand plaintiff or defendant," Maurice replied, coolly. "Give me my crust of bread and liberty."

"Fortunate for you that you have your crust of bread," growled Sir Henry, "but at the rate you are going you will never provide yourself with a slice of world cheese."

To-night, perhaps for the first time, Maurice Clissold felt that life was a mistake. His friend and comrade had been more necessary to him than he could have believed, for he had never quite accepted James as his equal in intellect. He had had his own world of thought, which the careless lad never entered. But now that the boy was gone he felt that shadowy darkened by his loss.

"Would to Heaven I could stand face to face with his murderer!" he said to himself; "one of us two should go down, never to rise again!"

CHAPTER XIV.

"Truth is truth, to the end of time."

Mr. Pergament went back to London by a train which left Eborsham at half-past five in the afternoon, half an hour after the termination of the inquest. Churchill went to the station with his solicitor, saw him into the railway carriage, and only left the platform when the train had carried Mr. Pergament away on his road to London. It was an understood thing that Pergament and Pergament were to keep the Penwyn estate in their hands, and that Churchill's interests were henceforward to be their interests. To Pergament and Pergament, indeed, it was as if James Penwyn had never existed, so completely did they transfer their allegiance to his successor.

Churchill walked slowly away from the station, seemingly somewhat at a loss how to dispose of his time. He might have gone back to London with Mr. Pergament, certainly, for he had no further business in the city of Eborsham. But for some sufficient reason of his own he had chosen to remain, although he was not a little anxious to see Madge Bellingham, whom he had not met since the change in his fortunes. He had written to her before he left London, to announce that fact—but briefly—feeling that any expression of pleasure in the altered circumstances of his life would show badly in black and white. He had expressed himself properly grieved at his cousin's sad death, but had affected no exaggerated affliction. Those clear dark eyes of Madge's seemed to be looking through him as he wrote.

"I wonder if it is possible to keep a secret from her?" he thought. "She has a look that pierces my soul—such utter truthfulness."

He had ordered his dinner for eight, and it was not yet six, so he had ample leisure for loitering. He went back to Lowgate and out through the bar to the dull, quiet road where James met his death. Churchill Penwyn wanted to see the spot where the murder had been committed.

He had heard it described so often that it was easy enough for him to find it. A few ragged bushes of elder and blackberry divided the low marshy ground from the road just at this point. From behind these bushes the murderer had taken his aim,—at least that was the theory of the police. Between the road and the river the herbage was sour and scant, and the cattle that browsed thereon had a solitary and dejected look, as if they knew they were shut out from the good things of this life. They seemed to be the odds and ends of the animal creation, and to have come there accidentally. A misanthropical donkey, a lean cow or two, some gaunt, ragged-looking horses, a bony pig, scattered wide apart over the narrow tract of sward along the low bank of the river.

Mr. Penwyn contemplated the spot thoughtfully for a little while, as if he would fain have made out something which the police had failed to discover, and then strolled across the grass to the river-bank. The gloomy solitude of the scene seemed to please him,

"TRUTH IS TRUTH, TO THE END OF TIME." 155

for he walked on for some distance, meditative and even moody. Fortune brings its own responsibilities; and a man who finds himself suddenly exalted from poverty to wealth is not always gay.

He was strolling quietly along the bank, his eyes bent upon the river, with that dreaming gaze which sees not the thing it seems to contemplate, when he was startled from his reverie by the sound of voices near at hand, and looking away from the water perceived that he had stumbled on a gipsy encampment. There were the low arched tents—mere kennels under canvas, where the dusky tribe burrowed at night or in foul weather—the wood fire—the ever-simmering pot —the litter of ashes, and dirty straw, and bones, and a broken bottle or two—the sinister-browed vagabond lying on his stomach like the serpent, smoking his grimy pipe, and scowling at any chance passer by— the half-naked children playing among the rubbish, the women sitting on the ground plaiting rushes into a door-mat. All these Churchill's eye took in at a glance—something more, too, perhaps, for he looked at one of the women curiously for a moment, and slackened his leisurely pace.

She put down her mat, rose, and walked beside him.

"Let me tell your fortune, pretty gentleman," she began, with the same professional sing-song in which she had addressed James Penwyn a few days before. It was the same woman who stopped the late Squire of Penwyn lower down the river bank.

"I don't want my fortune told, thank you. I know what it is pretty well," replied Churchill, in his calm, cold voice.

"Don't say that, pretty gentleman. No one can look into the urn of fate."

"And yet you and your tribe pretend to do it," said Churchill.

"We study the stars more than others do, and learn to read 'em, my noble gentleman. I've read something in the stars about you since the night your cousin was murdered."

"And pray what do the stars say of me?" inquired Churchill, with a scornful laugh.

"They say that you're a kind-hearted gentleman at bottom, and will befriend a poor gipsy."

"I'm afraid they're out in their reckoning, for once in a way. Perhaps it was Mercury you got the information from. He's a notorious trickster. And now, pray, my good woman," turning to see that they were beyond ken of the rest, "what did you mean by sending me a letter to say you could tell me something about my cousin's death? If you really have any information to give, your wisest course is to carry it directly to the police; and if your information should lead to the discovery of the murderer, you may earn a reward that will provide for you for the rest of your life."

His eyes were on the woman's face as he spoke, with that intent look with which he was accustomed to read the human countenance.

"I've thought of that," answered the gipsy, "and I was very near going and telling all I knew to the police the morning after the murder, but I changed my mind about it when I heard you were here; I thought it might be better for me to see you first."

"I can't quite fathom your motive. However, as

I am willing to give two hundred pounds reward for such information as may lead to the apprehension and conviction of the murderer, you may have come to the right person in coming to me; only, I tell you frankly, that, deeply as I am interested in the punishment of my cousin's assassin, I had rather not be troubled about details. I won't even ask the nature of your information. Take my advice, my good soul, and carry it to the police. They are the people to profit by it; they are the people to act upon it."

"Yes, and cheat me of the reward after all, choke me off with a five-pound note, perhaps. I know too much of the police to be over-inclined to trust 'em."

"Is your information conclusive?" asked Churchill; "certain to lead to the conviction of the murderer?"

"I won't say so much as that, but I know it's worth hearing, and worth paying for."

"You may as well tell me all about it, if you don't like to tell the police."

"What, without being paid for my secret? No, my pretty gentleman, I'm not such a fool as that."

"Come," said Churchill, with a laugh, "what does your knowledge amount to? Nothing, I dare say, that every one else in Eborsham doesn't share. You know that my cousin has been murdered, and that I am anxious to find the murderer."

"I know more than that, my noble gentleman."

"What then?"

"I know who did it."

Churchill turned his quick glance upon her again, searching, incredulous, derisive.

"Come," he said, "you don't expect to make me

believe that you know the criminal, and let him slip, and lose your chance of the reward? You are not that kind of woman."

"I don't say that I've let him slip, or lost my chance of profiting by what I know. Suppose the criminal was some one I'm interested in—some one I shouldn't like to see come to harm?"

"In that case you shouldn't come to me about it. You don't imagine that I am going to condone my cousin's murder? But I believe your story is all a fable."

"It's as true as the planets. We have been encamped here for the last week, and on the night of the murder we'd all been at the races. Folks are always kind to gipsies upon a racecourse, and there was plenty to eat and drink for all of us—perhaps a little too much drink,—and when the races were over I fell asleep in one of the booths, among some straw in a corner where no one took any notice of me. My son Reuben—him, as you saw yonder just now—was in the town, up to very little good, I dare say, and left me to take care of myself; and when I woke it was late at night, and the place was all dark and quiet. I didn't know how late it was till I came through the town and found all the lights out, and the streets empty, and heard the cathedral clock strike two. I walked slow, and the clock had struck the half-hour before I got through the Bar. I was dead tired standing and walking about the racecourse all day, and as I came along this road I saw some one walking a little way ahead of me. He walked on, and I walked after him, keeping on the other side of the way, and in the shadow of the hedge about a hundred yards behind him, and all at once I heard a shot fired, and saw him drop down. There was no one to give the alarm to, and no good in giving it if he was dead. I kept on in the shadow till I came nearly opposite where he lay, and then I slipped down into the ditch. There was no water in it, nothing but mud and slime and duckweed, and such like; and I squatted there in the shadow and watched."

"Like some toad in its hole," said Churchill. "Common humanity would have urged you to try to help the fallen man."

"He was past help, kind gentleman. He dropped without a groan, never so much as moaned as he lay there. And it was wiser for me to watch the murderer so as to be able to bear witness against him, when the right time came, than to scare him away by skreeking out like a raven."

"Well, woman, you watched and saw—what?"

"I saw a man stooping over the murdered gentleman; a tall man in a loose overcoat, with a scarf muffled round his neck. He put his hand in the other one's bosom, to feel if his heart had left off beating, I suppose, and drew it out again bloody. I could see that, even in the dim light betwixt night and morning, for I've something of a cat's eye, your honour, and am pretty well used to seeing in the dark. Candles ain't over plentiful with our people. He held up his hand dripping with blood, and pulled a white handkerchief out of his pocket with the other hand to wipe the blood off."

Churchill turned and looked her in the face, for the first time since she had begun her narrative.

"Come," he said, "you're overdoing the details.

Your story would sound more like truth if it were less elaborate."

"I can't help the sound of it, sir. There's not a word I'm saying that I wouldn't swear by, to-morrow, in a court of justice."

"You've kept your evidence back too long, I'm afraid. You ought to have given this information at the inquest. A jury would hardly believe your story now."

"What, not if I had proof of what I say?"

"What proof, woman?"

"The handkerchief with which the murderer wiped those blood-stains off his hands!"

"Pshaw!" exclaimed Churchill, contemptuously. "There are a hundred ways in which you might come possessed of a man's handkerchief. Your tribe lives by such petty plunder. Do you suppose that you, a gipsy and a vagabond, would ever persuade a British jury to believe your evidence, against a gentleman?"

"What!" cried the woman eagerly, "then you know it was a gentleman who murdered your cousin?"

"Didn't you say so just this minute?"

"Not I, my noble gentleman. I told you he was tall, and wore an overcoat. That's all I told you about him."

"Well, what next?"

"He wiped the blood off his hand, then put the handkerchief back in his pocket, as he thought; but I suppose he wasn't quite used to the work he was doing, for in his confusion he missed the pocket and let the handkerchief fall into the road. I didn't give him time to find out his mistake, for while he was stooping over the dead man, emptying his pockets, I crept across the road, got hold of the handkerchief, and slipped back to my hiding-place in the ditch again. I'm light of foot, you see, your honour, though an old woman."

"What next?"

"He opened the dead man's purse, emptied it, and put the contents in his own waistcoat pocket. Then he crammed watch and purse down into the ditch— the same ditch where I was hiding, but a little way off,—took a stick which he had broken off the hedge, and thrust it down into the mud under the weeds, making sure, I suppose, that no one could ever find it there. When he had done this, he pulled himself together, as you may say, and hurried off as fast as he could go, panting like a hunted deer, across the swampy ground and towards the river, where they found his footsteps afterwards. I think it would have been cleverer of him if he'd left his victim's pockets alone, and let those that found the body rob it, as they'd have been pretty sure to do. Yet it was artful of him to clean the pockets out, so as to make it seem a common case of highway robbery with violence."

"What did you do with the handkerchief?"

"Took it home with me, to that tent yonder, that's what we call home, and lighted an end of candle, and smoothed out the handkerchief to see if there was any mark upon it. Gentlemen are so particular about their things, you see, and don't like to get 'em changed at the wash. Yes, there the mark was, sure enough. The name in full—Christian and surname. It was as much as I could do to read 'em, for the blood-stains."

"What was the name?"

"That's my secret. Every secret has its price, and

I've put a price on mine. If I was sure of getting the reward, and not having the police turn against me, I might be more ready to tell what I know."

"You're a curious woman," said Churchill, after a longish pause. "But I suppose you've some plan of your own?"

"Yes, your honour, I have my views."

"As to this story of yours, even supported by the evidence of this handkerchief which you pretend to have found, I doubt very much if it would have the smallest weight with a jury. I do not, therefore, press you to bring forward your information; though as my cousin's next of kin, it is of course my duty to do my best to bring his assassin to justice."

"That's just what I thought, your honour."

"Precisely. And you did quite right in bringing the subject before me. It will be necessary for me to know when and where I can find you in future, so that when the right time comes you may be at hand to make your statement."

"We are but wanderers on the face of the earth, kind gentleman," whined the gipsy. "It isn't very easy to find us when you want us."

"That's what I've been thinking," returned Churchill, musingly. "If you had some settled home, now? You're getting old, and must be tired of roving, I fancy. Sleeping upon straw, under canvas, in a climate in which east winds are the rule rather than the exception. That sort of thing must be rather trying at your time of life, I should imagine."

"Trying! I'm racked with the rheumatics every winter, your honour. My bones are not so much bones as gnawing wolves — they torment me so.

Sometimes I feel as if I could chop off my limbs willingly, to be quit of the pain in 'em. A settled home—a warm bed—a fireside—that would be heaven to me."

"Well, I'll think about it, and see what can be done for you. In the meantime I'll give you a trifle to ward off the rheumatism."

He opened his purse, and gave the woman a bank note, part of an advance made him by Mr. Pergament that morning. The gipsy uttered her usual torrent of blessings—the gratitude wherewith she was wont to salute her benefactors.

"Have you ever been in Cornwall?" asked Churchill.

"Lord love your honour! there isn't a nook or a corner in all England where I haven't been!"

"Good. If you happen to be in Cornwall any time during the next three months, you may look me up at Penwyn Manor."

"Bless you, my generous gentleman, it won't be very long before you see me."

"Whenever you please," returned Churchill, with that air of well-bred indifference which he wore as a badge of his class. "Good afternoon."

He turned to go back to the city, leaving the woman standing alone by the river brink, looking after him; lost in thought, or lost in wonder.

CHAPTER XV.

"They shall pass, and their places be taken."

THE letter which told Miss Bellingham that her lover was master of Penwyn seemed to her almost like the end of a fairy tale. Lady Cheshunt had dropped in to afternoon tea only a quarter of an hour before the letter arrived, and Madge was busy with the old Battersea cups and saucers, and the quaint little Wedgwood teapot, when the accomplished serving man, who never abated one iota of his professional solemnity because his wages were doubtful, presented Churchill's letter on an antique salver.

"Put it on the table, please," said Madge, busy with the tea-service, and painfully conscious that the dowager's eye was upon her. She had recognised Churchill's hand at a glance, and thought how daring, nay, even impudent it was of him to write to her. It was mean of him to take such advantage of her weakness that Sunday morning, she thought. True, that in one fatal moment she had let him discover the secret she was most anxious to hide; but she had given him no right over her. She had made him no promise. Her love had been admitted hypothetically. "If we lived in a different world. If I had myself only to consider," she had said to him; which meant that she would have nothing to do with him under existing circumstances.

She glanced at Viola, that fragile Sèvres china

beauty, with her air of being unfitted for the vulgar uses of life.

"Poor child! For her sake I ought to marry Mr. Balecroft, that pompous Manchester merchant; or that vapid young fop, Sir Henry Featherstone," she thought, with a sigh.

"Read your letter, my dear love," said Lady Cheshunt, leaning over the tray to put an extra lump of sugar into her cup, and scrutinizing the address of that epistle which had brought the warm crimson blood to Madge Bellingham's cheeks and brow. The good-natured dowager permitted herself this breach of good breeding, in the warmth of her affection for Madge. The handwriting was masculine, evidently. That was all Lady Cheshunt could discover.

Miss Bellingham broke the seal, trying to look composed and indifferent, but after hurriedly reading Churchill's brief letter, gave a little cry of horror.

"Good heavens! it is too dreadful!" she exclaimed.

"What is too dreadful, child?"

"You remember what we were talking about last Saturday night, when you took so much trouble to warn me against allowing myself to—to entangle myself—I think that's what you called it—with Mr. Penwyn."

"With the poor Mr. Penwyn. I remember, perfectly; and that letter is from him—the man has had the audacity to propose to you? You may well say it is too dreadful."

"His cousin has been murdered, Lady Cheshunt— his cousin, Mr. James Penwyn."

"And your man comes into the Penwyn estate,"

cried the energetic dowager. "My dearest Madge, I congratulate you! Poor young Penwyn! A boy at school, or a lad at the University, I believe. Nobody seems to know much about him."

"He has been murdered. Shot from behind a hedge by some midnight assassin. Isn't that dreadful?" said Madge, too much shocked by the tidings in her lover's letter to consider the difference this event might make in her own fortunes. She could not be glad all at once, though that one man whom her heart had chosen for its master was raised from poverty to opulence. For a little while at least, she could only think of the victim.

"Very dreadful!" echoed Lady Cheshunt. "The police ought to prevent such things. One pays highway rates, and sewer rates, and so forth, till one is positively ruined, and yet one can be murdered on the very high road one pays for, with impunity. There must be something wrong in the legislature. I hope things will be better when our party comes in. Look at that child Viola, she's as white as a sheet of paper —just as if she were going to faint. You shouldn't blurt out your murders in that abrupt way, Madge."

Viola gave a little hysterical sob, and promised not to faint this time. She was but a fragile piece of human porcelain, given to swooning at the slightest provocation. She went round to Madge, and knelt down by her, and kissed her fondly, knowing enough of her sister's feelings to comprehend that this fatal event was likely to benefit Madge.

"Odd that I did not see anything of this business in the papers," exclaimed Lady Cheshunt. "But then

I only read the *Post*, and that does not make a feature of murders."

"Papa is at Newmarket," said Viola, "and Madge and I never look at the papers, or hear any news while he is away."

Madge sat silent, looking at Churchill's letter till every word seemed to burn itself into her brain. The firm, straight hand, the letters long and narrow, and a little pointed—something like that wonderful writing of Joseph Addison's—how well she knew it!

"And yet he *must* have been agitated," thought Madge. "Even his quiet force of character could not stand against such a shock as this. After what she said to me, too, last Sunday—to think that wealth and position should have come to him so suddenly. There seems something awful in it."

Lady Cheshunt had quite recovered her habitual gaiety by this time, and dismissed James Penwyn's death as a subject that was done with for the moment, merely expressing her intention of reading the details of the event in the newspapers at her leisure.

"And so, my dear Madge, Mr. Penwyn wrote to you immediately," she said. "Doesn't that look *rather* as if there were some kind of understanding between you?"

"There was no understanding between us, Lady Cheshunt, except that I could never be Mr. Penwyn's wife while he was a poor man. He understood that perfectly. I told him in the plainest, hardest words, like a woman of the world as I am."

"You needn't say that so contemptuously, Madge. I'm a woman of the world, and I own it without a blush. What's the use of living in the world if you don't acquire worldly wisdom? It's like living ever so long in a foreign country without learning the language, and implies egregious stupidity. And so you told Churchill Penwyn that you couldn't marry him on account of his poverty! and you pledged yourself to wait ten or twenty years for him, I suppose, and refuse every decent offer for his sake?"

"No, Lady Cheshunt, I promised nothing."

"Well, my dear, Providence has been very good to you; for, no doubt, if Mr. Penwyn had remained poor you'd have made a fool of yourself sooner or later for his sake, and gone to live in Bloomsbury, where even I couldn't have visited you, on account of my servants. One might get over that sort of thing one's self, but coachmen are so particular where they wait."

Her ladyship rattled on for another quarter of an hour, promised Madge to come and stay at Penwyn Manor with her by and by, congratulated Viola on her sister's good fortune, hoped that her dear Madge would make a point of spending the season in London when she became Mrs. Penwyn; while Madge sat unresponsive, hardly listening to this flow of commonplace, but thinking how awful fortune was when it came thus suddenly, and had death for its herald. She felt relieved when Lady Cheshunt gathered up her silken train for the last time, and went rustling downstairs to the elegant Victoria which appeared far too fairy-like a vehicle to contain that bulky matron.

"Thank Heaven she's gone!" cried Madge. "How she does talk!"

"Yes, dear, but she is always kind," pleaded Viola, "and so fond of you."

Madge put her arms round the girl and kissed her passionately. That sisterly love of hers was almost the strongest feeling in her breast, and all Madge's affections were strong. She had no milk-and-water love.

"Dearest!" she said softly, "how happy we can be now! I hope it isn't wicked to be happy when fortune comes to us in such a dreadful manner."

"You do care a little for Mr. Penwyn, then, dear?" said Viola, without entering upon this somewhat obscure question.

"I love him with all my heart and soul."

"Oh, Madge, and you never told me!"

"Why tell you something that might make you unhappy? I should never have dreamt of marrying Churchill but for this turn in Fortune's wheel. I wanted to make what is called a good marriage, for your sake, darling, more than for my own. I wanted to win a happy home for you, so that when your time came to marry you might not be pressed or harassed by worldly people as I have been, and might follow the dictates of your own heart."

"Oh, Madge, you are quite too good," cried Viola, with enthusiasm.

"And we may be very happy, mayn't we, my pet?" continued the elder, "living together at a picturesque old place in Cornwall, with the great waves of the Atlantic rolling up to the edge of our grounds—and in London sometimes, if Churchill likes—and knowing no more of debt and difficulty, or cutting and contriving so as to look like ladies upon the income of ladies' maids. Life will begin afresh for us, Viola."

"Poor papa!" sighed Viola, "you'll be kind to him, won't you, Madge?"

"My dearest, you know that I love him. Papa will be very glad, depend upon it, and he will like to go back to his old bachelor ways, I dare say, now that he will not be burthened with two marriageable daughters."

"When will you be married, Madge?"

"Oh, not for ever so long, dear; not for a twelvemonth, I should think. Churchill will be in mourning for his cousin, and it wouldn't look well for him to marry soon after such a dreadful event."

"I suppose not. Are you to see him soon?"

"Very soon, love. Here is his postscript." Madge read the last lines of her lover's letter: "'I shall come back to town directly the inquest is over, and all arrangements made, and my first visit shall be to you.'"

"Of course. And you really, really love him, Madge?" asked Viola, anxiously.

"Really, really. But why ask that question, Viola, after what I told you just now?"

"Only because you've taken me by surprise, dear; and—don't be angry with me, Madge—because Churchill Penwyn has never been a favourite of mine. But of course now I shall begin to like him immensely. You're so much better a judge of character than I am, you see, Madge, and if you think him good and true——"

"I have never thought of his goodness or his truth," said Madge, with rather a gloomy look. "I only know that I love him."

CHAPTER XVI.

"There is a history in all men's lives."

UPON his return to London, Churchill lost very little time before presenting himself in Cavendish Row. He did not go there on the day of his cousin's funeral. That gloomy ceremonial had unfitted him for social pleasures, above all for commune with so bright a spirit as Madge Bellingham. He felt as if to go to her straight from that place of tombs would be to carry the atmosphere of the grave into her home. The funeral seemed to affect him more than such a solemnity might have been supposed to affect a man of his philosophical temper. But then these quiet, reserved men—men who hold themselves in check, as it were—are sometimes men of deepest feeling. So Mr. Pergament thought as he stood opposite the new master of Penwyn in the vault at Kensal Green, and observed his pallid face, and the settled gloom of his brow.

Churchill drove straight back to the Temple with Mr. Pergament for his companion, that gentleman being anxious to return to New Square for his afternoon letters, before going down to his luxurious villa at Beckenham, where he lived sumptuously, or—as his enemies averred—battened, ghoul-like, on the rotten carcasses of the defunct chancery suits which he had lost. From Kensal Green to Fleet Street seemed an interminable pilgrimage in that gloomy vehicle. Mr. Pergament and his client had exhausted their conversational powers on the way to the cemetery, and now on the return home had but little to say for themselves. It was a blazing summer afternoon—an August day which had slipped unawares into June through an error in the calendar. The mourning coach was like a locomotive oven; the shabby suburban thoroughfares seemed baking under the pitiless sky. Never had the Harrow Road looked dustier; never had the Edgware Road looked untidier or more out at elbows than to-day.

"How I detest the ragged fringe of shabby suburbs that hangs round London!" said Mr. Penwyn. It was the first remark he had made after half an hour's thoughtful silence.

His only reply from the solicitor was a gentle snore, a snore which sounded full of placid enjoyment. Perhaps there is nothing more dreamily delightful than a stolen doze on a sultry afternoon, lulled by the movement of wheels.

"How the fellow sleeps!" muttered Mr. Penwyn, almost savagely. "I wish I had the knack of sleeping like that."

It is the curse of these hyper-active intellects to be strangers to rest.

The carriage drew up at one of the Temple gates at last, and Mr. Pergament woke with a start, jerked into the waking world again by that sudden pull-up.

"Bless my soul!" exclaimed the lawyer. "I was asleep!"

"Didn't you know it?" asked Churchill, rather fretfully.

"Not the least idea. Weather very oppressive.

Here we are at your place. Dear me! By the way, when do you think of going down to Penwyn?"

"The day after to-morrow. I should like you to go with me and put me in formal possession. And you may as well take the title-deeds down with you. I like to have those things in my own possession. The leases you can of course retain."

Mr. Pergament, hardly quite awake as yet, was somewhat taken aback by this request. The title-deeds of the Penwyn estate had been in the offices of Pergament and Pergament for half a century. This new lord of the manor promised to be sharper even than the old squire, Nicholas Penwyn, who among some ribald tenants of the estate had been known as Old Nick.

"If you wish it, of course—yes—assuredly," said Mr. Pergament; and on this, with a curt good day from Churchill, they parted.

"How property changes a man!" thought the solicitor, as the coach carried him to New Square. "That young man looks as if he had the cares of a nation on his shoulders already. Odd notion his, wanting to keep the title-deeds in his own custody. However, I suppose he won't take his business out of our hands,—and if he should, we can do without it."

* * * * * *

Churchill went up to his chambers, on a third floor. They had a sombre and chilly look in their spotless propriety, even on this warm summer afternoon. The rooms were on the shady side of the way, and saw not the sun after nine o'clock in the morning.

Very neatly kept and furnished were those bachelor

apartments, the sitting-room, at once office and living-room, the goods and chattels in it perhaps worth five-and-twenty pounds. An ancient and faded Turkey carpet, carefully darned by the deft fingers of a jobbing upholstress, whom Churchill sometimes employed to keep things in order; faded green cloth curtains; an old oak knee-hole desk, solid, substantial, shabby, with all the papers upon it neatly sorted—the inkstand stainless, and well supplied; a horsehair-covered armchair, high backed, square, brass-nailed, of a remote era, but comfortable withal; armless chairs of the same period, with an unknown crest emblazoned on their mahogany backs; a battered old bookcase, filled with law books, only one shelf reserved for that lighter literature which soothes the weariness of the student; every object as bright as labour and furniture polish could make it, everything in its place; a room in which no ancient spinster, skilled in the government of her one domestic, could have discovered ground for a complaint.

Churchill looked round the room with a thoughtful smile—not altogether joyous—as he seated himself in his arm-chair, and opened a neat cigar-box on the table at his side.

"How plain the stamp of poverty shows upon everything!" he said to himself, "the furniture the mere refuse of an auction-room, furbished and polished into decency; the faded curtains, where there is hardly any colour visible except the neutral tints of decay; the darned carpet—premeditated poverty, as Sheridan calls it—the mark of the beast shows itself on all. And yet I have known some not all unhappy hours in this room—patient nights of study—the fire of ambition—the sunlight of hope—hours in which I deemed that fame and fortune were waiting for me down the long vista of industrious years—hours when I felt myself strong in patience and resolve! I shall think of these rooms sometimes in my new life—dream of them perhaps—fancy myself back again."

He sat musing for a long time—so lost in thought that he forgot to light the cigar which he had taken from his case just now. He woke from that long reverie with a sigh, gave his shoulders an impatient shrug, as if he would have shaken off ideas that troubled him, and took a volume at random from a neat little bookstand on his table—where about half a dozen favourite volumes stood ranged, all of the cynical school—Rabelais, Sterne, Goethe's "Faust," a volume of Voltaire,—not books that make a man better—if one excepts Goethe, whose master-work is the Gospel of a great teacher. Under that outer husk of bitterness how much sweetness! With that cynicism, what depth of tenderness!

Churchill's hand lighted unawares upon "Faust." He opened the volume at the opening of that mightiest drama, and read on—read until the wearied student stood before him, tempting destiny with his discontent—read until the book dropped from his hand, and he sat, fixed as a statue, staring at the ground, in a gloomy reverie.

"After all, discontent is your true tempter—the fiend whose whisper for ever assails man's ear. Who could be wiser than Faust? and yet how easy a dupe! Well, I have my Margaret, at least; and neither man nor any evil spirit that walks the earth in shape impalpable to man shall ever come between us two."

Churchill lighted his cigar, and left his quiet room, which seemed to him just now to be unpleasantly occupied by that uncanny poodle which the German doctor brought home with him. He went to the Temple Gardens, and walked up and down by the cool river, over which the mists of evening were gently creeping, like a veil of faintest grey. It was before the days of the embankment, and the Templars still possessed their peaceful walk on the brink of the river.

Here Churchill walked till late, thinking,—always thinking,—property has so many cares; and then, when other people were meditating supper, went out into Fleet Street to a restaurant that was just about closing, and ordered his tardy dinner. Even when it came he seemed to have but a sorry appetite, and only took his pint of claret with relish. He was looking forward eagerly to the morrow, when he should see Madge Bellingham, and verily begin his new life. Hitherto he had known only the disagreeables of his position —the inquest—the funeral. To-morrow he was to taste the sweets of prosperity.

CHAPTER XVII.

"Death could not sever my soul and you."

Churchill Penwyn lost little of that morrow to which he had looked forward so eagerly. He was in Cavendish Row at eleven o'clock, in the pretty drawing-room, among brightly bound books and music, and flowers, surrounded by colour, life, and sunshine, and with Madge Bellingham in his arms.

For the first few moments neither of them could speak, they stood silent, the girl's dark head upon her lover's breast, her cheek pale with deepest feeling, his strong arms encircling her.

"My own dear love!" he murmured, after a kiss that brought the warm blood back to that pale cheek. "My very own at last! Who would have thought when we parted that I should come back to you so soon, with altered fortunes?"

"So strangely soon," said Madge. "Oh, Churchill, there is something awful in it."

"Destiny is always awful, dearest. She is that goddess who ever was, and ever will be, and whose veil no man's hand has ever lifted. We are blind worshippers in her temple, and must take the lots she deals from her inscrutable hand. We are among her favoured children, dearest, for she has given us happiness."

"I refused to be your wife, Churchill, because you were poor. Can you quite forgive that? Must I not seem to you selfish and mercenary, almost contemptible, if I accept you now?"

"My beloved, you are truth itself. Be as nobly frank to-day as you were that day I promised to win fame and fortune for your sake. Fortune has come without labour of mine. It shall go hard with me if fame does not follow in the future. Only tell me once more that you love me, that you rejoice in my good fortune, and will share it and—bless it?"

He made a little pause before the last two words, as if some passing thought had troubled him.

"You know that I love you, Churchill," she answered, shyly. "I could not keep that secret from you the other day, though I would have given so much to hide the truth."

"And you will be my wife, darling, the fair young mistress of Penwyn?"

"By and by, Churchill. It seems almost wrong to talk of our marriage yet awhile. That poor young fellow, your cousin, he may have been asking some happy girl to share his fortune and his home—to be mistress of Penwyn—only a little while ago."

"Very sad," said Churchill, "but the natural law. You remember what the father of poets has said— 'The race of man is like the leaves on the trees.'"

"Yes, Churchill, but the leaves fall in their season. This poor young fellow has been snatched away in the blossom of his youth — and by a murderer's hand."

"I have heard a good deal of that sort of talk since his death," remarked Mr. Penwyn, with a cloudy look. "I thought you would have a warmer greeting for me than lamentations about my cousin. But for his death I should not have the right to hold you in my arms, to claim you for my wife. You rejected me on account of my poverty; yet you bewail the event that has made me rich."

Miss Bellingham withdrew herself from her lover's arms with an offended look.

"I would rather have waited for you ten years than that fortune should have come to you under such painful circumstances," she said.

"Yes, you think so, I dare say. But I know what a woman's waiting generally comes to — above all when she is one of the most beautiful women in London. Madge, don't sting me with cold words, or cold looks. You do not know how I have yearned for this hour."

She had seated herself by one of the little tables, and was idly turning the leaves of an ivory-bound volume. Churchill knelt down beside her, and took the white ringed hand away from the book, and covered it with kisses—and put his arm round her as she sat—leaning his head against her shoulder, as if he had found rest there, after long weariness.

"Have some compassion upon me, darling," he pleaded. "Pity nerves that have been strained, a mind that has been overtaxed. Do not think that I have not felt this business. I have felt it God alone knows how intensely. But I come here for happiness. Time enough for troublous thoughts when you and I are apart. Here I would remember nothing—know nothing but the joy of being with you, to touch your hand, to hear your voice, to look into those deep, dark eyes."

There was nothing but love in the eyes that met his gaze now—love unquestioning and unmeasured.

"Dearest, I will never speak of your cousin again if it pains you," Madge said, earnestly. "I ought to have been more considerate."

She pushed back a loose lock from the broad forehead where the hair grew thinly, with a gentle caressing hand; timidly, for it was the first time she had touched her lover's brow, and there was something of a wife's tenderness in the action.

"Churchill," she exclaimed, "your forehead burns as if you were in a fever. You are not ill, I hope?"

"No, dear, not ill. But I have been over-anxious, over-excited, perhaps. I am calm now, happy now, Madge. When shall I speak to your father? I want to feel myself your acknowledged lover."

"You can speak to papa whenever you like, Churchill. He came home last night from Newmarket. I know he will be glad to see you either here or at his club."

"And our marriage, Madge, how soon shall that be?"

"Oh, Churchill, you cannot wish it to be soon, after———"

"But I do wish it to be soon; as soon as it may be with decency. I am not going to pretend exaggerated grief for the death of a kinsman of whom I hardly knew anything. I am not going to sit in sackcloth and ashes because I have inherited an estate I never expected to own, in order that the world may look on approvingly, and say, 'What fine feelings! what tenderness of heart!' Society offers a premium for hypocrisy. No, Madge, I will wear crape on my hat for just three months, and wait just three months for the crowning happiness of my life; and then we will be married, as quietly as you please, and slip away by some untrodden track to a Paradise of our own, some one fair scene among the many lovely spots of earth which has not yet come into fashion for honeymoons."

"You do not ask my terms — but dictate your own," said Madge, smiling.

"Dear love, are we not one in heart and hope from this hour? and must we not have the same wishes, the same thoughts?"

"You have no trousseau to think about, Churchill."

"No, a man hardly considers matrimony an occasion for laying in an unlimited stock of clothes, though I may indulge in a new suit or two in honour of my promotion. Seriously, dearest, do not trouble yourself to provide a mountain of millinery. Mrs. Penwyn shall have an open account with as many milliners and silk-mercers as she pleases."

"You may be sure that I shall not have too expensive a trousseau, and that I shall not run into debt," said Madge, blushing.

And so it was settled between them that they were to be married before the end of September, in time to begin their new life in some romantic corner of Italy, and to establish themselves at Penwyn before Christmas and the hunting season. Churchill had boasted friends innumerable as a penniless barrister, and this circle was hardly likely to become contracted by the change in his fortunes. Everybody would want to visit him during that first winter at Penwyn.

The lovers sat together for hours, talking of their future, opening their hearts to each other, as they had never dared to do before that day. They sat, hand clasped in hand, on that very sofa which Lady Cheshunt's portly form had occupied when she read Madge her lecture.

Viola was out riding with some good-natured friends who had a large stable, and gave the Miss Bellinghams a mount as often as they chose to accept that favour. It was much too early for callers. Sir Nugent never came upstairs in the morning. So Madge and her lover had the cool, shadowy rooms to themselves, and sat amidst the perfume of flowers, talking of their happy life to come. All the small-talk of days gone by, those many conversations at evening parties, flower shows, picture galleries, seemed as nothing compared with these hours of earnest talk; heart to heart, soul to soul; on one side, at least, without a thought of reserve.

Time flew on his swiftest wing for these two. Madge started up with a little cry of surprise when Viola dashed into the room, looking like a lovely piece of waxwork in a riding habit and chimney-pot hat.

"Oh, Madge, we have had such a round; Ealing, Willesden, Hendon, and home by Finchley.—I beg your pardon, Mr. Penwyn, I didn't see you till this moment. This room is so dark after the blazing sunshine. Aren't you coming down to luncheon? The bell rang half an hour ago, and poor Rickson looks the picture of gloom. I dare say he wants to clear the table and compose himself for his afternoon siesta."

Madge blushed, conscious of having been too deep in bliss for life's common sounds to penetrate her Paradise—in a region where luncheon bells are not.

"You'll stay to luncheon, Churchill, won't you?" she said—and Viola knew it was all settled.

Miss Bellingham would not have called a gentleman by his Christian name unless she had been engaged to be married to him.

Viola got hold of her sister's hand as they went downstairs, and squeezed it tremendously.

"I shall sit down to luncheon in my habit," she said, "if you don't mind, for I'm absolutely famishing."

That luncheon was the pleasantest meal Churchill Penwyn had eaten for a long time. Not an aldermanic banquet by any means, for Sir Nugent seldom lunched at home, and the young ladies fared but simply in his absence. There was a cold chicken left from yesterday's dinner, minus the liver-wing, a tongue, also cut, a salad, a jar of apricot jam, some dainty little loaves from a German bakery, and a small glass dish of Roquefort cheese. The wines were Medoc and sherry.

The three sat a long time over this simple feast, still talking of their future;—the future which Viola was to share with the married people.

"Have you ever seen Penwyn Manor?" she asked, after having declared her acceptance of the destiny that had been arranged for her.

"Never," answered Churchill. "It was always a sore subject with my father. His father had not treated him well, you see; he married when he was little more than a boy, and was supposed to have married badly, though my mother was as good a woman as ever bore the name of Penwyn. My grandfather chose to take offence at the marriage, and my father resented the slight put upon his wife so deeply that he never crossed the threshold of Penwyn Manor House again. Thus it happened that I was brought up with very little knowledge of my kindred, or the birthplace of my ancestors. I have often thought of going down to Cornwall to have a look at the old place, without letting anybody know who I was; but I have been too busy to put the idea into execution."

"How different you will feel going there as master!" said Viola.

"Yes, it will be a more agreeable sensation, no doubt."

It was between three and four o'clock when Churchill left that snug little dining-room to go down to Sir Nugent's club in St. James's Street, in the hope of seeing that gentleman and making all things straight without delay.

"Come back to afternoon tea, if you can," said Viola, who appeared particularly friendly to her future brother-in-law.

"If possible, my dear Viola—I may call you Viola, I suppose, now?"

"Of course. Are we not brother and sister henceforward?"

"Well, dear, have you been trying to like him?" asked Madge, when her lover had departed.

"Yes, and I found it quite easy, you darling Madge! He seemed to me much nicer to-day. Perhaps it was because I could see how he worships you. I never saw two people so intensely devoted. Prosperity suits him wonderfully; though that cloudy look which I have often noticed in him still comes over his face by fits and starts."

"He feels his cousin's awful death very deeply."

"Does he? That's very good of him when he profits so largely by the calamity. Well, dearest, I mean to like him very much; to be as fond of him as if he really were my brother."

"And he will be all that a brother could be to you, dear."

"I don't quite know that I should care about that," returned Viola, doubtfully; "brothers are sometimes nuisances. A brother-in-law would be more likely to be on his good behaviour, for fear of offending his wife."

*　　*　　*　　*　　*　　*

Churchill succeeded in lighting upon Sir Nugent at his club. He was yawning behind an evening paper in the reading-room when Mr. Penwyn found him. His greeting was just a shade more cordial than it had always been, but only a shade, for it was Sir Nugent's rule to be civil to everybody. "One never knows when a man may get a step," he said; and, in a world largely composed of younger sons and heirs presumptive, this was a golden rule.

Sir Nugent expressed himself profoundly sympathetic upon the subject of James Penwyn's death. He was perfectly aware of Churchill's business with him that afternoon, but affected the most Arcadian innocence.

Happily Churchill came speedily to the point.

"Sir Nugent," he began, gravely, "while I was a

struggling man I felt it would be at once presumption and folly to aspire to your daughter's hand; but to be her husband has been my secret hope ever since I first knew her. My cousin's death has made a total change in my fortune."

"Of course, my dear fellow. It has transformed you from a briefless barrister into a prosperous country gentleman. Pardon me if I remark that I might look higher for my eldest daughter than that. Madge is a woman in a thousand. If it had been her sister, now—a good little thing, and uncommonly pretty— but I have no lofty aspirations for her."

"Unhappily for your ambitious dreams, Sir Nugent, Madge is the lady of my choice, and we love each other. I do not think you ought to object to my present position—the Penwyn estate is worth seven thousand a year."

"Not bad," said the baronet, blandly, "for a commoner. But Madge could win a coronet if she chose; and I confess that I have looked forward to seeing her take her place in the peerage. However, if she really likes you, and has made up her mind about it, any objections of mine would be useless, no doubt; and as far as personal feeling goes there is no one I should like better for a son-in-law than yourself."

The two gentlemen shook hands upon this, and Sir Nugent felt that he had not let his handsome daughter go too cheap, and had paved the way for a liberal settlement. He asked his future son-in-law to dinner, and Churchill, who would not have foregone that promised afternoon tea for worlds, chartered the swiftest hansom he could find, drove back to Cavendish Row, spent an hour with the two girls and a little bevy of feminine droppers-in, then drove to the Temple to dress, and reappeared at Sir Nugent's street door just as the neighbouring clocks chimed the first stroke of eight.

"Bless the young man, how he do come backwards and forwards since he's come into his estates!" said the butler, who had read all about James Penwyn's death in the papers. "I always suspected that he had a sneaking kindness for our eldest young lady, and now it's clear they're going to keep company. If he's coming in and out like this every day, I hope he'll have consideration enough to make it worth my while to open the door for him."

* * * * *

"I hope you are not angry with me, papa," said Madge, by and by, after her lover had bid them good night and departed, and when father and daughter were alone together.

"Angry with you? no, my love, but just a trifle disappointed. This seems to me quite a poor match for a girl with your advantages."

"Oh, papa, Churchill has seven thousand a year: and think of our income."

"My love, that is not the question in point. What I have to think of is the match you might have made, had it not been for this unlucky infatuation. There is Mr. Balecroft, with his palace in Belgravia, a picture gallery worth a quarter of a million, and a superb place at Windermere——"

"A man who drops his h's, papa—complains of being 'ot!"

"Or Sir Henry Featherstone, one of the oldest families in Yorkshire, with twelve thousand a year."

"And not an idea which he has not learnt from his trainer or his jockey! Oh, papa, don't forget Tennyson's noble line,—

'Cursed be the gold that gilds the straightened forehead of the fool!'"

"All very well for poets to write that sort of stuff, but a man in my position doesn't like to see his daughter throw away her chances. However, I suppose I mustn't complain. Penwyn Manor is a nice enough place, I dare say."

"You must come to stay with me, papa, every year."

"My love, that kind of place would be the death of me, except for a week in October. I suppose there are plenty of pheasants?"

"I dare say, papa. If not, we'll order some."

"Well, it might have been worse," sighed Sir Nugent.

"You'll let Viola live with me when I am married, papa, won't you?" pleaded Madge, coaxingly, as if she were asking a tremendous favour.

"My dear child, with all my heart," replied her father, with amiable promptitude. "Where could she be so well off? In that case I shall give up housekeeping as soon as you are married. This house has always been a plague to me, taxes, repairs, no end of worry. I used to pay a hundred and fifty pounds a year for my rooms in Jermyn Street, and the business was settled. Bless you, my darling. You have always been a comfort to your poor old father."

And thus blandly, with an air of self-sacrifice, did Sir Nugent Bellingham wash his hands of his two daughters.

CHAPTER XVIII.

"What great ones do, the less will prattle of."

A YEAR had gone by since James Penwyn met his death by the lonely river at Eborsham, and again Maurice Clissold spent his summer holiday in a walking tour. This time he was quite alone. Pleasant and social though he was, he did not make friendships lightly or quickly. In the year that was gone he had found no friend to replace James Penwyn. He had plenty of agreeable acquaintances, knew plenty of men who were glad to dine with him or to give him a dinner. He was famous already, in a small way, at the literary club where he spent many of his evenings when he was in London, and men liked to hear him talk, and prophesied fair things for his future as a man of letters, all the more surely because he was not called upon to write for bread, but could follow the impulse that moved him, and wait, were it ever so long, for the moment of inspiration; never forced to spur the jaded steed, or work the too willing horse to death.

Not one among the comrades he liked well enough for a jovial evening, or a cosy dinner, had crept into his heart like the lad he had sworn to cherish in the ears of a dying woman five years ago. So when the roses were in bloom, and London began to look warm and dusty, and the parks had faded a little from their vernal green, Maurice Clissold set forth alone upon a voyage of adventure, with a pocket Shakespeare and a quire or so of paper in his battered, old leathern knapsack, and just so much clothing and linen as might serve him for his travels.

Needless to say that he avoided that northern city of Eborsham, where such sudden grief had come upon him, and all that route which he had trodden only a year ago with the light-hearted, hopeful lad who now slept his sweetest sleep in one of the vaults at Kensal Green, beside the mother he had loved and mourned.

Instead of northward, to the land of lakes and mountains, Maurice went due west. Many a time had he and James Penwyn talked of the days they were to spend together down at the old place in Cornwall, and behold! that visit to Penwyn Manor, deferred in order that James should see the Lake country, was destined never to be paid. Never were those two to walk together by the Atlantic, never to scale Tintagel's rugged height, or ramble among the rocks of Bude.

Maurice had a curious fancy for seeing the old home from which death had ousted James Penwyn. He might have gone as a visitor to the Manor House had he pleased, for Churchill had been extremely civil to him when they last met at the funeral, and had promised him a hearty welcome to Penwyn whenever he liked to come there; but Mr. Clissold infinitely preferred to go as an unknown pedestrian—knapsack on shoulder—having first taken the trouble to ascertain that Churchill Penwyn and his beautiful young wife were in London, where they had, for this season, a furnished house in Upper Brook Street. He saw their names in the list of guests at a fashionable reception, and knew that the coast would be clear, and that he could roam about the neighbourhood of his dead friend's ancestral home without let or hindrance. He went straight to Plymouth by an express train, crossed the Tamar, and pursued his journey on foot, at a leisurely pace, lingering at all the prettiest spots—now spending a day or two at some rustic wayside inn—sketching a little, reading a little, writing a little, thinking and dreaming a great deal.

It was an idle fancy that had brought him here, and he gave a free rein to all other idle fancies that seized him by the way. It was a morbid fancy, perhaps, for it must needs be but a melancholy pleasure, at best, to visit the domain which his friend had never enjoyed, to remember so many boyish schemes unfulfilled, so many bright hopes snapped short off by the shears of Atropos.

The long blue line of sea, and the wide moorland were steeped in the golden light of a midsummer afternoon when Maurice drew near Penwyn Manor. The scene was far more lonely than he had imagined it. Measureless ocean stretched before him, melting into the hazy summer sky—sea and heaven so near of a colour that it was hard to tell where the water ended and the sky began—measureless hills around him—and, except the white sheep yonder, making fleecy dots upon the side of the topmost hill, no sign of life. He had left the village of Penwyn behind him by a good two miles, but had not yet come in sight of the Manor House, though he had religiously followed the track pointed out to him by the hostess of the little inn—a mere cottage—where he left his knapsack, and where he had been respectfully informed that he could not have a bed.

"At the worst I can sleep on the lee side of one of these hills," he said to himself. "It can hardly be very cold, even at night, in this western climate."

He walked a little further on, upon a narrow footpath high above the sea level. On his right hand there were wide corn-fields, with here and there an open tract of turnip or mangold; on his left only the wild moorland pastures, undulating like a sea of verdure. The ground had dipped a little while ago, and as it rose again, with a gentle ascent, Maurice Clissold saw the chimney-stacks of the Manor House between him and the sea.

It was a substantial-looking house, built of greyish stone, a long low building, with grounds that stretched to the edge of the cliff, sheltered by a belt of fir and evergreen oak. The blue sea showed in little patches of gleaming colour through the dark foliage, and the spicy odour of the pines perfumed the warm, still air. In its utter loneliness the house had a gloomy look, despite the grandeur of its situation, on this bold height above the sea. The grounds were extensive, but to Maurice Clissold they seemed somewhat barren; orderly, beyond doubt, and well timbered, but lacking the smiling fertility, the richness of ornament, which a student of Horace and Pliny desired in his ideal garden.

But Mr. Clissold did not make acquaintance with he inside of the shrubbery or gardens without some little difficulty. His footpath led him ultimately into a villanous high road, just in front of the gates of Penwyn, so the landlady of the village inn had not sent him astray. There was a lodge beside the gate, a square stone cottage, covered with myrtle, honeysuckle, and roses, from which emerged an elderly female, swarthy of aspect, her strongly marked countenance framed in a frill cap, which gave an almost grotesque look to that tawny visage.

"Can I see the house and grounds, ma'am?" asked Maurice, approaching this somewhat grim-looking personage with infinite civility.

He had a vague idea that he must have seen that face before, or imagined it in a dream, so curiously did it remind him of some past occasion in his life—what, he knew not.

"The house is never shown to strangers," answered the woman.

"I know Mr. Penwyn, and will leave my card for him."

"You'd better apply to the housekeeper. As to the grounds, my granddaughter will take you round, if you like.—Elspeth," called the woman, and a black-eyed girl of twelve appeared at the cottage door, like a sprite at a witch's summons.

"Take this gentleman round the gardens," said the old woman, and vanished, before Maurice could quite make up his mind as to whether he had seen a face like that in actual flesh and blood or only on a painter's canvas.

The girl, who had an impish look, he thought, with her loose black locks, scarlet petticoat, and scanty scarlet shawl pinned tightly across her bony shoulders, led the way through a wild-looking shrubbery, where huge blocks of granite lay among the ferns, which grew with rank luxuriance between the straight pine-stems. A sandy path wound in and out among trees and shrubs, till Maurice and his guide emerged upon a spacious lawn at the back of the house, whose many windows blinked at them, shining in the western sun. There were no flower-beds on the lawn, but there was a small square garden, in the Dutch style, on one side of the house, and a bowling-green on the other. A terraced walk stretched in front of the windows, raised three or four feet above the level of the lawn, and guarded by a stone balustrade somewhat defaced by time. A fine old sundial marked the centre of the Dutch garden, where the geometrical flower-beds were neatly kept, and where Maurice found a couple of gardeners, elderly men both, at work, weeding and watering in a comfortable, leisurely manner.

"What a paradise for the aged!" thought Maurice; "the woman at the lodge was old, the gardeners are old, everything about the place is old, except this impish girl, who looks the oldest of all, with her evil black eyes and vinegar voice."

Mr. Clissold had not come so far without entering into conversation with the damsel. He had asked her a good many questions about the place, and the people to whom it belonged. But her answers were of the briefest, and she affected the profoundest ignorance about everything and everybody.

"You've not been here very long, I suppose, my girl," he said at last, with some slight sense of irritation, "or you'd know a little more about the place."

"I haven't been here much above six months."

"Oh! But your grandmother has lived here all her life, I dare say?"

"No, she hasn't. Grandmother came when I did."

"And where did you both come from?"

"Foreign parts," answered the girl.

"Indeed! you both speak very good English for people who come from abroad."

"I didn't say we were foreigners, did I?" asked the girl, pertly. "If you want to ask any more questions about the place or the people, you'd better ask 'em of the housekeeper, Mrs. Darvis; and if you want to see the house you must ask lief of her; and this is the door you'd better ring at, if you want to see her."

They were at one end of the terrace, and opposite a half-glass door which opened into a small and darksome lobby, where the effigies of a couple of ill-used ancestors frowned from the dusky walls, as if indignant at being placed in so obscure a corner. Maurice rang the bell, and after repeating that operation more than once, and waiting with consummate patience for the result, he was rewarded by the appearance of an elderly female, homely, fresh-coloured, comfortable-looking, affording altogether an agreeable contrast to the tawny visage of the lodge-keeper, whose countenance had given the traveller an unpleasant feeling about Penwyn Manor.

Mr. Clissold stated his business, and after spelling over his card and deliberating a little, Mrs. Darvis consented to admit him, and to show him the house.

"We used to show it to strangers pretty freely till the new Squire came into possession," she said, "but he's rather particular. However, if you're a friend of his——"

"I know him very well; and poor James Penwyn was my most intimate friend."

"Poor Mr. James! I never saw him but once, when he came down to see the place soon after the old Squire's death. Such a frank, open-hearted young gentleman, and so free-spoken. It was a terrible blow to all of us down here when we read about the murder. Not but what the present Mr. Penwyn is a liberal master and a kind landlord, and a good friend to the poor. There couldn't be a better gentleman for Penwyn."

"I am glad to hear you give him so good a character," said Maurice.

The girl Elspeth had followed him into the house, uninvited, and stood in the background, open-eyed, with her thin lips drawn tightly together, listening intently.

"As for Mrs. Penwyn," said the housekeeper, "why, she's a lady in a thousand! She might be a queen, there's something so grand about her. Yet she's so affable that she couldn't pass one of the little children at the poor school without saying a kind word; and so thoughtful for the poor that they've no need to tell her their wants, she provides for them beforehand."

"A model Lady Bountiful," exclaimed Maurice.

"You may run home to your grandmother, Elspeth," said Mrs. Darvis.

"I was to show the gentleman the grounds," answered the damsel, "he hasn't half seen 'em yet."

In her devotion to the service she had undertaken, the girl followed at their heels through the house, absorbing every word that was said by Mrs. Darvis or the stranger.

The house was old, and somewhat gloomy, belonging to the Tudor school of architecture. The heavy stonework of the window-frames, the lozenge-shaped mullions, the massive cross-bars, were eminently adapted to exclude light. Even what light the windows did admit was in many places tempered by stained glass emblazoned with the arms and mottoes of the Penwyn family, in all its ramifications, showing how it had become entangled with other families, and bore the arms of heiresses on its shield, until that original badge, which Sir Thomas Penwyn, the crusader, had first carried atop of his helmet, was almost lost among the various devices in a barry of eight.

The rooms were spacious, but far from lofty, the chimney-pieces of carved oak and elaborate workmanship, the paneling between mantel-board and ceiling richly embellished, and over all the principal chimney-pieces appeared the Penwyn arms and motto, "*J'attends.*"

There was much old tapestry, considerably the worse for wear, for the house had been sorely neglected during that dreary interval between the revolution and the days of George the Third, when the Penwyn family had fallen into comparative poverty, and the fine old mansion had been little better than a farmhouse. Indeed, brawny agricultural labourers had eaten their bacon and beans and potato pasty in the banqueting hall, now the state dining-room, handsomely furnished with plain and massive oaken furniture by the old Squire, Churchill's grandfather.

This room was one of the largest in the house, and looked towards the sea. Drawing-room, music-room, library, and boudoir were on the garden side, with windows opening on the terrace. The drawing-room and boudoir had been refurnished by Churchill, since his marriage.

"The old Squire kept very little company, and

hardly ever went inside any of those rooms," said Mrs. Darvis. "In summer he used to sit in the yew-tree bower, on the bowling-green, after dinner; and in winter he used to smoke his pipe in the steward's room, mostly, and talk to his bailiff. The dining-room was the only large room he ever used, so when Mr. Churchill Penwyn came he found the drawing-room very bare of furniture, and what there was was too shabby for his taste, so he had that and the boudoir furnished, after the old style, by a London upholsterer, and put a grand piano and a harmonium in the music-room; and the drawing-room tapestry is all new, made by the Goblins, Mrs. Penwyn told me, which, I suppose, was only her fanciful way of putting it."

The dame opened the door as she spoke, and admitted Maurice into this sacred apartment, where the chairs and sofas were shrouded with holland.

The tapestry was an exquisite specimen of that patient art. Its subject was the story of Arion. The friendly dolphin, and the blue summer sea, the Greek sailors, Periander's white-walled palace, lived upon the work. Triangular cabinets of carved ebony adorned the corners of the room, and were richly furnished with the Bellingham bric-à-brac, the only dower Sir Nugent had been able to give his daughter. The chairs and sofas, from which Mrs. Darvis lifted a corner of the holland covering for the visitor's gratification, were of the same dark wood, upholstered with richest olive-green damask, of mediæval diaper pattern. Window-curtains of the same sombre hue harmonized admirably with the brighter colours of the tapestry. The floor was darkest oak, only covered in the centre with a Persian carpet. The boudoir, which opened out of the drawing-room, was furnished in exactly the same style, only here the tapestried walls told the story of Hero and Leander.

"I believe it was all Mrs. Penwyn's taste," said the housekeeper, when Maurice had admired everything. "'Her rooms upstairs are a picture—nothing out of character with the house,' the head upholsterer said. 'There's so few ladies have got any notion of character,' he says. 'They'll furnish an old manor-house with flimsy white and gold of the Lewis Quince style, only fit for a drawing-room in the Shamps Eliza; and if you ask them why, they'll say because it's fashionable, and they like it. Mrs. Penwyn is an artist,' says the upholsterer's foreman."

Maurice did not hurry his inspection, finding the housekeeper communicative, and the place full of interest. He heard a great deal about the old Squire, Nicholas Penwyn, who had reigned for forty years, and for whom his dependents had evidently felt a curious mixture of fear, respect, and affection.

"He was a just man," said Mrs. Darvis, "but stern; and it was but rarely he forgave any one that once offended him. It took a good deal to offend him, you know, sir; but when he did take offence, the wound rankled deep. I've heard our old doctor say the Squire had bad flesh for healing. He never got on very well with his eldest son, Mr. George, though he was the handsomest of the three brothers, and the best of them too, to my mind."

"What made them disagree?" asked Maurice. They had made the round of the house by this time, and the traveller had seated himself comfortably on a broad window-seat in the entrance hall, a window through which the setting sun shone bright and warm. Mrs. Darvis sat on a carved oak bench by the fireplace, resting after her unwonted exertions. Elspeth stood at a respectful distance, her arms folded demurely in her little red shawl, listening to the housekeeper's discourse.

"Well, you see, sir," returned Mrs. Darvis, in her slow, methodical way, "the old Squire would have liked Mr. George to stop at home, and take an interest in the estate, for he was always adding something to the property, and his heart and mind were wrapped up in it, as you may say. Folks might call him a miser, but it was not money he cared for; it was land, and to add to the importance of the family, and to bring the estate back to what it had been when this house was built. Now Mr. George didn't care about staying at home. It was a lazy, sleepy kind of life, he said, and he had set his heart upon going into the army. The Squire gave way at last, and bought Mr. George a commission, but it was in a foot regiment, and that went rather against the grain with the young gentleman, for he wanted to go into the cavalry. So they didn't part quite so cordial like as they might have done when Mr. George joined his regiment and went out to India."

"You were here at the time, I suppose?"

"Lord love you, sir, I was almost born here. My mother was housekeeper before me. She was the widow of a tradesman in Truro, very respectably connected. Mrs. Penwyn, the Squire's lady, took me for her own maid when I was only sixteen years of age, and I nursed her all through her last illness twelve years afterwards, and when my poor mother died I succeeded her as housekeeper, and I look forward to dying in the same room where she died, and where I've slept for the last twenty years, when my own time comes, please God."

"So the Squire and his eldest son parted bad friends?"

"Not exactly bad friends, sir; but there was a coolness between them; anybody could see that. Mr. George—or the Captain, as we used generally to call him after he went into the army—hadn't been gone a twelvemonth before there was a quarrel between the Squire and his second son, Mr. Balfour, on account of the young gentleman marrying beneath him, according to his father's ideas. The lady was a brewer's daughter, and the Squire said Mr. Balfour was the first Penwyn who had ever degraded himself by marrying trade. Mr. Balfour was not much above twenty at the time, but he took a high hand about the matter, and never came to Penwyn Manor after his marriage."

"How was it that the eldest son never married?" asked Maurice.

"Ah, sir, 'thereby hangs a tale,' as the saying is. Mr. George came home from India after he'd been away above ten years, and had distinguished himself by his good conduct and his courage, people told me who had read his name in the papers during the war. He looked handsomer than ever, I thought, when he came home, though he was browned by the sun; and he was just as kind and pleasant in his manner as he had been when he was only a lad. Well, sir, the Squire seemed delighted to have him back again, and made a great deal of him. They were always together about the place, and the Squire would lean on his son's arm sometimes, when he had walked a long way and was a trifle tired. It was the first time any one had ever seen him accept anybody's support. They used to sit over their wine together of an evening, talking and laughing, and as happy as father and son could be together. All of us—we were all old servants—felt pleased to see it; for we were all fond of Mr. George, and looked to him as our master in days to come."

"And pray how long did this pleasant state of things endure?"

"Two or three months, sir; and then all at once we saw a cloud. Mr. George began to go out shooting early in the morning—it was the autumn season just then—and seldom came home till dark; and the Squire seemed silent and grumpy of an evening. None of us could guess what it all meant, for we had heard no high words between the two gentlemen, till all at once, by some roundabout way, which I can't call to mind now, the mystery came out. There was an elderly gentleman living at Morgrave Park, a fine old place on the other side of Penwyn village, with an only daughter, an heiress, and very much thought of. Mr. Morgrave and his daughter had been over to luncheon two or three times since Mr. George came home, and he and the Squire had dined at Morgrave Park more than once; and I suppose Miss Morgrave and our Mr. George had met at other places, for they seemed quite friendly and intimate. She was a fine-looking young lady, but rather masculine in her ways—very fond of dogs and horses, and such like, and riding to hounds all the season through. But whatever she did was right, according to people's notions, on account of her being an heiress."

"And George Penwyn had fallen in love with this dashing young lady?"

"Not a bit of it, sir. It came to our knowledge, somehow, that the Squire wanted Mr. George to marry her, and had some reason to believe that the young lady would say 'yes,' if he asked her. But Mr. George didn't like her. She wasn't his style, he said; at which the Squire was desperately angry. 'Join Penwyn and Morgrave, and you'll have the finest estate in the county,' he said, 'an estate fit for a nobleman. A finer property than the Penwyns owned in the days of James the First.' Mr. George wouldn't listen. 'I see what it is,' the Squire cried, in a rage, 'you want to disgrace me by some low marriage, to marry a shop-keeper's daughter, like your brother Balfour. But, by heavens! if you do, I'll alter my will, and leave the estate away from my race! It didn't matter so much in Balfour's case, neither he nor his are ever likely to be masters here, but I won't stand rebellion from you! I won't have a pack of kennel-born mongrels rioting here when I'm mouldering in my grave!'"

"What a sweet old gentleman!"

"Mr. George swore that he had no thought of making a low marriage, no thought of marrying at all yet awhile. He was happy enough as he was, he said, but he wouldn't marry a woman he didn't like, even to please his father. So they went on pretty quietly together for a little while after this, the Squire grumpy, but not saying much. And then Mr. George went up to London, and from there he went to join his regiment in Ireland, where they were stationed after they came from India, and he was about at different places for two or three years, during which time Miss Morgrave got married to a nobleman, much to the Squire's vexation. But I'm afraid I'm tiring you, sir, with such a long story."

"Not at all. I like to hear it."

"Well, Mr. George came back one summer. He was home on leave for a little while before he went on foreign service, and he and the Squire were pretty friendly again. It was a very hot summer, and Mr. George used to spend most of his time out of doors, fishing or idling away the days somehow. The Squire had a bad attack of gout that year, and was kept pretty close in his room. You couldn't expect a young man to sit indoors all day, of course, but I've often wondered what Master George could find to amuse him among these solitary hills of ours, or down among the rocks by the sea. He stayed all through the summer, however, and seemed happy enough, and at the beginning of the winter he went away to join his regiment, which was ordered off to Canada. I was thankful to remember afterwards that he and the Squire parted good friends."

"Why?" asked Maurice.

"Because they were never to meet again. Mr. George was killed in a fight with the savages six months after he went away. I remember the letter coming that brought the news one fine summer evening. The Squire was standing in this hall, just by that window, when Miles, the old butler, gave him the letter. He just read the beginning of it, and fell down as if he had been struck dead. It was his first stroke of apoplexy, and he was never quite the same afterwards, though he was a wonderful old gentleman to the last."

CHAPTER XIX.

"Farewell," quoth she, "and come again to-morrow."

THE old housekeeper's eyes were dim as she finished her story of the heir of Penwyn.

"He was the best of all," she said; "Mr. Balfour we saw very little of after he grew up, being the youngest to marry and leave home; Mr. James was a kind, easy-going young fellow enough; but Mr. George was everybody's favourite, and there wasn't a dry eye among us when the Squire called us together after his illness, and told us how his son had died. 'He died like a gentleman—upholding the honour of his Queen and his country, and the name of Penwyn,' said the master, without a tremble in his voice, though it was feebler than before the stroke, 'and I am proud to think of him lying in his far-off grave, and if I were not so old I would go over the sea to kneel beside my poor boy's resting-place before I die. He displeased me once, but we are good friends now, and there will be no cloud between us when we meet in another world.'"

Here Mrs. Darvis was fairly overcome, much to the astonishment of the girl Elspeth, whose uncanny black eyes regarded her with a scornful wonder. Maurice noticed that look.

"Sweet child," he said to himself. "What a charming helpmeet you will make for some honest peasant in days to come, with your amiable disposition!"

He had taken his time looking at the old house, and listening to the housekeeper's story. The sun was low, and he had yet to find a lodging for the night. He had walked far since morning, and was not disposed to retrace his steps to the nearest town, a place called Seacomb, consisting of a long straggling street, with various lateral courts and alleys, a market-place, parish church, lock-up, and five dissenting chapels of various denominations. This Seacomb was a good nine miles from Penwyn Manor.

"Perhaps you'd like to see the young Squire's portrait," said Mrs. Darvis, when she had dried those tributary tears.

"The young Squire?"

"Mr. George. We used to call him the young Squire sometimes."

"Yes, I should like to have a look at the poor fellow, now you've told me his history."

"It hangs in the old Squire's study. It's a bit of a room, and I forgot to show it to you just now."

Maurice followed her across the hall to a small door in a corner, deeply recessed and low, but solid enough to have guarded the Tolbooth, one would suppose. It opened into a narrow room, with one window looking towards the sea. The wainscot was almost black with age, the furniture, old walnut wood, of the same time-darkened hue. There was a heavy old bureau, brass handled and brass clamped; a book-case, a ponderous writing desk, and one capacious arm-chair, covered with black leather. The high, narrow chimney-piece was in an angle of the room, and above this hung the portrait of George Penwyn.

It was a kit-kat picture of a lad in undress uniform, the face a long oval, fair of complexion, and somewhat feminine in delicacy of feature, the eyes dark blue. The rest of the features, though sufficiently regular, were commonplace enough; but the eyes, beautiful alike in shape and colour, impressed Maurice Clissold. They were eyes which might have haunted the fancy of girlhood, with the dream of an ideal lover; eyes in whose somewhat melancholy sweetness a poet would have read some strange life-history. The hair, a pale auburn, hung in a loosely waving mass over the high narrow brow, and helped to give a picturesque cast to the patrician-looking head.

"A nice face," said Maurice, critically. "There is a little look of my poor friend James Penwyn, but not much. Poor Jim had a gayer, brighter expression, and had not those fine blue-grey eyes. I fancy Churchill Penwyn must be a plain likeness of his uncle George. Not so handsome, but more intellectual-looking."

"Yes, sir," assented Mrs. Darvis. "The present Squire is something like his uncle, but there's a harder look in his face. All the features seem cut out sharper; and then his eyes are quite different. Mr. George had his mother's eyes; she was a Trevillian, and one of the handsomest women in Cornwall."

"I've seen a face somewhere which that picture reminds me of, but I haven't the faintest notion where," said Maurice. "In another picture, perhaps. Half one's memories of faces are derived from pictures, and they flash across the mind suddenly, like a recollection of another world. However, I mustn't stand prosing here, while the sun goes down yonder. I have to find a lodging before nightfall. What is the nearest place, village, or farmhouse, where I can get a bed, do you think, Mrs. Darvis?"

"There's the 'Bell,' in Penwyn village."

"No good. I've tried there already. The landlady's married daughter is home on a visit, and they haven't a bed to give me for love or money."

Mrs. Darvis lapsed into meditation.

"The nearest farmhouse is Trevanard's, at Borcel End. They might give you a bed there, for the place is large enough for a barrack, but they are not the most obliging people in the world, and they are too well off to care about the money you may pay them for the accommodation."

"How far is Borcel End?"

"Between two and three miles."

"Then I'll try my luck there, Mrs. Darvis," said Maurice, cheerily. "It lies between that and sleeping under the open sky."

"I wish I could offer you a bed, sir; but in my position——"

"As custodian such an offer would be a breach of good faith to your employers. I quite understand that, Mrs. Darvis. I come here as a stranger to you, and I thank you kindly for having been so obliging as to show me the house."

He dropped a couple of half-crowns into her hand as he spoke, but these Mrs. Darvis rejected most decidedly.

"Ours has never been what you can call a showplace, sir, and I've never looked for that kind of perquisite."

"Come, young one," said Maurice, after taking

leave of the friendly old housekeeper, "you can put me into the right road to Borcel End, and you shall have one of these for your reward."

Elspeth's black eyes had watched the rejection of the half-crowns with unmistakable greed. Her sharp face brightened at Maurice's promise.

"I'll show you the way, sir," she said; "I know every step of it."

"Yes, the lass is always roaming about, like a wild creature, over the hills, and down by the sea," said Mrs. Darvis, with a disapproving air. "I don't think she knows how to read or write, or has as much Christian knowledge as the old jackdaw in the servants' hall."

"I know things that are better than reading and writing," said Elspeth, with a grin.

"What kind of things may those be?" asked Maurice.

"Things that other people don't know."

"Well, my lass, I won't trouble you by sounding the obscure depths of your wisdom. I only want the straightest road to Trevanard's farm. He is a tenant of this estate, I suppose, Mrs. Darvis?"

"Yes, sir. Michael Trevanard's father was a tenant of the old Squire's before my time. Old Mrs. Trevanard is still living, though stone-blind, and hardly right in her head, I believe."

They had reached the lobby door by this time, the chief hall door being kept religiously bolted and barred during the absence of the family.

"I shall come and see you again, Mrs. Darvis, most likely, before I leave this part of the country," said Maurice, as he crossed the threshold. "Good evening."

A Strange World. I.

"You'll be welcome at any time, sir. Good evening."

Elspeth led the way across the lawn, with a step so light and swift that it was as much as Maurice could do to keep pace with her, tired as he was, after a long day afoot. He followed her into the pine wood. The trees were not thickly planted, but they were old and fine, and their dense foliage looked inky black against a primrose-coloured sky. A narrow footpath wound among the tall black trunks, only a few yards from the edge of the cliff, which was poorly guarded by a roughly fashioned timber railing, the stakes wide apart. The vast Atlantic lay below them, a translucent green in the clear evening light, melting into purple far away on the horizon.

Maurice paused to look back at Penwyn Manor House, the grave, substantial old dwelling-house which had seen so little change since the days of the Tudors. High gable ends, latticed windows gleaming in the last rays of the setting sun; stone walls moss-darkened and ivy-shrouded, massive porch, with deep recesses, and roomy enough for a small congregation; mighty chimney-stacks, and quaint old iron weathercock, with a marvellous specimen of the ornithological race pointing its gilded beak due west.

"Poor old James! what good days we might have had here!" sighed Maurice, as he looked back at the fair domain. It seemed a place saved out of the good old world, and was very pleasant to contemplate after the gimcrack palaces of the age we live in—in which all that architecture can conjure from the splendour of the past is more or less disfigured by the tinsel of the present.

"Dear old James, to think that he wanted to marry

that poor little actress girl, and bring her to reign down here, in the glow and glory of those stained-glass windows—gorgeous with the armorial devices of a line of county families! Innocent, simple-hearted lad! wandering about like a prince in a fairy tale, ready to fall in love with the first pretty girl he saw by the roadside, and to take her back to his kingdom."

"If you want to see Trevanard's farm before dark you must come on, sir," said Elspeth.

Maurice took the hint, and followed at his briskest pace. They were soon out of the pine grove, which they left by a little wooden gate, and on the wild wide hills, where the distant sheepbell had an eerie sound in the still evening air.

Even the gables of the Manor House disappeared presently as they went down a dip in the hills. Far off in a green hollow, Maurice saw some white buildings—scattered untidily near a patch of water, which reflected the saffron-hued evening sky.

"That's Trevanard's," said Elspeth, pointing to this spot.

"I thought as much," said Maurice, "then you need go no further. You've fairly earned your fee."

He gave her the half-crown. The girl turned the coin over with a delighted look before she put it in her pocket.

"I'll go to Borcel End with you," she said. "I'd as lief be on the hills as at home—sooner, for grandmother is not over-pleasant company."

"But you'd better go back now, my girl, or it'll be dark long before you reach home."

Elspeth laughed, a queer impish cachination, which made Maurice feel rather uncomfortable.

"You don't suppose I'm afraid of the dark," she said, in her shrill young voice, so young and yet so old in tone. "I know every star in the sky. Besides, it's never dark at this time of year. I'll go on to Borcel End with you. May be you mayn't get accommodated there, and then I can show you a near way across the hills to Penwyn village. You might get shelter at one of the cottages anyhow."

"Upon my word you are very obliging," said Maurice, surprised by this show of benevolence upon the damsel's part.

"Do you know anything about this Borcel End?" he asked, presently, when they were going down into the valley.

"I've never been inside it," answered Elspeth, glibly, more communicative now than she had been an hour or two ago, when Churchill questioned her about the house of Penwyn. "Mrs. Trevanard isn't one to encourage a poor girl like me about her place. She's a rare hard one, they say, and would pinch and scrape for a sixpence; yet dresses fine on Sundays, and lives well. There's always good eating and drinking at Borcel End, folks say. I've heard tell as it was a gentleman's house once, before old Squire Penwyn bought it, and that there was a fine park round the house. There's plenty of trees now, and a garden that has all gone to ruin. The gentleman that owned Borcel spent all his money, people say, and old Squire Penwyn bought the place cheap, and turned it into a farm, and it's been in the hands of the Trevanards ever since, and they're rich enough to buy the place three times over, people say, if Squire Penwyn would sell it."

"I don't suppose I shall get a very warm welcome if this Mrs. Trevanard is such a disagreeable person," said Maurice, beginning to feel doubtful as to the wisdom of asking hospitality at Borcel End.

"Oh, I don't know about that. She's civil enough to gentlefolks, I've heard say. It's only her servants and such like she's so stiff with. You can but try."

They were at the farm by this time. The old house stood before them—a broad stretch of greensward in front of it, with a pool of blackish-looking water in the middle, on which several broods of juvenile ducks were swimming gaily.

The house was large, the walls rough-cast, with massive timber framework. There was a roomy central porch, also of plaster and timber, and this and a projecting wing at each end of the house gave a certain importance to the building. Some relics of its ancient gentility still remained, to show that Brocel End had not always been the house of a tenant farmer. A coat of arms, roughly cut on a stone tablet over the front door, testified to its former owner's pride of birth; and the quadrangular range of stables, stone-built, and more important than the house, indicated those sporting tastes which might have helped to dissipate the fortunes of a banished and half-forgotten race. But Borcel End, in its brightest day, had never been such a mansion as the old Tudor Manor House of Penwyn. There was a homeliness in the architecture which aspired to neither dignity nor beauty. Low ceilings, square latticed windows, dormers in the roof, and heavy chimney-stacks. The only beauty which the place could have possessed at its best was the charm of rusticity—an honest, simple English home.

To-day, however, Borcel End was no longer at its best. The stone quadrangle, where the finest stud of hunters in the county had been lodged, was now a straw-yard for cattle; one side of the house was overshadowed by a huge barn, built out of the *débris* of the park wall; a colony of jovial pigs disported themselves in a small enclosure which had once been a maze. A remnant of hedgerow, densest yew, still marked the boundary of this ancient pleasance, but all the rest had vanished beneath the cloven hoof of the unclean animal.

Though the farmyard showed on every side the tokens of agricultural prosperity, the house itself had a neglected air. The plaster walls, green and weather-stained, presented the curious blended hues of a Stilton cheese in prime condition, the timber seemed perishing for want of a good coat of paint. Poultry were pecking about close under the latticed windows, and even in the porch, and a vagabond pigling was thrusting his black nose in among the roots of one solitary rose bush which still lingered on the barren turf. Borcel End, seen in this fading light, was hardly a homestead to attract the traveller.

"I don't think much of your Borcel End," said Maurice, with a disparaging air. "However, here goes for a fair trial of west-country hospitality."

CHAPTER XX.

"O'er all there hung a shadow and a fear."

Mr. Clissold entered the porch, scattering the affrighted fowls right and left. As they sped cackling away, the house door, which had stood ajar, was opened wider by a middle-aged woman, who looked at the intruder frowningly. "We never buy anything of pedlars," she said, sharply. "It's no use coming here."

"I'm not a pedlar, and I haven't anything to sell. I am going through Cornwall on a walking tour, and want to find a place where I could stop for a week or so, and look about the country. I am prepared to pay a fair price for a clean homely lodging. The housekeeper at Penwyn Manor told me to try here."

"Then she sent you on a fool's errand," replied the woman; "we don't take lodgers."

"Not as a rule perhaps, but you might strain a point in my favour, I dare say."

Maurice Clissold had a pleasant voice and a pleasant smile. Mrs. Trevanard looked at him doubtfully, softened in spite of herself by his manner. And then no Trevanard was ever above earning an honest penny. They had not grown rich by refusing chances of small profits.

"Come, mother," cried a cheery voice from within, while she was hesitating, "you can ask the gentleman to come in and sit down a bit, anyhow. That won't make us nor break us."

"You can walk in and sit down, sir, if you like," said Mrs. Trevanard, with a somewhat unwilling air.

Maurice crossed the threshold, and found himself in a large stone-paved room, which had once been the hall, and was now the living room. The staircase, with its clumsy, black-painted balustrades, shaped like gouty legs, occupied one side of the room; on the other yawned the mighty chimney, with a settle on each side of the wide hearth, a cosy retreat on winter's nights. The glow of the fire had a comfortable look even on this midsummer evening.

A young man—tall, broad-shouldered, good-looking, clad in a suit of velveteen which gave him something the air of a gamekeeper—stood near the hearth cleaning a gun. He it was who had spoken just now—Martin Trevanard, the only son of the house, and about the only living creature who had any influence with his mother. Pride ruled her, religion, or bigotry, had power over her, gold was the strongest influence of all. But of all the mass of humanity there was but one unit she cared for besides herself, and that one was Martin.

"Sit down and make yourself at home, sir," said the young man, heartily. "You've walked far, I dare say."

"I have," answered Maurice, "but I don't want to rest anywhere until I am sure that I can get a night's shelter. There was no room for me at the 'Bell' at Penwyn, but I left my knapsack there, thinking I should be forced to go back to the village anyhow. It was an afterthought coming on here. Oh, by the way, there's a girl outside, the lodge-keeper's daughter, who has been my guide so far, and wants to know my fate before she goes home. What can you do with me, Mrs. Trevanard? I'm not particular. Give me a truss of clean hay in one of your barns, if you're afraid to have me in the house."

"Don't be ill-natured, old lady," said the young man, "the gentleman is a gentleman. One can see that with half an eye."

"That's all very well, Martin; but what will your father say to our taking in a stranger, without so much as knowing his name?"

"My name is Clissold," said the applicant, taking a card out of his pocket-book and throwing it on the polished beechwood table, the only handsome piece of furniture in the room. A massive oblong table, big enough for twelve or fourteen people to sit at. "There are my name and address. And so far as payment in advance goes,"—he put a sovereign down beside the card—"there's for my night's accommodation and refreshment."

"Put your money in your pocket, sir. You're a friend of Mr. Penwyn's, I suppose?" asked Mrs. Trevanard, still doubtful.

"I know the present Mr. Penwyn, but I cannot call myself his friend. The poor young fellow who was murdered, James Penwyn, was my nearest and dearest friend, my adopted brother."

"Let the gentleman stop, mother. We've rooms enough, and to spare, in this gloomy old barrack. A fresh face always brightens us up a little, and it's nice to hear how the world goes on. Father's always satisfied when you are. You can put the gentleman in that old room at the end of the corridor. You needn't be frightened, sir, there are no ghosts at Borcel End," added Martin Trevanard, laughing.

His mother still hesitated—but after a pause she said, "Very well, sir. You can stop to-night, and as long as you please afterwards at a fair price—say a guinea a week for eating, drinking, and sleeping, and a trifle for the servant when you go away."

Even in consenting the woman seemed to have a lingering reluctance, as if she were giving assent to something which she felt should have been refused.

"Your terms are moderation itself, madam, and I thank you. I'll send away my small guide."

He went out to the porch where Elspeth sat waiting—no doubt a listener to the conversation. Maurice rewarded her devotion with an extra sixpence, and dismissed her. Away she sped through the gathering gloom, light of foot as a young fawn. Maurice felt considerably relieved by the comfortable adjustment of the lodging question. He seated himself in an arm-chair by the hearth, and stretched out his legs in the ruddy glow, with a blissful sense of repose.

"Is there such a thing as a lad about the place who would go to the 'Bell' at Penwyn to fetch my knapsack for a consideration?" he asked.

There was a cowboy who would perform that service, it seemed. Martin went out himself to look for the rustic Mercury.

"He's a good-natured lad, my son," said Mrs. Trevanard, "but full of fancies. That comes of idleness, and too much education, his father says. His grandmother yonder never learned to read or write, and 'twas she and her husband made Borcel End what it is."

Following the turn of Mrs. Trevanard's head, Maurice perceived that an object which in the obscurity of the room he had taken for a piece of furniture was in reality a piece of humanity—a very old woman, dressed in dark garments, with only a narrow white border peeping from under a cowl-shaped black silk cap, a dingy red handkerchief pinned across her shoulders, and two bony hands, whose shrivelled fingers moved with a mechanical regularity in the process of stocking knitting.

"Ay," said a quivering voice. "I can't read or write—that's to say I couldn't even when I had my sight—but between us, Michael and I made Borcel what it is. Young people don't understand the old ways—they have servants to wait upon 'em, and play the harpsichord—but little good comes of it."

"Is she blind?" asked Maurice of the younger Mrs. Trevanard, in a whisper.

The old woman's quick ear caught the question.

"Stone blind, sir, for the last eighteen years. But the Lord has been good to me. I've a comfortable home and kind children, and they don't turn me out of doors, though I'm such a useless creature."

A gloomy figure in that dark corner beyond the glow of the fire. Maurice felt that the room was less comfortable somehow, since he had discovered the presence of this old woman, with her sightless orbs, and never-resting fingers, long and lean, weaving her endless web, gloomy as Clotho herself.

A plump, ruddy-cheeked maid-servant came bustling in with preparations for supper, making an agreeable diversion after this sad little episode. She lighted a pair of tall tallow candles in tall brass candlesticks, which feebly illumined the large low room. The wainscoted walls were blackened by smoke and time, and from the cross-beams that sustained the low ceiling hung a grove of hams, while flitches of bacon adorned the corners, where there was less need of headway. Every object in the room belonged to the useful rather than the beautiful. Yet there was something pleasant to Maurice's unaccustomed eye in the homely old-world comfort of the place.

He took advantage of the light to steal a glance at the face of his hostess, as she helped the servant to lay the cloth and place the viands on the table. Bridget Trevanard was about fifty years of age, but there were few wrinkles on the square brow, or about the eyes and mouth. She was tall, buxom, and broad-shouldered; a woman who looked as if she had few feminine weaknesses, either moral or physical. The muscular arm and broad open chest betokened an almost virile strength. Her skin was bright and clear, her nose broad and thick, but fairly modelled of its kind, her under lip full, and firm as if wrought in iron, the upper lip long, straight, and thin. Her eyes were dark brown, bright and hard, with that sharp penetrating look which is popularly supposed to see through deal boards, and even stone walls on occasion. So at least thought the servants at Borcel End.

A model farmer's wife, this Mrs. Trevanard, a severe mistress, yet not unjust or unkind, a proud woman, and in her own particular creed something of a zealot. A woman who loved money, not so much for its own sake, as because it served the only ambition she had ever cherished, namely, to be more respectable than her neighbours. Wealth went a long way towards this superior respectability, therefore did Mrs. Trevanard toil and spin, and never cease from labour in the pursuit of gain. She was the motive power of Borcel End. Her superlative energy kept Michael Trevanard, a somewhat lazy man by nature, a patient slave at the mill. Martin was the only creature at Borcel who escaped her influence. For him life meant the indulgence of his own fancies, with just so much work as gave him an appetite for his meals. He would drive the waggon to the mill, or superintend the men at hay-making and harvest. He rather liked attending market, and was a good hand at a bargain, but to the patient drudgery of every-day cares young Trevanard had a rooted objection. He was good-looking, good-natured, walked well, sang well, whistled better than any other man in the district, and was a general favourite. People said that the good blood of the old Trevanards showed in young Martin.

CHAPTER XXI.

"He cometh not," she said.

When the supper-table was ready, the servant girl ran to the porch and rang a large bell, which was kept under one of the benches—a bell that pealed out shrilly over the silent fields. This summons brought home Michael Trevanard, who appeared in about five minutes, pulling down his shirt-sleeves, and carrying his coat over his arm, while some stray wisps of hay which hung about his hair and clothes indicated that he had but that moment left the yard where they were building a huge stack, which Maurice had seen looming large through the dusk as he approached Borcel.

"We've stacked the fourteen acre piece, mother," said the farmer, as he pulled on his coat, "and a fine stack it is, too, as sweet as a hazel nut. No fear of mildew this year. And now I'll give myself a wash——"

He stopped, surprised at beholding a stranger standing by his hearth. Maurice had risen to receive the master of the house.

Martin explained the traveller's presence.

"We've taken to lodging-letting since you've been out, father," he said, in his easy way. "This gentleman wants to stay here and to look about the country round for a few days, and as mother thought he'd be company for me, and knew you wouldn't have any objection, she said yes. Mr. Clissold, that's the gentleman's name, is a friend of the family up yonder." An upward jerk of Martin's head indicated the Manor House.

"Any friend of the Squire's, or any one your mother thinks proper to accommodate, my lad, she's missus here," answered Mr. Trevanard. "You're kindly welcome, sir."

The farmer went out to some back region, whence was immediately heard an energetic pumping and splashing, and a noise as of a horse being rubbed down, after which Mr. Trevanard reappeared, lobster-like of complexion, and breathing hard after his rapid exertions.

He was a fine-looking man, with a face which might fairly be supposed to show the blood of the Trevanards, for the features were of a patrician type, and the broad open brow inspired at once respect and confidence. That candid countenance belonged to a man too incapable of deceit to be capable of suspicion; a man whom an artful child might cheat with impunity, a man who could never have grown rich unaided.

Mr. and Mrs. Trevanard, their son, and their guest, sat down to supper without delay; but the old blind mother still kept her seat in the shadowy corner, and eat her supper apart. It consisted only of a basin of broth, sprinkled with chopped parsley, which the old woman sipped slowly, while the rest were eating their substantial meal.

Maurice had eaten nothing since noon, and did ample justice to the lordly round of corned beef, and home-cured chine, the freshly gathered lettuces, and even the gooseberry pie and clotted cream. He and Martin talked all supper-time, while the house-mother carved, and the farmer abandoned himself to the pleasures of the table, and drank strong cider with easy enjoyment after the toilsome day.

"There's no place like a hay-field for making a man thirsty," he said, by way of apology, after one of his deep draughts; "and I can't drink the cat-lap mother sends to the men."

Martin talked of field sports and boating. He had a little craft of his own, four or five tons burden, and was passionately fond of the water. By and by the conversation drifted round to the Squire of Penwyn.

"He rides well," said Martin, "but I don't believe he's over-fond of hunting, though he subscribes handsomely to the hounds. I never knew such a fellow for doing everything liberally. He's bound to be popular, for he's the best master they ever had at the Manor."

"And is he popular?" asked Maurice.

"Well, I hardly know what to say about that. I only know that he ought to be. People are so hard to please. There are some say they liked the old Squire best, though he wasn't half so generous, and didn't keep any company worth speaking of. He had a knack of talking to people and making himself one of them that went a long way. And then some people remember Mr. George, and seem to have a notion that this man is an interloper. He oughtn't to have come into the property, they say. Providence never could have meant the son of the youngest son to have Penwyn. They're as full of fancies as an egg is full of meat in our parts."

"So it seems. Mrs. Penwyn is liked, I suppose?"

"Yes, she made friends with the poor people in no time. And then she's a great beauty; people go miles to see her when she rides to covert with her husband. There's a sister, too, still prettier to my mind."

Martin promised to show his new friend all that was worth seeing for twenty miles round Borcel. He would have the dog-cart ready early next morning, directly after breakfast, in fact, and six o'clock was breakfast-time at the farm. Maurice was delighted with the friendly young fellow, and thought that he had stumbled upon a very agreeable household.

Mrs. Trevanard was somewhat stern and repellent in manner, no doubt, but she was not absolutely uncivil, and Mr. Clissold felt that he should be able to get on with her pretty well.

She had said grace before meat, and she stopped the two young men in their talk presently, and offered a thanksgiving after the meal. It was a long grace, Methodistical in tone, with an allusion to Esau's mess of pottage, which was brought in as a dreadful example of gluttony.

After this ceremonial Mrs. Trevanard went upstairs to superintend the preparation of the stranger's apartment. The grandmother vanished at the same time, spirited away by the serving wench, who led her out by a little door that opened near her corner, and the three men drew round the hearth, lighted their pipes, and smoked and talked in a very friendly fashion for the next half hour or so. They were talking merrily enough when Mrs. Trevanard came downstairs again, candle in hand. She had taken out one of the old silver candlesticks which had been part of her dower, in order to impress the visitor with a proper notion of her respectability.

"Your room's ready, Mr. Clissold," she said, "and here's your bedroom candle."

Maurice took the hint, and bade his new friends good night. He followed Mrs. Trevanard up the broad, bulky old staircase, and to the end of a corridor. The room into which she led him was large, and had once been handsome, but some barbarian had painted the oak paneling pink, and the wood carving over the fireplace had been defaced by the industrious knives of several generations of schoolboys; there was a good deal of broken glass in the lattices, and a general air of dilapitude. A fire burned briskly in the wide basket-shaped grate, and, though it brightened the room, made these traces of decay all the more visible.

"It's a room we never use," said Mrs. Trevanard, "so we haven't cared to spend money upon it. There's always enough money wanted for repairs, and we haven't need to waste any upon fanciful improvements. The place is dry enough, for I take care to open the windows on sunny days, and there's nothing better than air and sun to keep a room dry. I had the fire lighted to-night for cheerfulness' sake."

"You are very kind," replied Maurice, pleased to see his knapsack on a chair by the bed, "and the room will do admirably. It looks the pink of cleanliness."

"I don't harbour dirt, even in unused rooms," answered Mrs. Trevanard. "It needs a mistress's eye to keep away cobwebs and vermin, but I've never spared myself trouble that way. Good night, sir."

"Good night, Mrs. Trevanard. By the way, you've no ghosts here, I think your son said?"

"I hope both you and he know better than to believe any such rubbish, sir."

"Of course; only this room looks the very picture of a haunted chamber, and if I were capable of believing in ghosts I should certainly lie awake on the look-out for one to-night."

"Those whose faith is surely grounded have no such fancies, sir," replied Mrs. Trevanard, severely, and closed the door without another word.

"The room looks haunted, for all that," muttered Maurice, and then involuntarily repeated those famous lines of Hood's,—

> "O'er all there hung a shadow and a fear;
> A sense of mystery the spirit daunted,
> And said, as plain as whisper in the ear,
> The place is haunted!"

The bedstead was a four-poster, with tall, spirally twisted posts, and some dark drapery, shrunken with age, and too small for the wooden framework. There was an old-fashioned press, or wardrobe, of black wood, whose polished surface reflected the firelight. A three-cornered wash-hand stand, and a clumsy-looking chest of drawers between the windows, surmounted by a cracked looking-glass, completed the furniture of the room. The boards were uncarpeted, and showed knots and dark patches in the worm-eaten wood, which a morbid fancy might have taken for the traces of some half-forgotten murder.

"Not a cheerful-looking room by any means, even with the aid of that blazing fire," thought Maurice.

15*

He opened one of the casements and looked out. The night air was soft and balmy, perfumed with odours of clover and the newly stacked hay. The Atlantic lay before him, shining under the great red moon, which had but just risen. A pleasanter prospect this than the bare walls of faded, dirty pink, the black clothes-press, and funereal four-poster.

Maurice lingered at the window, his arms folded on the broad ledge, his thoughts wandering idly— wandering back to last year and the moonlight that had shone upon the cathedral towers of Eborsham, the garden of the "Waterfowl" Inn, and the winding river.

"Poor James!" he mused, "how happy that light-hearted fellow might have been at Penwyn Manor!— how happy, and how popular! He would have had the knack of pleasing people, with that frank, easy kindness of his, and would have made friends of half the county. And if he had married that actress girl? A folly, no doubt; but who knows if all might not have ended happily? There was nothing vulgar or low about that girl—indeed, she had the air of one of Nature's gentlewomen. It would have been a little difficult for her to learn all the duties of a *châtelaine*, perhaps—how to order a dinner, and whom to invite —the laws of precedence—the science of morning calls. But if James loved her, and chose her from all other women for his wife, why should he not have been happy with her? I was a fool to oppose his fancy, still more a fool for leaving him. He might be alive now, perhaps, but for that wild-goose journey of mine."

Here his thoughts took another turn. They went

back to that train of circumstances which had brought about his absence from Eborsham on the night of James Penwyn's murder.

It was past midnight when Maurice Clissold roused himself from that long reverie, and prepared for peaceful slumber in the funereal bed. His fire had burned low by this time, and the red glow of the expiring embers was drowned in the full splendour of the risen moon, whose light silvered the bare boards, and brought into strong relief those stains and blotches upon the wood which looked so like the traces of ancient murder. The bed was luxurious, for there was no stint of feathers at Borcel End; yet Maurice wooed the god of sleep in vain. He began to think that there must be some plumage of game birds mingled with the stuffing of his couch, and that, soft and deep as it was, this was one of those beds upon which a man could neither sleep nor die comfortably.

"I ought to be tired enough to sleep on a harder bed than this, considering the miles I've walked to-day," he thought.

It may have been that he was over-tired, or it may have been that flood of silver light streaming through the diamond-panes of yonder lattice. Whatever might be the reason of his restlessness, sleep came not to straighten his unquiet limbs, or to steep his wandering thoughts in her cool waters of forgetfulness.

He heard a distant clock—in the hall where he had supped, most likely—strike two, and just at this time a gentle drowsiness began to steal over him. He was just falling deep down into some sleepy hollow, soft as a bed of poppies, when his door was opened by a cautious hand, and a light footstep sounded on the floor. He was wide awake in a minute, and without moving from his recumbent position, drew the dark curtain back a little way and looked towards the door. The shadow of the curtain fell upon him as he lay, and the bedstead looked unoccupied.

"The ghost!" he said to himself, with rather an awful feeling. "I knew there must be one in such a room—or perhaps the house is on fire, and some one has come to warn me."

No; that wanderer through the deep of night had evidently no business with Mr. Clissold—nay, was unconscious of, or indifferent to, the fact of his existence. The figure slowly crossed the floor, with a light step, but a little sliding noise, as of a foot ill-shod—a slipper down at heel.

It came full into the moonlight presently, between the bedstead and the two windows.

"Ay, verily a ghost," thought Maurice, with a feeling like ice-cold water circulating slowly through every artery in his body.

Never had he seen, or conceived within his mind, a figure more spectral, yet with a certain wild beauty in its ghastliness. He raised himself in his bed, still keeping well within the shadow of the curtains, and watched the spectre with eyes which seemed endowed with a double power of vision in the thrilling intensity of that moment.

The spectre was a woman's form; tall, slender—nay, so wasted that it seemed almost unnaturally tall. The face was death-pale in that solemn light, the eyes large and dark, the hair ebon-black and falling in long loose masses over the white garment, whose folds were straight as those of a winding-sheet. So might the dead, risen from a new-made grave, have looked.

The figure went straight to one of the casements—that furthest from the bed, and at right angles with it—unfastened the hasp, and flung the window wide open. She drew a chair close to the open window, and kneeled upon it, resting her arms on the sill, and leaning out of the window, as if watching for some one to come, thought Maurice, that frozen blood of his beginning to thaw a little.

"Those actions seem too deliberate and real for a ghost," he told himself. "Phantoms must surely be soundless. Now I heard the slipshod feet upon the floor. I heard the scrooping of the chair. I can see a gentle heaving of the breast under that shroud-like garment. Ergo my visitor is not a ghost. Who can she be? Not Mrs. Trevarand assuredly, nor the old blind grandmother, nor the buxom lass who waited on us at supper. I thought those were all the womenkind in the house."

A heavy sigh from that unearthly-looking intruder startled him, a sigh so long, so full of anguish, so like the utterance of some lost soul in pain! Difficult not to yield to superstitious fear as he gazed at that kneeling figure, with its long dark hair, and delicate profile, sharply outlined against the black shadow of the deep-sunk casement.

Again came the sigh, despairing, desolate.

"Oh, my love, my love, why don't you come back to me?"

The words broke like a cry of despair from those pale lips. Not loud was the sorrowful appeal, but so full of pain that it touched the listener's heart more deeply than the most passionate burst of louder grief could have done.

"Dear love, you promised, you promised me. How could I have lived if I had not thought you would come back?"

Then the tone changed. She was no longer appealing to another, but talking to herself, hurriedly, breathlessly, with ever increasing agitation.

"Why not to-night? Why shouldn't he come back to-night? He was always fond of moonlight nights. He promised to be true to me, and stand by me, come what might. No harm should ever come to me. He swore that, swore it with his arms round me, his eyes looking into mine. No man could be false, and yet look as he looked, and speak as he spoke."

Silence for a brief space, and then a sudden cry—a sharp anguish-stricken cry, as of a broken heart.

"Who said he was dead and gone, dead and gone years ago? The world wouldn't look as bright as it does if he were dead. He loved the moonlight. Could you shine, false moon, if he were dead?" Again a pause, and then a slower, more thoughtful tone, as if doubts disturbed that demented brain. "Was it last year he used to come, last year when we were so happy together—last year when———"

A sudden burst of tears interrupted the sentence. The woman's face fell forward on her folded arms, and the frail body was shaken by her sobs.

Maurice Clissold no longer doubted his visitant's humanity.

This was real grief, perchance real madness. For a little while he had fancied it a case of somnambulism. But the eyes which he had seen lifted despairingly to that moonlit sky had too much expression for the eyes of a somnambulist.

For a long time—or time that seemed long to Clissold's mind—the woman knelt by the window, now silent, motionless as an inanimate figure, now talking rapidly to herself, anon invoking that absent one whose broken promises were perhaps the cause of her wandering wits. Never had the young man beheld a more piteous spectacle. It was as if one of Wordsworth's most pathetic pastorals were here realized. His heart ached at the sound of those heart-broken sighs. This flesh and blood sorrow moved him more deeply than any spectral woe. This was no ghostly revisitant of earth, who acted over agonies dead and gone, but a living, loving woman, who mourned a lost or a faithless lover.

At last, with one farewell look seaward, as if it were along yon moonlit track across the waves she watched for the return of her lover, this new Hero turned from the casement, closed it carefully and quietly, and then slowly left the room. Maurice heard that slipshod foot going slowly along the passage, until the sound dwindled and died in the distance.

He fancied sleep would have been impossible after such a scene as this, but perhaps that overstrained attention of the last hour had exhausted his wakefulness, for he fell off presently into a sound slumber, from which he was only awakened by a friendly voice outside his door saying, "Six o'clock, Mr. Clissold. If you want the long round I promised you last night we ought to start at seven."

"All right," answered Maurice, as gaily as if no

uncanny visitor had shortened his slumbers. "I'll be with you in half an hour."

He kept his word, and was down in the hall, or family sitting-room, just in time to hear the noisy old eight-day clock strike the half-hour, with a slow and laborious movement of its inward anatomy, as if fast subsiding into dumbness and decrepitude. Mr. Trevanard had breakfasted an hour ago, and gone forth to his haymakers. Mrs. Trevanard was busy about the house, but the old blind grandmother sat in her corner, plying those never-resting needles, just as she had sat, just as she had knitted last night; with no more apparent share or interest in the active life around her than the old clock had.

There was a liberal meal ready for the stranger. Last night's round of beef, and a Cornish ham, archetype of hams, adorned the board, but were only intended as a reserve force in case of need, while the breakfast proper consisted of a dish of broiled ham and eggs, and another of trout, caught a hundred yards or so from the house that morning. Home-baked bread, white and brown, a wedge of golden honeycomb, and a plate of strawberries counted for nothing.

Both young men did justice to the breakfast, which they eat together, making the best use of the half-hour allotted for the meal, and not talking so much as they had done last night at the more leisurely evening repast.

"I hope you slept pretty well," said Martin, when he had taken the edge off a healthy appetite, and was trifling with a slice of beef.

"Not quite so well as I ought to have done in so

comfortable a bed. My brain was a little over-active, I believe."

"Ah, that's a complaint I don't suffer from. Father says I haven't any brains. I tell him brains don't grow at Borcel End. One year is so like another that we get to be a kind of clockwork, like poor old granny yonder. We get up every morning at the same hour, look out of our windows to see what sort of weather it is, eat and drink, and walk about the farm, and go to bed again, without using our minds at all from the beginning to the end of the business. Father and I brighten up a little on market days, but for the rest of our lives we might just as well be a couple of slow-going machines."

"There is nothing drowsy or mechanical about your mother's nature, I should think, in spite of the quiet life you all lead here."

"No, mother's mind is a candle that would burn to waste in a dark cellar. Her blood isn't poppy-juice, like the Trevanards'. Do you know that my father has never been as far as Plymouth one way, or as far as Penzance the other way, in his life? He has no call to go, he says, so he doesn't go. He squats here upon his land like a toad, and would if his life was to be threescore and ten centuries instead of as many years."

"You would like a different kind of life, I dare say," suggested Maurice.

The young man's bright eye reminded him of a caged squirrel's—a wild, freeborn creature, longing for the liberty of forests and untrodden groves.

"Yes, if I could have chosen my own life, I would have been a soldier, like George Penwyn."

"To die by the hands of savages."

"Yes, they say he had a hard death, that those copper-coloured devils scalped him—tied him to a tree—tortured him. His soldiers went mad with revenge, and roasted some of the miscreants alive afterwards, I believe; but that wouldn't bring the captain to life again."

"Do you remember him!"

"Well. He used to come fishing in our water; the very stream that trout came out of this morning. I was a little chap of eight or nine years old when the Captain was last home, and used to catch flies for him, and carry his basket and loaf about with him half the day through; and many a half-crown has he given me, for he was an open-handed fellow always, and one of the handsomest, pleasantest young men I ever remember seeing—when I say young, I suppose he must have been past thirty at this time, for he was the oldest of the three brothers, and Balfour, the youngest, had been married ever so many years. But here's the trap, and we'd better be off; good-bye, granny."

The old woman gave a hoarse chuckle of response, marvellously like the internal rumbling of the ancient clock.

"Good morning, ma'am," said Maurice, anxious to be civil; but of his salutation the dame took no notice.

The horse, though clumsily built, and not unacquainted with the plough, was a good goer. The two young men had soon left Borcel End behind them, down in its sleepy hollow, and were driving over the fair green hills.

"Now to fathom the mystery of last night's adventure," thought Maurice, when they were out of sight of Borcel. "I think I can venture to speak pretty freely to this good-natured young man."

He meditated a few minutes, and then began the attack.

"When you asked me at breakfast how I rested last night, I didn't give you quite a straightforward answer," he said. "There was a reason for my not getting a full allowance of sleep, which I didn't care to speak of till you and I were alone."

"Indeed," said Martin Trevanard, looking round at him sharply. "What was that?"

There was a lurking anxiety in that keen glance of scrutiny, Maurice Clissold thought.

"Some one came into my room in the dead of the night—a woman," he said. "At first I almost thought she was a ghost. I was never so near yielding to superstitious terror in my life. But I soon discovered my mistake, and that she was only a living, suffering fellow-creature."

"I am very sorry such a thing should have happened," said Martin, gravely. "She ought to be better taken care of. The person you saw must have been my unfortunate sister."

"Your sister?"

"Yes. She is ten years older than I, and not quite right in her mind. But she is perfectly harmless—has never in her life attempted to injure any one—not even herself, poor soul, though her own existence is dreary enough; and neither my father nor my mother will consent to send her away to be taken care of. Our old doctor sees her now and then, and doesn't call her mad. She is only considered a little weak in her intellect."

"Has she been so from childhood?" asked Maurice.

"Oh dear no. She went to school at Helstone, and was quite an accomplished young woman, I believe—played the piano, and painted flowers, and was brought up quite like a young lady; never put her hand to dairy work, or anything of the kind. She was a very handsome girl in those days, and father and mother were uncommonly proud of her. I can just remember her when she left school for good. I was always hanging about her, and I used to think she was like a beautiful princess in a fairy tale. She was very good to me, told me fairy stories, and sung to me in the twilight. Many a time I've fallen asleep in her lap, lulled by her sweet voice, when I was a little chap of eight or nine. There were only us two, and she was very fond of me. Poor Muriel!"

"What was it brought about such a change in her?"

"Well that's a story I've never quite got to the bottom of. It's a sore subject even with father, who's easy enough to deal with about most things. And as to mother, you have but to mention Muriel's name to make her look like thunder. Yet she's never unkind to the poor soul. I know that."

"Does your sister live among you when you are alone?"

"No, she has a little room over granny's, with a little old-fashioned staircase leading up to it. A room quite cut off from the rest of the house. You can't reach it except by going through granny's bedroom, which is on the ground-floor, you must understand, on account of the old lady's weak legs. Now one of poor Muriel's fancies is to roam about the house in the middle of the night, especially moonlight nights, for the moonlight makes her wakeful. So, as a rule, granny locks her door of a night. However, I suppose last night the old lady forgot, in consequence of the excitement caused by your arrival, and that's how you happened to have such an uncomfortable time."

"You haven't told me even the little you do know as to the cause of your sister's state."

"Haven't I? All I know is what my father told me once. She was crossed in love, it seems—loved some one rather above her in station—and never got over it. That comes of being constant to one's first fancy."

"You say she lives in a room by herself. Does she never have air or exercise?"

"Do you imagine us barbarians? Yes, she roams about the old neglected garden at the back of the house, just as she pleases, but never goes beyond. She has a pretty clear notion that that is her beat, poor girl, and I've never known her break bounds. Mother fetches her indoors at sunset, and gives her her supper, and sees that she's comfortable for the night, and tries to keep her clothes decent and tidy, but the poor soul tears them sometimes when her melancholy fit is upon her."

CHAPTER XXII.

"And I shall be alone until I die."

THE image of that white-robed figure, pallid face, and ebon hair haunted Maurice Clissold throughout the day, though his day was very pleasant, and Martin Trevanard the most cheerful of companions. They halted at various villages, explored old parish churches, where tarnished and blackened brasses told of mitred abbots, and lords of the soil, otherwise unrecorded and forgotten. Clissold was learned in church architecture, and not a gargoyle escaped his keen eye. Martin was pleased to exhibit the interesting features of his native land, and listened deferentially to Maurice's disquisitions on brasses, fonts, and piscinæ.

They stopped at a wayside inn, lunched heartily on bread and cheese and cider, and were altogether as companionable as young men can well be. Martin had read about half a dozen books since he left Helstone grammar school, but those were of the highest character, and he had them in his heart of hearts. Shakespeare, Pope, and Byron were his poets; Fielding, Goldsmith, and Scott his only romances.

From Shakespeare and Scott he had learned history, from Fielding and Goldsmith he had caught the flavour of wit and humour that are dead as the Latin classics. Thus Clissold found, not without a touch of surprise, that the farmer's son was no unworthy companion for a man who had made literature his profession.

On their homeward round they pulled up at Penwyn Church, which stood high and dry on the green hill-side, midway between the village and the manor, and looked like a church that had fallen from the sky, so completely was it out of everybody's way. Tradition insisted that in the Middle Ages there had been a village close to the church, but no trace of that vanished settlement remained. There stood the temple, square-towered, with crocketed finials at the four angles of the tower. There lay its ancient slumberous graveyard on the slope of the hill, the dead for ever basking in the southern sun, which, in this midsummer weather, seemed to have power enough to warm them back to life again.

Here Maurice saw the resting-place of the Penwyns, almost as old as the church itself, a vault so large that these lords of the soil seemed to have a whole crypt to themselves. Very mouldy, and cold and dark, was this last abode of the squires and their race. Here he saw also the parish registers, which contained a concise synopsis of the history of the Penwyns since the Middle Ages, how they had been christened, married, and buried.

"James ought to have been brought down here," said Maurice, when they were in the churchyard, where the deep soft grass was full of field flowers, and the air of sweet homely odours; "not in that mouldy old crypt with his ancestral dust, but here amongst this thymy grass, face to face with the sun and the sea, and with the skylark singing above his grave. It would have been ever so much better than Kensal Green."

It was eight o'clock when they drove down into

the valley, where the old white house and its numerous barns and outbuildings looked like a village nestling in that grassy hollow. The scene looked just the same as last night, when Maurice Clissold approached it for the first time—the same stillness upon all things, the same low yellow light in the western sky, the same red glow from the hall fire, the same changeless figure of the old grandmother in her high-backed leather-covered arm-chair, half hidden in the shadow of the corner where she sat.

It wanted an hour to supper, and Mr. Trevanard was struggling with some accounts at a table by one of the windows, where he had the last of the dying daylight.

"Hope you've had a pleasant day, sir," he said, without looking up from his papers, or relaxing the frown with which he contemplated a long column of figures. "Take a pull of that cider after your drive; it's only just drawn.—You might give me a hand with these accounts, Martin. I never was a dab at figures."

"All right, father, we'll soon tot 'em up."

Martin sat down by his father, and took the pen out of his hand. Maurice refreshed himself with a draught of cider, and then went to the porch.

"I should like to take a look round the place between this and supper-time, if you don't mind, Mr. Trevanard," he said.

"Look where you please, sir, you're free and welcome. You'll hear the supper-bell at nine o'clock."

Maurice lighted a cigar as he left the porch, and prepared for a contemplative, dreamy stroll, one calm hour of solitude before the day was done.

He avoided the stackyard, and did not honour the various families of black and white piglings, in divers stages of infancy and adolescence, with his attention. He made a circuit of the pond, and went round to the back of the homestead, where lay that neglected garden which he had seen from the distance. At this midsummer-time it was a wilderness of verdure, and flowers ran wild. Great lavender bushes, forests of unpruned roses, tall white lilies, syringa, carnations, weeds, and blossoms, growing as they would. Moss-grown paths, a broken sundial fallen across a bed of heart's-ease and mignonette. Beyond the flower-garden there was a still deeper wilderness of hazel, quinces, and alders, which drew their chief sustenance from a shallow pool, whose dark shining surface was almost hidden by the spreading branches, the grey old trunks, the thick screen of leaves, through which the light came dimly even at noon.

A delightful spot for a meditative poet. Maurice was charmed with garden and wilderness, and lighted a second cigar on the strength of his discovery of the alder and quince grove.

It was not easy walking here by reason of the undergrowth of St. John's-wort, fern, and briar, which made a dense jungle, but after a little exploration Mr. Clissold came upon a narrow footpath, evidently well trodden, which wound in and out among the old grey trunks, and under the hazel boughs, till it brought him to the brink of the water.

The pool was wider than he had thought, but so covered with water-lilies that the dark water only showed in patches through that thick carpet of shining leaves. Just such a pool as a stranger might easily walk into unawares. Maurice pulled up in time, and seated himself on the gnarled trunk of an alder, whose roots straggled deep down into the water, among sedges and innocent harmless cresses. Here he slowly pulled at his cigar, abandoning himself to such thoughts as a poet has in such a scene and such an hour.

The last yellow gleam of the sun shone faintly behind the low thick trees, and through the one break in the wood the distant sea-line showed darkly grey, just where ocean merged into sky.

"I should write better verses if I lived here for a year," thought Maurice, musing upon a certain volume which he meant to give the world by and bye. He hardly knew whether there would be much in it worthy the world's acceptance. It was only the outpouring of a strong, fresh soul, a soul that had known its share of human sorrow, and done a brave man's battle with care.

He was deep in a reverie that had led him very far away from Borcel End when he heard a rustling of the branches near him, and turned quickly round, expecting to see Martin Trevanard.

The face that looked at him from between the parted hazel boughs startled him almost as much as that white-robed figure last night. It was the face he had seen in the moonlight, and which he saw now with peculiar distinctness in the clear grey light—a wan white face, with large dark eyes—a face which once must have been most beautiful. The dark eyes, the delicate features, were still beautiful, but the complexion was almost ghastly in its pallor, and the eyes were unnaturally bright. This was Muriel Trevanard.

Maurice thought she would have been frightened at sight of him, and would have hurried away. But, to his surprise, she came a little nearer him, cautiously, stealthily even, those restless eyes glancing right and left as she approached. There was a curious intensity in her gaze when her eyes fixed themselves at last upon his face, peering at him, scrutinizing him with something of her mother's keen look. One hand was lifted to her head to push back the wild mass of tangled hair, and the loose sleeve of her gown fell back from the white wasted arm. Face and body seemed alike wasted by the mind's consuming fire.

"You can tell me, perhaps," she said, in a quick eager voice, "others won't, they're too unkind, for they must know. You can tell me, I'm sure. When will he come back?"

"My poor soul, I would gladly tell you if I knew. But I don't even know whom you are talking of."

"Oh yes, you do. Mother knows. She told you, I dare say. I'm not going to tell his name. I promised to keep that secret, whatever it cost me to be silent, and I'm not going to break my promise. When is he coming back?"

She paused, looking at him with beseeching expectant eyes, as if she waited breathless for his answer.

"Is he ever coming back?"

She waited again.

"Indeed, Miss Trevanard, I know nothing about it."

"How dare you call me Miss Trevanard? That's not my name."

"Muriel, then."

"That's better. . He called me Muriel."

Her chin dropped on her breast, and she stood for a few moments looking down at the water, all her face softened by some sweet sad thought.

"He called me Muriel," she repeated. "Muriel, Muriel. I can hear his voice now. Hear it—yes, as plainly as I can see him when I close my eyes."

Again a pause, and then an eager question.

"How can he be dead when he is so near me? How can he be dead when I hear him and see him, and can even feel the touch of his hand upon my head, his lips upon my lips. He awakes me from my sleep sometimes with a kiss, but when I open my eyes he is gone. Was he always a spirit?"

She seemed unconscious of Maurice's presence as she moved a few paces further along the water's edge, always looking downward, in self-communion.

"My love, how can they say that you are dead, when I am waiting for you so patiently, and will wait for you to the end—wait till you come to take me away with you? It was to be little more than a year, you told me. Oh, God, what a long year!"

The anguish in that last ejaculation pierced the listener's heart as it had been pierced by her wild cry of sorrow last night. He followed her along the brink of the pool, put his arm round her shrunken form protectingly, and tried to comfort her as best he might, knowing so little of her grief.

"Muriel," he said gently, and her name so spoken seemed to have a softening influence upon her, "I am almost a stranger to this place and to you, but I would gladly be your friend if I could. Tell me if there is anything I can do to comfort you. Are you happy in your home, with your poor old grandmother? or would you rather be somewhere else?"

He wanted to find out if she was suffering from any sense of ill-usage, if she felt herself a prisoner and an alien in her father's house.

"No," she said, resolutely, "I must stay here. He will come and fetch me."

"But you speak sometimes as if you knew him to be dead. Is it not foolish, vain, to hope for that which cannot happen?"

"He is not dead. People have told me so on purpose to break my heart, I think. Haven't I told you that I see him very often?"

"Then why are you so unhappy?"

"Because he will not stay with me—because he does not come to fetch me away, as he promised, in a little more than a year—because he comes and goes like a spirit. Perhaps they are right, and he is really dead."

"Would it not be better to make up your mind to that, and to leave off watching for him. and roaming about the house at night?"

"Who told you that?" she asked, quickly.

"Never mind who told me. You see I know how foolish you are. Wouldn't it be wiser to try and go back to the common business of life, to bind up all that loose hair neatly, like a lady, and to try to be a comfort to your father and mother."

At that last word an angry cry broke from the pale lips.

"Mother!" echoed Muriel, "I have no mother. That woman yonder," pointing towards the house, "is my worst enemy. Mother! My mother!" with a bitter laugh. "Ask her what she has done with my child?"

That question came upon Maurice Clissold like a revelation. Here was a sadder story than he had dreamt of, a story which no word of Martin's had hinted at, a story of shame as well as of sorrow, perchance. He remained silent, troubled and perplexed by this new turn of affairs. His office of consoler, his attempt to smooth the tangled threads of a disordered brain, came to an end all at once.

The woman turned from him impatiently, muttering to herself as she went away. He followed her along the sinuous footpath, and across the garden, and watched her as she entered by a low half-glass door at the back of the house. He passed this door afterwards, and stole a glance through the glass into a large low room, where there was a fire burning— a room which he divined to be the grandmother's chamber.

An old-fashioned tent bedstead, with red and white chintz curtains, occupied one side of the room; a ponderous old arm-chair stood near the fireplace; a huge wooden chest made at once a seat and a receptacle for all kinds of household stores; a corner cupboard filled with crockery ware, and a small round table near the hearth, completed the catalogue of furniture.

Here, on the hearth-rug, sat Muriel, her wild hair falling about her face, her hands clasped upon her knees, her eyes bent gloomily upon the burning log.

The supper-bell rang from the porch on the other side of the homestead while Maurice was watching that melancholy figure by the hearth.

"She has taken away my appetite for supper," he said to himself, "and has almost set me against Borcel End."

That last speech of Muriel Trevanard's troubled him—"Ask her what she has done with my child?"

It set him thinking of dark stories of family pride and hidden crime. It took the flavour of enjoyment out of this rustic home, and imparted a taint of mystery and suspicion which poisoned the atmosphere.

CHAPTER XXIII.

"Surely, most bitter of all sweet things thou art."

Maurice Clissold keenly scrutinized Bridget Trevanard's face as they sat at supper that evening. Muriel's look of horror at the mention of her mother's name had inspired unpleasant doubts upon the subject of his hostess's character. He remembered how Elspeth had told him that Mrs. Trevanard was known as a hard woman; and he told himself that cruelty, or even crime, might be consistent with that hard nature which had won for the farmer's wife the reputation of a stern and exacting mistress. His closer examination of that face showed him no indication of lurking evil. That square, unwrinkled brow, those dark brown eyes, with their keen, straight outlook, denoted at least an honest nature. The firm lips, the square jaw, gave severity to the countenance—a resolute woman—a woman not to be turned from her purpose, thought Maurice, but a woman whom he could hardly imagine capable of crime.

And then why give credence to the rambling assertions of lunacy? It is the nature of madness to accuse the sane. Maurice tried to put the thought of Muriel's wild talk out of his mind; yet that awful question, "What has she done with my child?" haunted him.

He felt less desire to prolong his stay at Borcel. The restful tranquillity of the place seemed to have

"MOST BITTER OF ALL SWEET THINGS THOU ART." 251

departed. Muriel's fevered mind had its influence upon the atmosphere. He could not forget that she was near—wakeful, unhappy—waiting for the lover who was never to return to her.

He took good care to lock his door that night, and his slumbers were undisturbed. The next morning was devoted to a long ramble with Martin. They walked to a distant hill-side, where there were some Druidic remains well worth inspection; came back to the farm in time for the substantial early dinner, had a look at the haymakers dining plenteously in a great stone kitchen, and then retired to a field where the hay was cocked, to lie basking in the sun, with their faces seaward, dreaming away the summer afternoon.

Here Maurice told Martin the story of James Penwyn's death, and the brief love story which had come to so pitiful an ending.

"Poor child," he said, musingly, recalling his last interview with Justina, "I verily believe she loved him truly and honestly, and would have made him a good wife. I never saw a nobler countenance than that player girl's. I'm sorry I thrust myself between them with so much as one hard word."

"Was no one ever suspected of the murder?" asked Martin.

"Yes," replied Maurice, without taking his cigar from his lips, "I was for a little while."

This was rather startling. Martin Trevanard stared at his new acquaintance with a curious look for a moment or so, before he recovered himself.

"You were?"

"Yes. Didn't you know? My name was in the papers, but I believe they did me the favour to spell it wrong. Perhaps I ought to have mentioned the fact when I was asking Mrs. Trevanard to take me in. Yes, I, his bosom friend, was the only person they could pitch upon when they wanted to find the assassin. Yes, I have been in Eborsham gaol under suspicion as a murderer. The charge broke down at the inquest, and I came off with flying colours, I believe. Still there the fact remains. The Spinnersbury detectives put the crime down to me."

"It would need pretty strong proof to make *me* suspect you," said Martin, heartily.

"I was a good many miles away from the spot when that cursed deed was done, but it did not suit me to advertise my exact whereabouts to the world."

"Why not?"

"Because to have told the truth would have been to compromise a woman, the only one I ever loved, as a man loves one chosen woman out of all the world."

Martin threw away his unfinished cigar, turned himself about upon the haycock which he had chosen for his couch, and settled himself to hear something interesting, with a bright eager look in his dark eyes.

"Tell me all about it," he said.

"Bah! weak sentimentality," muttered Maurice, "I should only bore you."

"No, you wouldn't. I should like to hear it."

"Well, naming no names, and summing up the matter briefly, there will be no harm done. It is the story of a dead and buried folly, that's all; a hackneyed commonplace story enough."

He sighed, as if the recollection hurt him a little, dead as this old foolishness might be—sighed and looked seaward dreamily, as if he were looking back into the past.

"You must know that when I was a year or two younger, and life was fresher to me, I went a good deal into what people call society—didn't set my face against new acquaintances, dinner parties, dances, and so forth, as I do now. I've a fair income for a bachelor, belong to a good family, and can hold my own position well in a crowd. Now amongst the houses I visited in those days there were only two or three where I went from sheer honest regard for the people I visited. Among these was the house of a certain fashionable physician, not a hundred miles from Cavendish Square. He was a widower, with three daughters, the two elder thorough women of the world, and most delightful girls to know. We were chums from the outset. They drove me about in their barouche, made me useful as an escort at flower shows, a perambulatory catalogue at picture galleries, and we all three comprehended perfectly that I was not to dream of marrying either of them."

"Dangerous I should think," suggested Martin.

"Safe as the Tarpeian rock. My feelings for the dear girls were of a purely fraternal character from the first. I would as soon have bought the winner of the last Derby for a Park hack as had one of these two for my wife. I went shopping with them occasionally, twiddled my thumbs at Peter Robinson's while they turned over silks, and I knew the amount of millinery required for their sustenance. No, Martin, there was no peril here. Unluckily, there was the third daughter—a tender slip of a girl, hardly out of the schoolroom—a child who had her gowns meted out to her by her sisters, and wore perpetual white muslin for evening dress, and brown holland for morning. Good heavens! I can see her this moment, standing by the piano in her holland frock, with a blue ribbon twisted through her loose brown hair, and those divine hazel eyes looking at me pleadingly, as who should say, 'Be gentle to me, you see what a child I am.' No worldliness here—no ambition here—no avid desire of millinery—no set purpose of making a great marriage, I said to myself. Only innocence, and trustfulness, and childlike meekness. So I fell over head and ears in love with my friend's third daughter."

"Very natural," said Martin. "I don't see why it shouldn't have ended pleasantly."

"I didn't act like a sneak—make love to the girl behind her sisters' backs, and bide my time for winning her. I went to the doctor at once, told him what had happened, ventured to add that I thought my darling liked me, and asked his permission to offer her my hand. He hummed and hawed, said there was no one he would like better for a son-in-law; but his youngest child was really not out of the nursery, any question of an engagement was absurd. It seemed only yesterday that he had bought her a Shetland pony. However, he gave me to understand, in a general way, that I was free to come and go, so our intimacy knew no abatement. I still did the walking-stick business at flower shows, and the catalogue business at exhibitions, and made myself generally useful, seeing a good deal of my fair blossom-like maiden in the meanwhile. We met very often, sat together of an evening unnoticed when the room was full, and before long we knew that we loved each other, and we had sworn that for us two there should be no love but this. Papa might say what he liked about youth and foolishness and Shetland ponies. We were not impatient, we would wait for ever so many years, if necessary, but in good time we two should be one. Sweet and tender promises breathed in the twilight from lips too lovely to betray, dove-like eyes lifted shyly to mine, soft little hand resting so fondly within my arm! I laugh when I think of you, and how it all ended."

He did laugh bitterly, savagely almost, as he flung the stump of his cigar across the hay-cocks towards the sea. Martin waited in respectful silence, awed by this little gust of passion.

"Well, we were pledged to each other and happy. This went on for a year. Nobody took any notice of us, any more than if we had been children playing at lovers. We lived in a foolish Paradise of our own, at least I did. Heaven only knows what her thoughts may have been. One day, when I had been away from town for a week or so, I called in Cavendish Square, saw the two elder girls, and heard that my betrothed had gone for a long visit to some friends in Yorkshire, at a place called Tilney Longford, a fine old country seat. Papa had thought her looking pale and thin, and had sent her off at a day's notice. She might be away two or three months. Lady Longford was the kindest of women, and was always asking them to stay at her place. 'We can't go, of course,' they said, "with our large circle; but that child has no ties, and can stay as long as they like to keep her.'

"This was hard upon me. The privilege of correspondence was denied us, for I could not write my darling a clandestine letter. I went to the doctor a second time, and told him that I had waited a year, that I was so much deeper in love by every day of that blessed year, and urged him to receive me as his daughter's suitor. He treated the question rather more seriously than before, repeated his assurance that I was the very man he would have liked for a son-in-law, but added that he did not consider my income sufficiently large, or my profession sufficiently lucrative to allow of his entrusting his daughter's happiness to my care. 'My girls have been expensively brought up,' he said. 'You have no notion what they cost me. I have been too busy to teach them prudence. It has been easier for me to earn money for them to waste than to find leisure to check their extravagance. We live in too fast an age for the vulgar virtues.' I argued the point, but vainly, and told him that whatever decision he might arrive at, his youngest daughter and I had made up our minds to be true to each other against all opposition. 'I am sorry to hear that,' he replied, 'for it will oblige me to ask you to discontinue your visits here when my little girl comes back, a discourtesy which goes very much against the grain.' I left him in a white heat, went straight off to James Penwyn, and arranged a tour which we had been talking about ever so long. We were to walk through the north of England, and I was to coach poor Jim for his last struggle at Oxford. London was hateful to me now that my darling had left it, and James Penwyn's company the only society I cared for."

He paused, abandoned himself to the memory of that vanished past for a little, and then went on more hurriedly.

"It was at Eborsham, the morning before James Penwyn's murder, that I received the first and last letter I was ever to get from my love. She had addressed it to me at my London lodgings, and it had been travelling about after me for the last three weeks. Her first letter! I opened it with such a thrill of joy, thinking how divine it was of her to be so daring as to write to me. Such a broken-hearted letter!—telling me how a certain rich landowner, near Lady Longford's, had proposed to her—she broke into a parenthesis, a page long, to assure me she had never given him the faintest encouragement—and how everybody persuaded her to accept him, and how her father himself had come down to Tilney to lecture her into subjection. 'But it is all useless,' she said, 'I will marry no one but my own dear love; and, oh, please, write and tell me what I am to do.' Think what I must have felt, Trevanard, when I considered that the letter was three weeks old, and what persecution the poor little soul might have had to suffer in the interval."

"What did you do?"

"Can you ask me? I started off without a quarter of an hour's delay, and got to Tilney as soon as the trains would carry me. It was an abominable cross-country journey, and there I was eating my heart out at dismal junctions for half the day. It was past three o'clock when I ended my journey of something less than a hundred miles, and found myself at a detestable little station called Tilney Road, eight miles from Tilney Longford, and no conveyance of any kind to be had. I did the distance in something under two hours, and entered the park gates just as the church clock hard by was striking five."

"You went straight to the house?"

"No, I didn't want to bring trouble upon that poor child, so I prowled about the place like a poacher, skirting the carriage roads. Luckily for me, there was a right of way through the park, so I was able to get pretty close to the house without attracting any one's particular attention. I reflected that, unless the doctor was still there—not a likely thing for a man whose moments were gold—there was no one to recognise me except my poor pet. As I approached the gardens I heard laughter and fresh young voices, and a general hubbub, on the other side of the haw-haw which divided the park from a croquet lawn. There was a gaily striped marquee on one side of the lawn, a group of people taking tea under a gigantic cedar, and a double set of croquet players disporting on the level sward. My eyes were keen as a hawk's to distinguish my dearest in mauve muslin and an innocent little chip hat trimmed with daisies—I observed even details, you see—busily engaged with her attendant cavalier, and with no appearance of being bored by his society. Her fresh young laugh rang out silver-clear—that girlish laugh which had been one of her many charms, to my mind. 'That hardly sounds like a broken heart,' I said to myself."

He sighed, and waited for a minute or so, and then resumed in a harder voice,—

"Well, I was determined to form no judgment from appearances; and I could not stand on the other side of the haw-haw taking observations from the covert of an old hawthorn for ever, so I went round to the back of the house, waylaid a neat little Abigail, and asked her if she could find Miss Blank's maid for me. I accompanied my question with a fee which insured compliance, and my pretty one's handmaiden appeared presently at the gate where I was waiting. She remembered me among the intimates in Cavendish Square, and consented to give her mistress the note I scribbled on a leaf of my pocket-book: 'I hope I am not doing wrong, sir,' she said, 'but a young lady in my mistress's position cannot be too careful how she acts——' 'In what position?' I asked. 'Didn't you know, sir, my young lady is to be married the day after to-morrow?'"

"That was a facer!" exclaimed Martin.

"It wasn't a pleasant thing to hear, was it—with that letter in my pocket vowing eternal fidelity? The remembrance of that gay young laughter was hardly pleasant either. The man I had seen on the croquet lawn was a good-looking fellow enough; and then one man is so like another now-a-days. A woman may be constant to the type whilst she jilts the individual. I had written to my betrothed, asking her to meet me in the park at nine o'clock, by a certain obelisk which I had observed on my way. By nine she would be free, I fancied, in that half hour of liberty which the women get after dinner, while the men are talking politics and pretending to be very wise about claret."

"Did she come?"

"Yes, poor, pretty, shallow-hearted thing, looking very sweet in the moonlight, but tearful and trembling, as if she thought I should beat her. She sobbed out her wretched little story. Papa had been so kind, her elder sisters had badgered her. Poor Reginald, the lover, had been so good, so generous, so self-sacrificing, and it had ended as such things generally do end, I dare say. She was to be married to him the day after to-morrow. 'And oh, Maurice, pray give me back my letter,' she said, 'for I don't know what would become of me if it ever fell into Reginald's hands.'"

"How did you answer her?"

"With never a word. I tore the lying letter into atoms, and threw them away on the summer wind. I made my love a respectful bow and left her, never, I trust in God, to see her fair, false face again."

CHAPTER XXIV.

"We are past the season of divided ills."

IF any one had asked Maurice Clissold why he had bared old wounds in the dreamy restfulness of that June afternoon in the hayfield, and why he had chosen Martin Trevanard for his father-confessor, he would have been sorely puzzled to answer so natural a question. That inexpressible longing to talk of himself and his own sorrows which seizes upon men now and then had laid hold of him, and there had been a kind of bitter pleasure, a half-cynical enjoyment in going over that story of the dead past. There was something sympathetic about Martin, too, a man who might have been crossed in love himself, Maurice thought, or who at least had a latent capacity for sincerest passion. Friendship had proved a plant of rapid growth in the utter solitude of Borcel End. Maurice felt that he could talk to this young Trevanard very much as he had talked to James Penwyn, knowing very well that he might not be always understood when his flights of fancy went widest, but very sure of sympathy at all times.

That afternoon was Saturday, and on the following morning perfect rest reigned at Borcel End. Even the ducks seemed less noisy than usual, as if their own voices startled them unpleasantly in the universal silence. Mr. and Mrs. Trevanard came down to the eight o'clock breakfast, luxurious Sabbath hour, in their best clothes, the farmer seeming somewhat embarrassed by the burden of respectability involved in sleek new broad cloth and a buff waistcoat starched to desperation, Mrs. Trevanard stern and even dignified of aspect in her dark grey silk gown and smart Sunday cap.

"Would you like to go to church?" Martin asked, with some faint hesitation, lest his new friend, being something of a poet, should also be something of an infidel.

"By all means. You drive, I suppose, as it's so far?"

Penwyn church, that lonely church among the hills, was the nearest to Borcel, a good four miles off at least.

"Yes, we drive to church and back. Mother says it goes against her to have the horse out on the Sabbath, but the distance is more than she could manage."

The morning service began at half-past ten, so at half-past nine the dog-cart was at the door, for there was a good deal of walking up and down hill to be allowed for, driving in this part of the country being not altogether a lazy business. The two young men, who occupied the back seat, were continually getting up and down, and had walked about half the distance by the time they came to the quiet old church whose single bell clanged over the green hill-side.

"I'm blest if the Squire and Mrs. Penwyn haven't come back!" cried Martin, descrying a handsome landau and pair in front of them as they drew near the church.

"Are you sure that's the Penwyn carriage? They were not expected three days ago," said Maurice.

"Quite sure. We've no other gentry hereabouts, except the Morgrave Park people, and they hardly ever are at home. There is no doubt about it. That is Mr. Penwyn's carriage."

"Then I'll renew my acquaintance with him after church," said Maurice.

The old grey church, which he had explored two days ago, had quite a gay look in its Sunday guise. The farmers' wives and daughters in their fine bonnets —the villagers, with their sunburnt faces and Sabbath cleanliness—the servants from the Manor, occupying two pews under the low gallery, within which dusky recess the livery of Churchill Penwyn's serving-men gleamed gaily, while the bonnets of the maids, all more or less in the last Parisian fashion, made the shadowy corner a perfect flower-bed. And most important of all, in a large square pew in the chancel appeared the Manor House family—Churchill, gentlemanlike and inscrutable, with his pale, thoughtful face, and grave grey eyes—Madge, looking verily the young queen of that western land—and Viola, fair and flower-like, a beauty to be worshipped so much the more for that frail loveliness which had a fatal air of evanescence.

"I'm afraid she won't live long," whispered Martin to his companion, in one of the pauses of the service, while the purblind old clerk was hunting for the antiquated psalm, Tate and Brady, which it was his duty to give out.

"Not Mrs. Penwyn? Why, she looks the picture of health," replied Maurice, in a similar undertone.

Martin coloured like a schoolboy justly suspected of felonious views in relation to apples.

"I meant the fair one," he gasped, "her sister."

"She! Ah! looks rather consumptive," replied Maurice, heartlessly.

The Borcel End and Manor House families met in the churchyard after the service — Borcel End respectful, and not intrusive — the Manor House kindly, cordial even, with no taint of patronage. In sooth, Michael Trevanard was the best tenant a landowner could have; a man who was always improving his holding, and paid his rent to the hour; a man to take the chair at audit dinners, and stumble through a proposal of his landlord's health.

"You didn't expect to see us so soon, did you, Mrs. Trevanard?" said Madge, with her bright smile; "but we all grew tired of town in the middle of the season."

"We're always glad to see you back," said Michael, screwing up his courage, and jerking out the words as if they were likely to choke him. "The place doesn't seem homelike when there's no family at the Manor House. You see we were accustomed to see the old Squire pottering about the place from year's end to year's end, and entering into every little bit of improvement we made; and as familiar, you know, as if he was one of ourselves. That spoiled us a bit, I make no doubt."

"It shall not be my fault if you do not come to consider me one of yourselves in good time, Mr. Trevanard," said Churchill kindly—kindly, but without that real heartiness which makes a country gentleman popular among his vassals.

Maurice was standing in the background, and it was only at this moment that Mr. Penwyn recognised him. Something like a spasm of pain changed his face for a moment, as if some unwelcome memory were suddenly brought back to him.

"Natural enough," thought Maurice. "The last time we met was at his cousin's funeral, and it is hardly a pleasant idea for any man that he stands in the shoes of the untimely dead."

That momentary flush of pain past, Mr. Penwyn welcomed the stranger in the land with exceeding cordiality.

"How long have you been in Cornwall, Mr. Clissold?" he asked. "You ought not to come to Penwyn without putting up at the Manor House."

"You are very good. I have been to the Manor House, and ventured to put forward my acquaintance with you as a reason why your faithful old housekeeper should let me see your house. I dare say she has forgotten to mention the fact."

"There has been scarcely time. We only arrived last night. Let me present you to my wife.—Madge, this is the Mr. Clissold of whom you have heard me speak; Mr. Clissold, Mrs. Penwyn, her sister Miss Bellingham."

Madge acknowledged the introduction with something less than her accustomed sweetness. Although Churchill was so thoroughly convinced of the man's innocence, Madge had not quite made up her mind that he was guiltless of his friend's blood. He had been suspected, and the taint clung to him yet.

Still when she looked at the dark earnest eyes, the open brow, the firm mouth with its expression of subdued power, the countenance on which thought had exercised its refining influence, she began to think that Churchill must be right in this opinion as in all other things, and that this man was incapable of crime.

So when, after questioning Mr. Clissold as to his whereabouts, Churchill asked him to go back to the Manor House with them for luncheon, and to bring his friend Martin Trevanard, Madge seconded the invitation. "If Mrs. Trevanard can spare her son for a few hours," she added graciously.

Mrs. Trevanard curtseyed, and thanked Mrs. Penwyn for her condescension, but added that she did not hold with young people keeping company with their superiors, and thought that Martin would be better at home in his own sphere.

"If I had ever seen good come of it I might think differently," said the farmer's wife with a gloomy look, "but I never have."

Martin looked angry, and his father embarrassed.

"I hope you'll excuse my wife for being so free-spoken," Mr. Trevanard said, in a rather clumsy apology. "She doesn't mean to be uncivil, but there are points ——" here he came aground hopelessly, and could only repeat in a feeble tone—"There are points."

"Thanks for your kind invitation, Mr. Penwyn," said Martin, still flushed with shame and anger, "but you see I'm not supposed to have a will of my own yet awhile, and must do as my mother tells me."

"Come along, old lady," said Michael, and after making their salaams to the quality, the Borcel End party retired to the dog-cart. The horse had been tethered on the sward near at hand, browsing calmly throughout the hour and a half service.

Maurice drove off with the Penwyns in the landau.

"What a very disagreeable person that Mrs. Trevanard seems!" said Madge. "I should think it could be hardly pleasant staying in her house, Mr. Clissold."

"She is eccentric rather than disagreeable, I think," replied Maurice, "a woman with a fixed idea which governs all her conduct. I had hard work to persuade her to let me stop at the farm, but she has been an excellent hostess. And her son Martin is a capital fellow—one of Nature's gentlemen."

"Yes, I liked his manner, except when he got so angry with his mother. But she was really too provoking, with her preachment about equality, more especially as these Trevanards belong to a good old Cornish family. Do they not, Churchill?"

"Yes, love. By Tre, Pol, and Pen, you may know the Cornish men. I believe these are some of the original Tres. Admirable tenants too. One can hardly make too much of them."

"Do you know anything about their daughter?" asked Maurice of Mr. Penwyn.

"Yes, I have heard of her, but never seen her. A poor half-witted creature, I believe."

"Not half-witted, but deranged. Her brain has evidently been turned by some great sorrow. From what I can gather she must have loved some one superior to her in rank, and been ill-treated by him. I fancy this is why Mrs. Trevanard says bitter things about inequality of station."

"An all-sufficient reason. I shall never feel angry with Mrs. Trevanard again," said Madge.

The Manor House looked much gayer and brighter to-day, with servants passing to and fro, great bowls of roses on all the tables, banks of flowers in the windows, new books scattered on the tables, holland covers banished to the limbo of household stores, and two pretty women lending the charm of their presence to the scene.

Never had Maurice Clissold seen husband and wife so completely happy, or more entirely suited to each other than these two seemed. Domestic life at Penwyn Manor House was like an idyl. Simple, unaffected happiness showed itself in every look, in every word and tone. There was just that amount of plenteousness and luxury in all things which makes life smooth and pleasant, without the faintest ostentation. A certain subdued comfort reigned everywhere, and Churchill in no wise fell into the common errors of men who have suffered a sudden elevation to wealth. He neither "talked rich," nor told his friends with a deprecating shrug of his shoulders that he had just enough for bread and cheese. In a word, he took things easily.

As a husband he was, in Viola's words, "simply perfect." It was impossible to imagine devotedness more thorough yet less obtrusive. His face never turned towards his wife without brightening like a landscape in a sudden gleam of sunlight. There was nothing that could be condemned as "spooning" between these married lovers, yet no one would fail to understand that they were all the world to each other.

Viola had long since altered her mind about Mr. Penwyn. From thinking him "not quite nice," she had grown to consider him adorable. To her he had been all generosity and kindness, treating her in every way as if she had been his own sister, and a sister well beloved. She had the prettiest possible suite of rooms at Penwyn, a horse of Churchill's own choosing, her own piano, her own maid, and more pocket-money than she had ever had in her life before.

"It comes rather hard upon Churchill to have two young women to provide for instead of one," Viola remarked to her sister; "but he is so divinely good about it"—she was a young lady who delighted in strong adverbs—"that I hardly realize what a sponge I am."

And then came sisterly embracings and protestations. Thus the Penwyn Manor people were altogether the happiest of families.

Maurice thoroughly enjoyed his day at Penwyn. After luncheon they all rambled about the grounds, Churchill and his wife always side by side, so that the guest had the pretty Miss Bellingham for his companion.

"It might be dangerous for another man," he said to himself, "but I've had my lesson. No more fair soft beauties for me. If ever I suffer myself to fall in love again it shall be with a girl who looks as if she could knock me down if I offended her. A girl with as much character in her face as the actress poor James was so fond of. Of the two I think I would rather have Clytemnestra than Helen. I dare say Menelaus believed his wife a pattern of innocence and purity till he woke one morning and found she had levanted with Paris."

Thus secure from the influence of her attractions Mr. Clissold made himself very much at home with Miss Bellingham. She showed him all the beauties of Penwyn, spots where a glimpse of the sea looked brightest through a break in the pine grove, hollows where the ferns grew deepest and greenest, and proved a very different guide from Elspeth.

"I have been through the grounds before," said Maurice, "but on that occasion my companion did not enhance the beauties of nature by the charm of her society."

"Who was your companion?"

"The granddaughter of the woman at the Lodge. Rather curious people, are they not?"

"Yes, I have often wondered how my brother came to pick them up, for they are not natives of the soil, as almost every one else is at Penwyn. But Churchill says the old woman is a very estimable person, well worthy of her post, so one can say no more about it."

When Maurice wanted to take leave, his new friends insisted that he should stay to dinner, Mr. Penwyn offering to send him home in a dog-cart. This favour, however, the sturdy pedestrian steadfastly declined.

"I am not afraid of a night walk across the hills," he said, "and am getting as familiar with the country about here as if I were to the manner born."

So he stayed, and assisted at Mrs. Penwyn's kettle-drum, which was held in the old Squire's yew-tree bower on the bowling-green, an arbour made of dense walls of evergreen, cool in summer, and comfortably sheltered in winter.

Here they drank tea, lazily enjoying the freshening breeze from the great wide sea, the sea which counts so many argosies for her spoil, the mighty Atlantic! Here they talked of literature and the world, and rapidly progressed in friendliness. But not one word was said of James Penwyn, who, save for that shot fired from behind a hedge, would have been master of grounds and bower, manor and all thereto belonging. That was a thought which flashed more than once across Maurice's mind.

"How happy these people seem in the possession of a dead man's goods!" he thought, "how placidly they enjoy his belongings, how coolly they accept fate's awful decree! Only human nature I suppose.

"'Les morts durent bien peu, laissons-les sous la pierre.'"

He stayed till ten o'clock, and left charmed with host and hostess.

Churchill Penwyn had been at his best all day, a man whose talk was worth hearing, and whose opinions were not feeble echoes of Saturday's literary journals. After dinner they had music, as well as conversation, and Madge played some of Mozart's finest church music—choice bits culled from the Masses.

"How long do you stay in Cornwall?" was the question at parting.

"About a week longer at Borcel End, I suppose. But I am my own master as to time. I have no legitimate profession—for I believe literature hardly comes under that head,—and am therefore something of a Bohemian: not in a bad sense, Miss Bellingham, so please don't look alarmed."

"Why not come to us instead of staying at Borcel End?" asked Churchill.

"You are too good. But I could hardly do that. When I offered myself to Mrs. Trevanard as a lodger, I said I should stay for a week or two, and she is just the kind of woman to feel wounded if I left her abruptly. And then, Martin and I are great friends. He is really one of the best fellows I ever met, except —except the friend I lost," he added, quickly and huskily, feeling that any allusion of that kind was ill-judged here.

"Well, you must do just as you please about it, but give us as much of your company as you can. We shall have a dinner next week, I believe."

"Saturday," said Madge.

"You will come to us then, of course. And as often in the meanwhile as you can."

"Thanks. The dinner-party is out of the question. I travel with a knapsack, and am three hundred miles from my dress suit. But if you will allow me to drop in now and then between this and Saturday I shall be delighted."

CHAPTER XXV.

"The drowsy night grows on the world."

THE advent of the Manor House family made life all the more pleasant to Mr. Clissold at Borcel End. It imparted variety to his existence, and the homely comfort of the farmhouse was agreeably contrasted by the refinement of Mr. Penwyn's surroundings. He dined at Penwyn twice during the week, and as he became more familiar with the interior of Churchill's home, only saw fresh proofs of its perfect happiness. Here were a man and a woman who made the most and the best of wealth and position, and shed an atmosphere of contentment around them.

With Martin for his companion, Maurice saw all that was worth seeing within the reach of Borcel End. They drove to Seacomb, the nearest market town, and explored the church there, which was old and full of interest. Here, in looking over the register for some name of world-wide renown, Maurice stumbled upon an entry that aroused his curiosity.

It was in the register of baptisms,—

"Emily Jane, daughter of Matthew Elgood, comedian, and Jane Elgood his wife." The date was just eighteen years ago.

"Matthew Elgood. That girl's father was Matthew," thought Maurice, "can it be the same man, I wonder? Yes, Matthew Elgood, comedian. There would hardly be two men of the same name and calling. His daughter must be the age of the child baptized here, for I remember James telling me that she was just seventeen."

The infant was certainly recorded in the register as Emily Jane, and the young actress's name was Justina. But Mr. Clissold concluded that this was merely a fictitious appellation, chosen for euphony. He made up his mind that the child entered in these old yellow pages, and the girl he had seen weeping for his friend's untimely death, were one and the same. Strange that the sweetheart of James Penwyn's choice had been born so near the cradle of his own race. It was as if there had been some subtle sympathy between these children of the same soil, and their hearts had gone forth to each other spontaneously.

"Is there a theatre at Seacomb?" asked Maurice, wondering how that quiet old town could have afforded a field for Mr. Elgood's talents.

"Not now," replied Martin. "There used to be, some years ago. The building exists still, but it has been converted into a chapel. It answers better than the theatre did, I believe."

The week came to an end. Maurice attended a second service at Penwyn Church, and paid a farewell visit to the Manor House on Sunday afternoon. This time he refused Mr. Penwyn's hearty invitation to dinner, and wished his new friends good-bye shortly after luncheon, with cordial expressions of friendship on both sides.

He walked across the hills, ruminating upon all that had happened since he first followed that track, with Elspeth for his guide. He had made acquaintance

CHAPTER XXV.

"The drowsy night grows on the world."

THE advent of the Manor House family made life all the more pleasant to Mr. Clissold at Borcel End. It imparted variety to his existence, and the homely comfort of the farmhouse was agreeably contrasted by the refinement of Mr. Penwyn's surroundings. He dined at Penwyn twice during the week, and as he became more familiar with the interior of Churchill's home, only saw fresh proofs of its perfect happiness. Here were a man and a woman who made the most and the best of wealth and position, and shed an atmosphere of contentment around them.

With Martin for his companion, Maurice saw all that was worth seeing within the reach of Borcel End. They drove to Seacomb, the nearest market town, and explored the church there, which was old and full of interest. Here, in looking over the register for some name of world-wide renown, Maurice stumbled upon an entry that aroused his curiosity.

It was in the register of baptisms,—

"Emily Jane, daughter of Matthew Elgood, comedian, and Jane Elgood his wife." The date was just eighteen years ago.

"Matthew Elgood. That girl's father was Matthew," thought Maurice, "can it be the same man, I wonder? Yes, Matthew Elgood, comedian. There would hardly be two men of the same name and calling. His daughter must be the age of the child baptized here, for I remember James telling me that she was just seventeen."

The infant was certainly recorded in the register as Emily Jane, and the young actress's name was Justina. But Mr. Clissold concluded that this was merely a fictitious appellation, chosen for euphony. He made up his mind that the child entered in these old yellow pages, and the girl he had seen weeping for his friend's untimely death, were one and the same. Strange that the sweetheart of James Penwyn's choice had been born so near the cradle of his own race. It was as if there had been some subtle sympathy between these children of the same soil, and their hearts had gone forth to each other spontaneously.

"Is there a theatre at Seacomb?" asked Maurice, wondering how that quiet old town could have afforded a field for Mr. Elgood's talents.

"Not now," replied Martin. "There used to be, some years ago. The building exists still, but it has been converted into a chapel. It answers better than the theatre did, I believe."

The week came to an end. Maurice attended a second service at Penwyn Church, and paid a farewell visit to the Manor House on Sunday afternoon. This time he refused Mr. Penwyn's hearty invitation to dinner, and wished his new friends good-bye shortly after luncheon, with cordial expressions of friendship on both sides.

He walked across the hills, ruminating upon all that had happened since he first followed that track, with Elspeth for his guide. He had made acquaintance with the interior of two families since then, in both of which he felt considerable interest.

"Churchill Penwyn must be a thoroughly good fellow," he said to himself, "or he would never have behaved so well as he has to me. It would have been so natural for him to be prejudiced against me by that business at Eborsham. But he has not only done me the justice to disbelieve the accusation from the very first; he has taken pains to let me see I am in no way damaged in his opinion by the suspicion that has attached to me."

Maurice had made up his mind to leave Borcel End next day. He had thoroughly explored the neighbourhood, and thoroughly enjoyed the tranquil pastoral life at the farmhouse, and he saw no reason for delaying his departure to fresher scenes. Mrs. Trevanard had heard of his resolution with indifference, her husband with civil regret, Martin with actual sorrow.

"I don't know how I shall get on when you are gone," he said. "It has been so nice to have some one to talk to, whose ideas rise above threshing-machines and surface drainage. Father's a good old soul, but he and I have precious little to say to each other. Now, with you, the longest day seems short. I think you've taught me more since we've been together than all I learnt at Helstone."

"No, Martin, I haven't taught you anything. I've only stirred up the old knowledge that was in you, hidden like stagnant water under duckweed," answered Maurice. "But we are not going to bid each other good-bye for ever. I shall come down to Borcel End again, you may be very sure, if your people will let me; and whenever you come to London you must take up your quarters with me, and I'll show you some of the pleasantest part of London life."

Maurice really regretted parting from the young man who had been the brightest and most light-hearted of companions, and he regretted leaving Borcel End without knowing a little more of Muriel Trevanard's history.

He had thought a good deal upon this family secret during the past week, though in all his wanderings about the old neglected garden, or down in the wilderness of hazel by the pond — and he had smoked many a cigar there in the interval — he had never again encountered Muriel. He had no reason to suppose there was any undue restraint placed upon her movements, or that she was unkindly treated by any one. Yet the thought that she was there, a part of the family, yet divided from it, banished from the home circle, yet so near, cut off from all the simple pleasures of her father's hearth, haunted him at all times. He was thinking of her this afternoon during his lonely walk across the hills. She was more in his thoughts than the people he had left.

It was past six o'clock when he entered the old hall at Borcel End, and he was struck at once by the quietude of the place. The corner where old Mrs. Trevanard was wont to sit was empty this evening. The hearth was newly swept, as it always seemed to be, and the fire, not unacceptable on this dull grey afternoon, burned bright and red. The table was laid with a composite kind of meal, on one side a small tea-tray, on the other the ponderous Sunday sirloin and a tempting salad, a meal prepared for himself,

Maurice felt sure. The maid-servant entered from the adjoining kitchen at the sound of his footsteps.

"Oh, if you please, sir, they're all gone to tea at Limestone Farm. Mr. Spurcombe, at Limestone, is an old friend of master's. And missus said if you should happen to come home before they did, would you please to make yourself comfortable, and I was to lay tea for you."

"Your mistress hardly expected me, I suppose?"

"I don't think she did, sir. She said she thought you'd dine up at Penwyn, most likely."

Maurice was not long about his evening meal. Perhaps he made shorter work of it than he might have done otherwise, perceiving that the maid was longing for the moment when she might clear the table, and slip away by the back door to her Sunday evening tryst. Maid-servants at Borcel were kept very close, and were almost always under the eye of their mistress, yet as a rule the Borcel End domestic always had her "young man." Maurice heard the back door shut, stealthily, and felt very sure that the kitchen was deserted. He drew his chair nearer to the hearth, lighted a cigar, and abandoned himself to idle thought.

CHAPTER XXVI.

"Good night, good rest. Ah! neither be my share."

Maurice Clissold sat for some time, smoking and musing by the hearth—sat till the light faded outside the diamond-paned windows, and the shadows deepened within the room. He might have sat on longer had he not been surprised by the opening of a door in that angle of the hall which was sacred to age and infirmity in the person of old Mrs. Trevanard.

It was the door of her room which had opened. "Have they come back yet?" asked her feeble old voice.

"No, ma'am," answered Maurice, "not yet. Can I do anything for you?"

"No, sir. It's the strange gentleman, Mr.—Mr.——"

"Clissold. Yes, ma'am. Won't you come to your old place by the fire?"

"No; I've my fire in here, thank you kindly. But the place seems lonesome when they're away. I'm not much of a one to talk myself, but I like to hear voices. The hours seem so long without them. You can come in, if you please, sir. My room is kept pretty tidy, I believe; I should fret if I thought it wasn't."

The old woman was standing on the threshold of the door opening between the two rooms. Maurice had risen to offer her assistance.

"Come in and sit down a bit," she said, pleased

at having found some one to talk to, for it was a notorious fact at Borcel End that old Mrs. Trevanard always had a great deal more to say for herself when her daughter-in-law was out of the way than she had in the somewhat freezing presence of that admirable housewife.

Maurice complied, and entered the room which he had observed through the half-glass door, a comfortable homely room enough, in the light of an excellent fire. Old Mrs. Trevanard required a great deal of warmth.

She went back to her arm-chair, and motioned her visitor to a seat on the other side of the hearth.

"It's very kind of you to be troubled with an old woman like me," she mumbled.

"I dare say you could tell me plenty of interesting stories about Borcel End if you were inclined, Mrs. Trevanard," said Maurice.

"Ah, there's few houses without a history; few women of my age that haven't seen a good deal of family troubles and family secrets. The best thing an old woman can do is to hold her tongue. That's what my daughter-in-law's always telling me. 'Least said, soonest mended.'"

"Ah," thought Maurice, "the dowager has been warned against being over-communicative."

Contemplating the room more at his leisure now than he had done from outside, he perceived a picture hanging over the chimney-piece which he had not noticed before. It was a commonplace portrait enough, by some provincial limner's hand, the portrait of a young woman in a gipsy hat and flowered damask gown—a picture that was perhaps a century old.

"Is that picture over the chimney a portrait of one of your son's family, ma'am?" asked Maurice.

"Yes. That's my husband's mother, Justina Trevanard."

Justina. The name startled him—so uncommon a name—and to find it here in the Trevanard family.

"That's a curious name," he said, "and one which recalls a person I met under peculiar circumstances. Have you had many Justinas in the Trevanard family since that day?"

"No, there was never anybody christened after her."

"I met your granddaughter in the garden the other night, Mrs. Trevanard," said Maurice, determined to find out whether this blind woman was a friend to Muriel, "and I was grieved to see her in so sad a condition."

"Muriel. Yes, poor girl, it's very sad—sad for all of us," answered the old woman, with a sigh, "saddest of all for her father. He was so proud of that girl—spared no money to make her a lady, and now he can't bear to see her. It wounds him too deep to see such a wreck. Yet he won't have her away from the house. He likes to know that she's near him, and as well cared for as she can be—in her state."

"It must have been a great sorrow that so changed her?"

"It was more sorrow than she could bear, poor child; though others have borne harder things."

"She was crossed in love, her brother told me."

"Yes, yes—crossed in love, that was it. The young man that she loved died young, and she was told of it suddenly. The shock turned her brain.

She had a fever, and every one thought she was going to die. She got the better of the illness, but her senses never came back to her. She's quite harmless, as you've seen, I dare say; but she has her fancies, and one is to think that the young man she was fond of is still alive, and that he'll keep his promise and come back to her."

Maurice told Mrs. Trevanard of his first night at Borcel End, and the intrusion which had shortened his slumbers.

"Ah, to think that she should have happened to find her way there that night, close as we keep her! My door is always locked, and she can't get out into the house without coming through this room; but I suppose that night I must have forgotten to take the key out of the door and put it under my pillow as I do mostly. And the poor child went roaming about the house by moonlight. That's an old trick of hers. The room where you sleep was her room once upon a time, and she always goes there if she gets the chance. It was unlucky that it should have happened the first night of your being here!"

"She is very fond of you, I suppose," said Maurice, anxious to hear more of one in whom he felt a strong interest.

"Yes, I think she likes me better than any one else now."

"Better even than her own mother?"

"Why, yes, she does not get on very well with her mother; she has odd fancies about her."

"I thought as much. I have heard her speak of a child. That was a mere delusion, I conclude."

"Yes, that was one of her fancies."

"Has Mrs. Trevanard never consulted any medical man upon the state of her daughter's mind?"

"Medical man," repeated the old woman, dubiously. "You mean a doctor, I suppose? Yes; Dr. Mitchell, from Seacomb, has seen the poor child many a time, and given her physic for this, that, and the other, but he says her mind will never be any different. There's no use worrying about that. He gives her stuff for her appetite sometimes, for she has but a poor appetite at the best. She's sorely wasted away from the figure she was once upon a time."

"She was a very beautiful girl, I have heard from Martin."

"Yes, I never saw a handsomer girl than Muriel when she came from school. It was all along of sending her to boarding school things went wrong."

"How do you mean?"

"Oh dear me, sir, you mustn't listen to my rambling talk, I'm a weak old woman, and I dare say my mind goes astray sometimes, just like Muriel's."

A light step sounded on the narrow stairs, a door in the paneling opened, and the figure Maurice had first seen in the spectral light of the moon came towards the hearth, and crouched down at the grandmother's knees. A slender figure, dressed in a light-coloured gown which looked white in the uncertain flare of the fire, a pale worn face, a mass of tangled hair.

Muriel took the old woman's withered hand, laid her hollow cheek against it, and kissed it fondly.

"Granny," she murmured, "patient, loving granny. Muriel's only friend."

Mrs. Trevanard smoothed the dark hair with her tremulous hand.

"How tangled it is, Muriel! Why won't you let me brush it, and keep it nice for you? My poor old hands can do that without the help of eyes."

"Why should it be made smooth or nice? He isn't coming back yet. See here, granny, you shall dress me the day he comes home—all in white—with myrtle in my hair, like a bride. I would have orange blossoms if I knew where to get any. There are some orange trees up at the Manor House. I'll ask him to bring me some. I was never dressed like a bride."

"Oh, Muriel, Muriel, so full of fancies!"

"Ah! but there are some of them real—too real. Where is the old cradle that my little brother used to sleep in?"

"I don't know, darling. In the loft, perhaps."

"They should have burnt it. I peeped into the loft one day, and saw it in a corner—the old cradle. It set me thinking—such strange thoughts!"

She remained silent for a few minutes, still crouching at her grandmother's knees, and with her hollow eyes fixed on the low fire.

"Didn't you hear a child cry?" she asked, suddenly, looking up with a listening face first at the old woman, then at Maurice. "Didn't you, granny?"

"No, love. I heard nothing."

"Didn't you, then?" to Maurice.

"No, indeed."

"Ah, you are all of you deaf. I hear that crying so often—a poor little feeble voice. It comes and goes like the wind in the long winter nights, but it sounds so distant. Why doesn't it come nearer? Why doesn't it come close to us, that we may take the child in and comfort it?"

"Ah, Muriel, Muriel, so full of fancies," repeated the old woman, like the burden of an ancient ballad.

The sound of doors opening, and loud voices, announced the return of the family.

"You'd better go back to the hall, sir. Bridget won't like to find you here with *her*," said Mrs. Trevanard in a hurried whisper, pointing to the figure leaning against her knees.

Maurice obeyed without a word. His last look at Muriel showed him the great haggard eyes gazing at the fire, the wasted hand clasped upon the grandmother's knee.

He left Borcel early next morning, Martin insisting upon bearing him company for the first few miles of his journey. He had paid liberally for his entertainment, rewarded the servant, and parted upon excellent terms with Mr. and Mrs. Trevanard and the blind grandmother. But he saw no more of Muriel, and it was with her image that Borcel End was most associated in his mind. When he was parting with Martin he ventured to speak of her, for the first time since that conversation in the dog-cart.

"Martin, I am going to say something which will perhaps offend you, but it is something I can't help saying."

"I don't think there's much fear of offence between you and me—at least not on my side."

"I am not so sure of that; some subjects are hazardous even between friends. You remember our talk about your sister? Well, I have seen her twice since then, never mind how or where; and I am more interested at her sad story than I can well express to you. It seems to me that there is something in that story which you, her only brother, ought to know, or, in a word, that she has need of your love and protection. Do not suppose for a moment that I would insinuate anything against your father and mother. They have doubtless done their duty to her according to their lights, but it is just possible that she has need of more active friendship, more sympathetic affection, than they can give. She clings to her old grandmother—a fading succour. When old Mrs. Trevanard dies, your sister will lose a natural nurse and protector. It will be your duty to lighten that loss for her, to interpose your love between her and the sense of desolation that may then arise. You are not angry with me for saying so much?"

"Angry with you? no, indeed! You set me thinking, that's all. Poor Muriel! I used to be so fond of her when I was a little chap, and perhaps I have thought too little about her of late years. My mother doesn't like any interference upon that point—doesn't even like me to talk of my poor sister, and so I've got into the way of taking things for granted, and holding my tongue. Honestly, if I had thought there was anything to be done for Muriel, that she could be better off than she is, or happier than she is, I should have been the first to make the attempt to bring about that improvement. But my mother has always told me there was nothing to be done except submit to the will of Providence."

"Your mother may be right, Martin; it is not for me, a stranger in your home, to gainsay her. But your sister's case seems to me most pitiful, and it will be long before I shall get her image out of my mind. If ever there should come a time when you may need the advice or the assistance of a man of the world upon that subject, be very sure my best services will be at your disposal. And whenever you come to London on business or on pleasure, remember that you are to make my home yours."

"I shall take you at your word. But you are more likely to come back to Borcel than I to come to London, for, mind, I count upon your coming next summer. And now you are so thick with the Manor House people you've some inducement for coming," added Martin, with the faintest touch of bitterness.

"There is temptation enough for me at Borcel End, Martin, without any question of the Manor House."

Martin shook his head incredulously.

"Miss Bellingham is too pretty to be left out of the question," he said.

"Miss Bellingham! A mere Dresden china beauty, a very fine specimen of human waxwork. I have told you my adventure in that line, Martin. I'm not likely to make a second venture."

They parted with the friendliest farewell, and Maurice felt that he was leaving something more than a chance acquaintance behind him at Borcel End.

CHAPTER XXVII.

"Such a lord is love."

NOTHING could be more perfect than that serenity which ruled the domestic life of Penwyn Manor. The judgment which Maurice Clissold had formed of that life, as seen from the outside, was fully confirmed by its inner every-day aspect. Mr. and Mrs. Penwyn had no company manners. They did not pose themselves before a stranger as model husband and wife, and settle their small differences at their leisure in the sanctuary of the lady's dressing-room or the gentleman's study. They had no differences, but lived in each other and for each other.

Yet, so impossible is perfect happiness to erring mortality, even here there was a hitch. Affection the most devoted, peace that knew not so much as a summer cloud across its fair horizon—these there were truly—but not quite happiness. Madge Penwyn had discovered somehow, by some subtle power of intuition given to anxious wives, that the husband she loved so fondly was not altogether happy, that he had his hours of lassitude and depression, when the world seemed to him, like Hamlet's world, "out of joint,"—his dark moments, when even she had no spell that could exorcise his demon.

Vainly she sought a cause for these changeful moods. Was he tired of her? Had he mistaken his own feelings when he chose her for his wife? No, even when most perplexed by his fitful spirits, she could not doubt his love. That revealed itself with truth's simple force. She knew him well enough to know that his love for her was the diviner half of his nature.

Once, on the eve of an event which was to complete the sacred circle of their home life, when her nature was most sensitive, and she clung to him with a pathetic dependence, Madge ventured to speak of her husband's intervals of gloom.

"I'm afraid there is something wanting even in your life, Churchill," she said, gently, fearful lest she should touch some old wound—"that you are not quite happy at Penwyn."

"Not happy! My dear love, if I am not happy here, and with you, there is no such thing as happiness for me. Why should I not be happy? I have no wish unfulfilled, except perhaps some dim half-formed aspiration to make my name famous—an idea with which most young men begin life, and which I can well afford to let stand over for future consideration, while I make the most of the present here with you."

"But, Churchill, you know that I would not stand between you and ambition. You must know how more than proud any success of yours would make me."

"Yes, dearest, and by and by I will put up for Seacomb, and try to make a little character in the House, for your sake," replied Mr. Penwyn, with a yawn. "It's a wonderful thing how ambitious a man feels while he has his living to win, and only his own wits to help him. Then, indeed, the distant blast of

Fame's trumpet is a sound that wakes him early in the morning, and keeps him at his post in the night watches. But then fame means income, position, the world's esteem, all the good things of life. The penniless struggler knows he must be Cæsar or nothing. Give the same man a comfortable estate like Penwyn, and fame becomes a mere addendum to his life, an ornament which vanity may desire, but which hardly weighs against the delight of idle days and nights that know not care. In short, darling, since I won fortune and you I have grown somewhat forgetful of the dreams I cherished when I was a struggling bachelor."

"Is it regret for those old dreams that makes you so gloomy sometimes, Churchill?"

"I do not regret them. I regret nothing. I am not gloomy," said Churchill, eagerly. "Never question my happiness, Madge. Joy is a spirit too subtle to endure a doubter's analysis. God forbid that you and I should be otherwise than utterly happy. Oh, my dear love, never doubt me; let us live for each other, and let me at least be sure that I have made your life all sunshine."

"It has never known a cloud since our betrothal, Churchill; except when I have thought you depressed and despondent."

"Neither depressed nor despondent, Madge, only thoughtful. A man whose early days have been for the most part given up to thinking must have his hours of thoughtfulness now and then. And perhaps my life here has smacked a little too much of the Lotus Land. I must begin to look about me, and take more interest in the estate,—in short, follow in the footsteps of my worthy grandfather, the old Squire; as soon as I can add the respectable name of father to my qualifications for the post."

That time came before the sickle had been put to the last patch of corn upon the uplands above Penwyn Manor. The halting bell of Penwyn Church rang out its shrill peal one August morning, and the little world within earshot of the Manor knew that the Squire rejoiced in the coming of his firstborn. There were almost as many bonfires in the district that summer night, outflaring the mellow harvest moon, as at Penzance on the eve of St. John the Evangelist. The firstborn was a son, whose advent the newspapers, local and metropolitan, duly recorded,—"At Penwyn Manor, August 25th, the wife of Churchill Penwyn, Esq., of a son (Nugent Churchill)." The new-comer's names had been settled beforehand.

"The sweet thing," exclaimed Lady Cheshunt, when she read the announcement in the reading-room of a German Kursaal. "I feel as if she had made me a grandmother."

And Lady Cheshunt wrote straight off to her silversmith, and ordered him to make the handsomest thing in christening cups, and sent a six-page letter to Mrs. Penwyn by the same post, requesting, in a manner that amounted to a command, that she might be represented by proxy as sponsor to the infant.

The child's coming gave new brightness to the domestic horizon. Viola was in raptures. This young nephew was the first baby that had ever entered into the sum of her daily life. She seemed to regard him as a phenomenon; very much as grave fellows of the

Zoological Society regarded the first hippopotamus born in Regent's Park.

Madge saw no more clouds on her husband's brow after that gentle remonstrance of hers. Indeed, he took pains to demonstrate his perfect contentment. His naturally energetic character re-asserted itself. He threw himself heart and soul into that one ambition of the old Squire, the improvement and aggrandizement of the Penwyn estate. He made a fine road across those lonely hills, and planted the land on both sides of it with Scotch and Norwegian firs, wherever there was ground available for plantation. The young groves arose, as if by magic, giving a new charm to the face of the landscape, and a new source of revenue to the lord of the soil. Mr. Penwyn also interested himself in the mining property, and finding his agent an easy-going, incapable sort of person, took the collection of the royalty into his own hands, much to the improvement of his income. People shrugged their shoulders, and said that the new Squire was just such another as "Old Nick," meaning the late Nicholas Penwyn. But careful as he was of his own interests, Churchill did not prove himself an illiberal landlord or a bad paymaster. Those plantations and new roads of his gave employment enough to use up all the available labour of the district, and impart new prosperity to the neighbourhood. When he suggested an improvement to a tenant he was always ready to assist in carrying it out. He renewed leases to good tenants upon the easiest terms, but was merciless in the expulsion of bad tenants. He was just one of those landlords who do most to improve the condition of an estate and the people on it, and in Ireland would inevitably have met with a violent death. The Celts of Western England took matters more quietly, abused him a good deal, owned that he was the right sort of man for the improvement of the soil, and submitted to fate which had given them King Stork, rather than King Log, for their ruler.

When the election came on, Mr. Penwyn put himself into nomination for Seacomb, and came in with flying colours. All the trading classes voted for him, out of self-interest. He had spent more money in the town than any one of his name had ever expended there. Madge's popularity secured the lower classes. Her schools were the admiration of the district, and she was raising up a model village between Old Penwyn and the Manor House. "Madge's Folly," Mr. Penwyn called the pretty cluster of cottages on the slope of the hill, but he allowed his wife to draw upon his balance to any extent she pleased, and never grumbled at the builder's bills, or troubled her by suggesting that the money she was laying out was likely to produce something less than two per cent.

So Churchill Penwyn wrote himself down M.P., and might be fairly supposed to have conquered all good things which fortune could bestow upon a deserving member of Burke's Landed Gentry. He had a fair young wife, who won love and honour from all who knew her. His infant heir was esteemed a model of all that is most excellent in babyhood. His sister-in-law believed in him as the most wonderful and admirable of husbands and men. His estate prospered, his plantations grew and flourished. The vast Atlantic itself was as a lake beneath his windows, and seemed to call him lord. No cloud, were it but the bigness of a man's hand, obscured the brightness of his sky.

Mr. and Mrs. Penwyn spent their second season in town with greater distinction than their first. More people were anxious to know them—more exalted invitation cards showered in upon them, and Churchill, who had been a successful man even in the days of his poverty, felt that he had then only tasted the skimmed milk of success, and that this which was offered to his lips to-day was the cream. There was a subtle difference in the manner of his reception by the same world now-a-days. If he had been only a country gentleman, with the ability to take a furnished house in Belgravia, the difference might have been slight enough; or, indeed, the advantage might have been on the side of the portionless barrister, with his way to make in life, and his chances of success before him. But Churchill's maiden speech had been a success. He had developed a special capacity for committees, had shown slow-going county members how to get through their work in about one-fifth of the time they had been in the habit of giving to it, had proved himself a master of railway and mining economics—in a word, without noise, or bluster, or assumption, had infused something of Transatlantic go-a-headishness into all the business to which he put his hand. Men in high places marked him as a young man worth cultivating, and thus, before the session was over, Churchill Penwyn had tasted the first-fruits of parliamentary success.

Perhaps if ever a man went in danger of being spoiled by a wife Churchill Penwyn was that man. Madge simply worshipped him. To hear him praised, to see him honoured, was to her of all praise and honour the highest. She shaped all the circumstances of her life to suit his interest and his convenience; chose her acquaintance at his bidding, would have given up the greatest party of the season to sit by his side in the dingy Eaton Square study, copying paragraphs out of a blue-book for his use and advantage. Churchill, on his side, was careful not to impose upon devotion so unselfish, and was never prouder than in assisting at his wife's small social triumphs. He chose the colours of her dresses, and took as much interest in her toilet as in the state of the mining market. He never seemed so happy as in those rare evenings which he contrived to spend alone with Madge, or in hearing some favourite opera with her, and going quietly home afterwards to a snug little *tête-à-tête* supper, while Viola was dancing to her heart's content under the wing of some good-natured chaperon, like Lady Cheshunt.

That friendly dowager was enraptured with her *protégée's* domestic life.

"My sweet love, you renew one's belief in Arcadia," she exclaimed to Madge, after her enthusiastic fashion. "I positively must buy you a crook and a lamb or two to lead about with blue ribbons. You are the simplest of darlings. To see how you worship that husband of yours puts me in mind of Baucis and what's-his-name, and all that kind of thing. And to think that I should have taken such trouble to warn you against this very man! But then who could imagine that young Penwyn would have been so good-natured as to die?"

"When are you coming to see me at the Manor,

Lady Cheshunt?" asked Madge, laughing at her friend's raptures. "You can form no fair idea of my domestic happiness in London. You must see me at home in my Arcadia, with my crook and flock."

"You dear child! I shall certainly come in August."

"I'm so glad. You must be sure to come before the twenty-fifth. That's Nugent's birthday, you know, and I mean to give a pastoral *fête* in honour of the occasion, and you will see all my cottagers and their children, and the rough miners, and discover what a curious kingdom we reign over in the West."

"My dearest love, I detest poor people, and tenants, and cottagers—but I shall come to see *you*."

CHAPTER XXVIII.

"Then streamed life's future on the fading past."

More than a year had gone by since Maurice Clissold had said farewell to Borcel End, and he had not yet found leisure to revisit that peaceful homestead. He had corresponded with Martin Trevanard regularly during the interval, and had heard all that was to be told of Borcel and its neighbourhood; how Mrs. Penwyn was daily becoming more and more popular, how her schools flourished, her cottagers thrived, her cottage gardens blossomed as the rose; and how Mr. Penwyn, though respected for his liberality and justice, and looked up to very much in his parliamentary capacity, had not yet found the knack of making himself popular. From time to time, in reply to Maurice's inquiries, Martin had written a few words about Muriel. She was always the same—there was no change. She was neither better nor worse, and the good old grandmother was very careful of her, and kept her from wandering about the house at night. Nothing had happened to disturb the even current of life at Borcel End.

This year that had gone had brought success, and, in some measure, fame, to Maurice Clissold. He had published the long-contemplated volume of verse, the composition whereof had been his labour and delight since he left the university. His were not verses "thrown off" in the leisure half-hours of a man whose occupations were more serious—verses to be apologized for, with a touch of proud humility, in a preface. They contained the full expression of his life. They were strong with all the strength of his manhood. Passion, fervour, force, intensity, were there; and the world, rarely slow to appreciate youthful fire, was quick to recognise their real power. Maurice Clissold slowly awoke to the fact that, under his *nom de plume*, he was famous. He had taken care not to affix his real name to that confession of faith—not to let all the world know that his was that inner life which a poet reveals half unconsciously, even when he writes about the shadows his fancy has created. In the story-poem which made the chief portion of his volume Maurice had, in some wise, told the story of his own passion, and his own disappointment. Pain and disillusion had given their bitter flavour to his verse; but happily for the poet's reputation, it was just that bitter-sweet—that sub-acid, which the lovers of sentimental poetry like. That common type of womanhood, fair and lovable, and only false under the pressure of circumstance, was here represented with undeniable vigour. The modern Helen, the woman whose passive beauty and sweetness are the source of tears and death, and whom the world forgives because she is mild and fair, here found a powerful limner. He had spared not a detail of that cruel portrait. It was something better than a miniature of that one girl who had jilted him. It was the universal image of weakly, selfish womanhood, yielding, unstable, caressing, dependent, and innately false.

Side by side with this picture from life he had set the ideal woman, pure, and perfect, and true, lovely in face and form, but more lovely in mind and soul. Between these two he had placed his hero, wayward, mistaken, choosing the poison-flower, instead of the sweet thornless rose, led through evil ways to a tragical end, comforted by the angel-woman only as chill death sealed his lips. Bitterness and sorrow were the dominant notes of the verse, but it was a pleasing bitter, and a melodious sadness.

There was a run on Mudie's for "A Life Picture, and other Poems," by Clifford Hawthorn. The book was widely reviewed, but while some critics hailed the bard as that real poet for whom the age had been waiting, others dissected the pages with a merciless scalpel, and denounced the writer as a profligate and an infidel. The fugitive pieces, brief lyrics some of them, with the delicate finish of a cabinet picture, won almost universal favour. In a word Maurice Clissold's first venture was a success.

He was not unduly elated. He did not believe in himself as the poet for whom the expectant age had been on the look-out. He had measured himself against giants, and was pretty clear in his estimate of his own powers. This pleasant taste of the strong wine of success made him only more intent upon doing better. It stimulated ambition, rather than satisfied it. Perhaps the adverse criticism did him most good, for it created just that spirit of opposition which is the best incentive to effort.

Very happy was the bachelor-poet's life in those days. He had lived just long enough to survive the pain of his first disappointment. It was a bitter memory still, but a memory which but rarely recurred to mar his peace. He had friends who understood him

—two or three real friends, who with his publisher alone knew the secret of his authorship. He had an occupation he loved, just enough ambition to give a stimulus to life, and he had not a care.

He had visited the Penwyns in Eaton Square several times during the course of the season, but he had been careful not to go to that very pleasant house too often. Afternoon tea in Mrs. Penwyn's drawing-room—the smaller drawing-room, with its wealth of flowers, was a most delightful manner of wasting an hour or so. But Maurice felt somehow that it was an indulgence he must not give himself too often. He had a lurking fear of Viola. She was very fair, and sweet and gentle, like the girl he had loved, and though he had, as yet, regarded her with only the most fraternal feeling—nay, a sentiment approaching indifference,—he had an idea that there might be peril in too much friendliness.

Dropping in one afternoon at the usual hour, he was pleased to see his own book on one of the gipsy tables.

"Have you read this 'Life Picture,' which the critics have been abusing so vigorously?" he asked.

"Yes, I saw it dreadfully cut up in the *Saturday Review*, so I thought it must be nice, and sent to the publishers for a copy," answered Madge. "I've had it down on my Mudie's list ever so long, without effect. It's a wonderful book. Viola and I were up till three o'clock this morning reading it together. Neither of us could wait. From the moment we began with that picture of a London twilight, and the two girls and the young lawyer sitting in a balcony talking, we were riveted. It is all so easy, so lifelike, so full of vigour and freshness and colour."

"The author would be very much flattered if he could hear you," said Maurice.

"The author—oh, I'm afraid he must be rather a disagreeable person. He seems to have such a bad opinion of women."

"Oh, Madge, his heroine is a noble creature!" cried Viola.

"Yes, but the woman his hero loves best is worthless."

"Well, I should like to know the author," said Viola.

"I don't think Churchill would get on very well with him," said Madge. And that to her mind made an end of the question.

The only people she sought were people after Churchill's own heart. This poet had a wildness in his ideas which the Squire of Penwyn would hardly approve.

* * * * * *

Among Mr. Clissold's literary acquaintance was a clever young dramatic author, whose work was just beginning to be popular. One afternoon at the club —a rather Bohemian institution for men of letters, in one of the streets off the Strand—this gentleman—Mr. Flittergilt—invited Maurice to assist at the first performance of his last comedietta at a small and popular theatre near at hand.

They dined together, and dropped in at the theatre just as the curtain was falling on a half-hour farce played while the house was filling. The piece of the evening came next. "No Cards," an original comedy in three acts; which announcement was quite enough to convince Maurice that the motive was adapted from Scribe, and the comic underplot conveyed from a Palais Royal farce.

"There's a new girl in my piece," said Mr. Flittergilt, on the tiptoe of expectation, "such a pretty girl, and by no means a bad actress."

"Where does she come from?"

"Goodness knows. It's her first appearance in London."

"Humph, comes to the theatre in her brougham, I suppose, and has her dresses made by Worth."

"Not the least in the world. She wore a shabby grey thing, which I believe you call alpaca, at rehearsal this morning, and she ran into the theatre, dripping like a naiad, in a waterproof—if you can imagine a naiad in a waterproof—having failed to get a seat in a twopenny omnibus."

"That is the prologue," said Maurice, with a slight shoulder-shrug. "Perhaps Madge was right, and that he really had a bad opinion of women."

He turned to the programme listlessly presently, and read the old names he knew so well, for this house was a favourite lounge of his.

"Is the piece really original, Jack?" he inquired of his friend.

"Well," said Mr. Flittergilt, pulling on a new glove, and making a wry face, perhaps at the tightness of the glove—perhaps at the awkwardness of the question—"I admit there was a germ in that last piece at the Vaudeville, which I have ripened and expanded, you know. There always is a germ, you see, Maurice.

It's only from the brains of a Jove that you get a full-grown Minerva at a rush."

"I understand. The piece is a clever adaptation. Why, what's this?"

It was a name in the programme which evoked that sudden question.

"Celia Flower, Miss Justina Elgood."

"Flittergilt," said Maurice, solemnly, "I know that young woman, and I regret to inform you that, though really a superior girl in private life, she is a very poor actress. If the fortunes of your piece are entrusted to her, I am sorry for you."

"If she acts as well to-night as she did this morning at rehearsal, I shall be satisfied," replied Mr. Flittergilt. "But how did you come to know her?"

Maurice told the story of those two days at Eborsham. "Poor child, when last I saw her she was bowed down with grief for my murdered friend. I dare say she has forgotten all about him by this time."

"She doesn't look like a girl who would easily forget," said the dramatist.

The curtain rose on one of those daintily furnished interiors which the modern stage realizes to such perfection. Flowers, birds, statuettes, pictures, a glimpse of sunlit garden on one side, and an open piano on the other. A girl was seated on the central ottoman, looking over a photograph album. A young man was in a half-recumbent position at her feet, looking up at her. The girl was Justina Elgood—the old Justina, and yet a new Justina—so wondrously had the overgrown girl of seventeen improved in womanly beauty and grace. The dark blue eyes, with their depth of thought and tenderness of expression, were alone unchanged. Maurice could have recognised the girl anywhere by those eyes.

The management had provided the costumes for the piece, and Justina, in her white silk dress, with its voluminous frills and flouncings, looked as elegant a young woman as one could desire to see offered up, Iphigenia-like, on the altar of loyalty at St. James's Palace, to be almost torn to pieces on a drawing-room day. Celia Flower is the heroine of the comedy, and this is her wedding morning, and this young man at her feet is a cousin and rejected lover. She is looking over the portraits of her friends, in order to determine which she shall preserve and which drop after marriage.

Mr. Flittergilt's comedy goes on to show that Celia's intended union is altogether a mistake, that she really loves the rejected cousin, that he honestly loves her, that nothing but misery can result from the marriage of interest which has been planned by Celia's relatives.

Celia is at first indifferent and frivolous, thinking more of her bridal toilet than of the bond which it symbolizes. Little by little she awakens to deeper thought and deeper feeling, and here, slender as Mr. Flittergilt's work is, there is scope for the highest art.

Curiously different is the actress of to-day from the girl whose ineptitude the strolling company at Eborsham had despised. There is a brightness and spontaneity about her comedy, a simple artless tenderness in her touches of sentiment, which show the untaught actress—the actress whose art has grown out of her own depth of feeling, whose acting is the outcome of a rich and thoughtful mind rather than the hard and dry result of tuition and study, or the mechanical art of imitation. Impulse and fancy give their bright brief flashes of light and colour to the interpretation, and the dramatist's creation lives and moves before the audience,—not a mere mouthpiece for smart sayings or graceful bits of sentiment—but a being with a soul, an original absolute creation of an original mind.

The audience are enchanted, Mr. Flittergilt is in fits of admiration of himself and the actress. "By Jove, that girl is as good as Nesbitt, and my dialogue is equal to Sheridan's!" he ejaculates, when the first act is over, and the rashly enthusiastic, without waiting for the end, begin to clamour for the author. And Maurice—well, Maurice sits in a brown study, far back in the box, and unseen by the actors, astride upon his chair, his arms folded upon the back of it, his chin upon his folded arms, the image of intense contemplation.

"By heaven, the girl is a genius," he says to himself. "I thought there was something noble about her, but I did not think two short years would work such a change as this."

At the end of the piece Justina was received with what it is the fashion to call an ovation. There were no bouquets thrown to her, for these floral offerings are generally pre-arranged by the friends and admirers of an actress, and Justina had neither friends nor admirers in all the great city to plan her triumph. She had conquered by the simple force of an art which was spontaneous and unstudied as the singing of a nightingale. Time and practice had made her mistress of the mechanism of her art, had familiarized her with the glare of the lights and the strange faces of the crowd, had made her as much at her ease on the stage as in her own room. The rest had come unawares, it had come with the ripening of her mind, come with the thoughtfulness and depth of feeling that had been the growth of that early disappointment, that first brief dream of love, with its sad sudden ending.

When the piece was over, and Justina and Mr. Flittergilt had enjoyed their triumph, and all the actors had been called for and applauded by a delighted audience, Maurice suddenly left the box. He had done nothing to help the applause; but had stood in his dark corner like a rock, while the little theatre shook with the plaudits of pit and gallery.

"Come, I say, that's rather cool," the dramatist muttered to himself. "He might have said something civil, anyhow; I was just going to ask him if he'd like to go behind the scenes, too." The accomplished Flittergilt had contented himself with bowing from his box, and he was now in haste to betake himself to the green-room, there to receive the congratulations of the company, and to render the usual meed of praise and thanks to the interpreters of his play.

The green-room at the Royal Albert Theatre was a very superior apartment to the green-room at Eborsham. It was small, but bright and comfortable-looking, with carpeted floor, looking-glasses over chimney-piece and console table, photographs and engraved portraits of popular actors and actresses upon the gaily papered walls, a cushioned divan all round the room, and nothing but the table and its appurtenances wanted to make the apartment resemble a billiard-room in a pleasant unpretentious country house.

Here, standing by the console table, and evidently quite at his ease, Mr. Flittergilt found his friend talking to the new actress. Mr. Clissold had penetrated to the sacred chamber somehow, without the dramatist's safe-conduct.

"How did you get here?" asked Flittergilt, annoyed.

"Oh, I hardly know. The old man at the stage door didn't want to admit me. I'm afraid I said I was Miss Elgood's brother, or something of that kind, I was so desperately anxious to see her."

He had been congratulating Justina on her developed talents. The girl's success had surprised herself more than any one else. She had been applauded and praised by provincial critics of late, but she had not thought that a London audience was so easily conquered. The dark eyes shone with a new light, for success was very sweet. In the background stood a figure that Maurice had not observed till just now, when he made way for Mr. Flittergilt.

This was Matthew Elgood, clad in the same greasy-looking frock coat, or just such a coat as that which he had worn two years ago at Eborsham, but smartened by an expanse of spotless shirt-front, which a side view revealed to be only frontage, and not an integral part of his shirt, and a purple satin cravat.

"How do you do, Mr. Elgood? Are you engaged here too?" asked Maurice.

"No, sir. There was no opening for a man of my standing. The pieces which are popular now-a-days are too flimsy to afford an opening for an actor of weight, or else they are one-part pieces written for some mannerist of the hour. The genuine old legitimate school of acting — the school which was fostered in the good old provincial theatres — is nowhere now-a-days. I bow to the inevitable stroke of Time. I was born some twenty years too late. I ought to have been the compeer of Macready."

"Your daughter has been fortunate in making such a hit."

"Ay, sir. The modern stage is a fine field for a young woman with beauty and figure, and when that young woman's talents have been trained and fostered by a man who knows his art, she enters the arena with the assurance of success. There was a time when the malignant called my daughter a stick. There was a time when my daughter hated the profession. But my fostering care has wrought the change which surprises you to-night. A dormant genius has been awakened — I will not venture to say by a kindred genius, lest the remark should savour of egotism."

"You are without occupation, then, in London, Mr. Elgood?"

"Yes, Mr. Clissold, but I have my vocation; I am here as guardian and protector of my innocent child."

"I told Miss Elgood two years ago that, if ever she came to London and needed a friend, my best services should be at her disposal. But her success of to-night has made her independent of friendship."

"I don't know about that, Mr. Clissold. You are a literary man, I understand, a friend of Mr. Flittergilt's, and you have doubtless some influence with dramatic critics. One can never have too much help of that kind. There is a malevolent spirit in the press which requires to be soothed and overcome by friendly influences. Beautiful, gifted as my daughter is, I feel by no means sure of the newspapers. Our unpretending domicile is at No. 27, Hudspeth Street, Bloomsbury, a lowly but a central locality. If you will favour us with a call I shall be delighted. Our Sunday evenings are our own."

"I shall lose no time in availing myself of your kind permission," said Maurice; and then he added in a lower tone, for Mr. Elgood's ear only, "I hope your daughter has got over the grief which that dreadful event at Eborsham occasioned her."

"She has recovered from the blow, sir, but she has not forgotten it. A curiously sensitive child, Mr. Clissold. Who could have supposed that so brief an acquaintance with your murdered friend could have produced so deep an impression upon that young mind? She was never the same girl afterwards. From that time she seemed to me to dwell apart from us all, in a world of her own. She became after a while more attentive to her professional duties—more anxious to excel—more interested in the characters she represented, and she began to surprise us all by touches of pathos which we had not expected from her. She engaged with Mr. Tilberry, of the Theatre Royal, Westborough, for the juvenile lead about six months after your young friend's death, and has maintained a leading position in the provinces ever since. 'Sweet are the uses of adversity, which, like the toad,' &c. Her genius seemed to have been called into being by sorrow. Good night, Mr. Clissold. I dare say Justina will be ready to go home by this time. If you *can* square any of the critics for us, you will discover that Matthew Elgood knows the meaning of the word gratitude."

Maurice promised to do his best, and that evening at his club near the Strand, used all the influence he had in Justina's favour. He found his task easy. The critics who had seen Mr. Flittergilt's new comedy were delighted with the new actress. Those who had been elsewhere, assisting at the production of somebody else's new piece, heard their brothers of the pen enthusiastic in their encomiums, and promised to look in at the Royal Albert Theatre on Monday.

To-night was Saturday. Maurice promised himself that he would call in Hudspeth Street to-morrow evening. He had another engagement, but it was one that could be broken without much offence. And he was curious to see the successful actress at home. Was she much changed from the girl he had surprised on her knees by the clumsy old arm-chair, shedding passionate tears for James Penwyn's death? He had thought her half a child in those days, and the possibilities of fame whereof he had spoken so consolingly very far away. And behold! she was famous already—in a small way, perhaps, but still famous. On Monday the newspapers would be full of her praises. She would be more immediately known to the world than he, the poet, had made himself yet. And she had already tasted the sweetness of applause coming straight from the hearts and hands of her audience, not filtered through the pens of critics, and losing considerable sweetness in the process.

* * * * * *

The illimitable regions of Bloomsbury have room enough for almost every diversity of domicile, from the stately mansions of Russell Square to the lowly abode of the mechanic and the charwoman. Hudspeth Street is an old-fashioned, narrow street of respectable and substantial-looking houses, which must once have been occupied by the professional classes, or have served as the private dwellings of wealthy traders, but which now are for the most part let off in floors to the shabby-genteel and struggling section of humanity, or to more prosperous mechanics, who ply their trades in the sombre paneled rooms, with their tall mantel-boards and deep-set windows.

The street lies between the oldest square of this wide district and a busy thoroughfare, where the costermongers have it all their own way after dark; but Hudspeth Street wears at all times a tranquil gloom, as if it had been forgotten somehow by the majority, and left behind in the general march of progress. Other streets have burst out into stucco, and masked their aged walls with fronts of plaster, as ancient dowagers hide their wrinkles under Bloom de Ninon or Blanc de Rosati. But here the dingy old brick façades remain undisturbed, the old carved garlands still decorate the doorways, the old extinguishers still stand ready to quench torches that have gone to light the dark corridors of Hades.

To Maurice Clissold on this summer evening— Sunday evening, with the sound of many church bells filling the air—Hudspeth Street seems a social study, a place worth half an hour's thought from a philosophical lounger, a place which must have its memories.

No. 27 is cleaner and brighter of aspect than its immediate neighbours. A brass plate upon the door announces that Louis Charlevin, artist in buhl and marqueterie, occupies the ground-floor. Another plate upon the doorpost bears the name of Miss Girdleston, teacher of music; and a third is inscribed with the legend, Mrs. Mapes, Furnished Lodgings, and has furthermore a little hand pointing to a bell, which Maurice rings.

The door is opened by a young person, who is evidently Mrs. Mapes's daughter. Her hair is too elaborate, her dress too smart, her manner too easy for a servant under Mrs. Mapes's dominion. She believes that Mr. Elgood is at home, and begs the visitor to step up to the second floor front, not troubling herself to precede and announce him.

Maurice obeys, and speeds with light footstep up the dingy old staircase. The house is clean and neat enough, but has not been painted for the last thirty years, he opines. He taps lightly at the door and some one bids him enter. Mr. Elgood is lying on a sofa, smoking luxuriously, with a glass of cold punch on the little table at his elbow. The Sunday papers lie around him. He has been reading the records of Justina's success, and is revelling in the firstfruits of prosperity.

Justina is sitting by an open window, dressed in some pale lavender-hued gown, which sets off the tall and graceful figure. Her head leans a little back against the chintz cushion of the high-backed chair, an open book lies on her lap. It falls as she rises to receive the visitor, and Maurice stoops to pick it up.

His own poem.

It gives him more pleasure, somehow, to find it in her hands than he derived from the praises of those two fashionable and accomplished women, Mrs. Penwyn and her sister. It touches him more deeply still to see that Justina's cheeks are wet with tears.

"She has been crying over some foolish poetry, instead of thanking Providence for such criticism as this," said Mr. Elgood, slapping his hand upon the *Sunday Times.*

END OF VQL. I.

PRINTING OFFICE OF THE PUBLISHER.

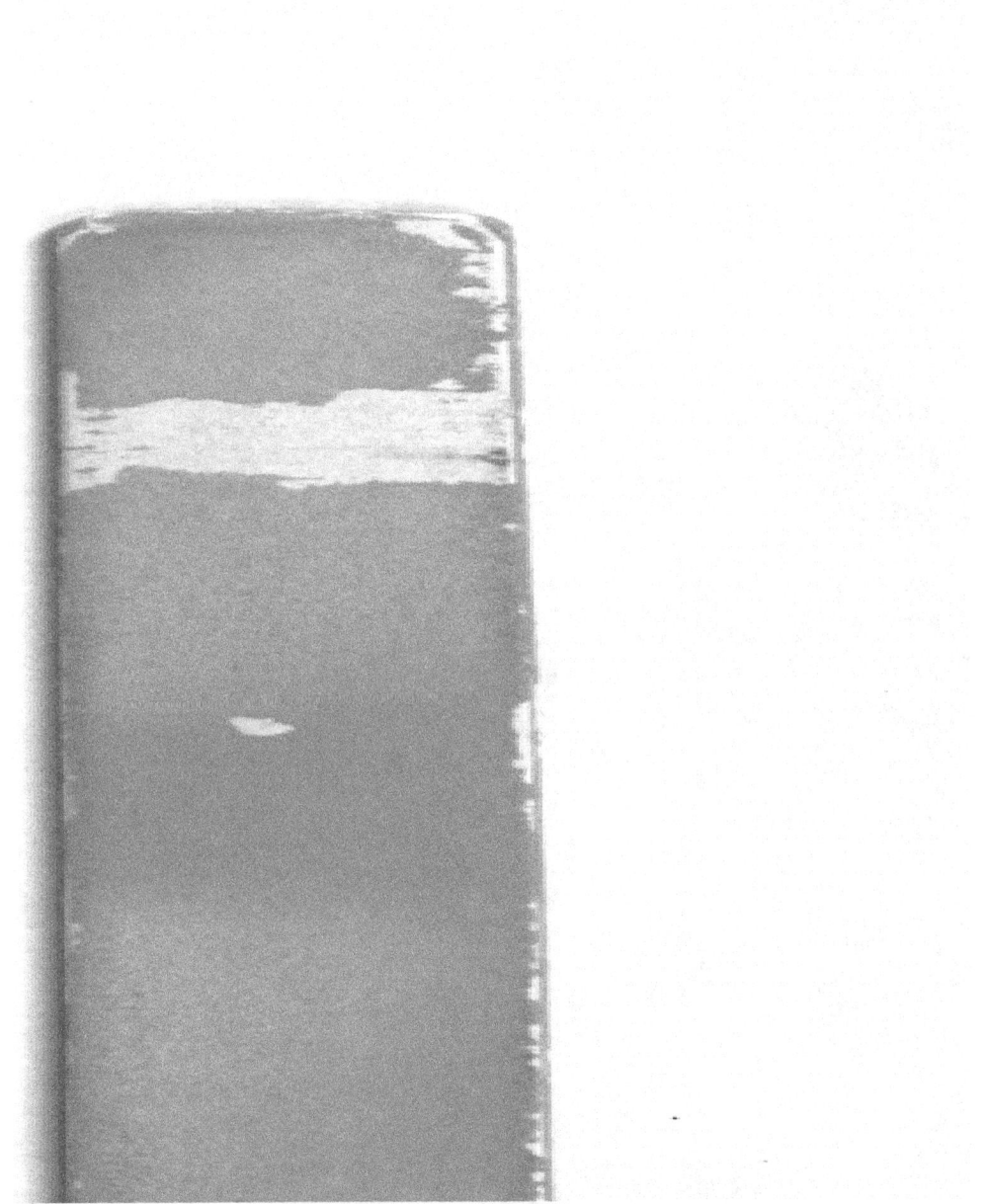

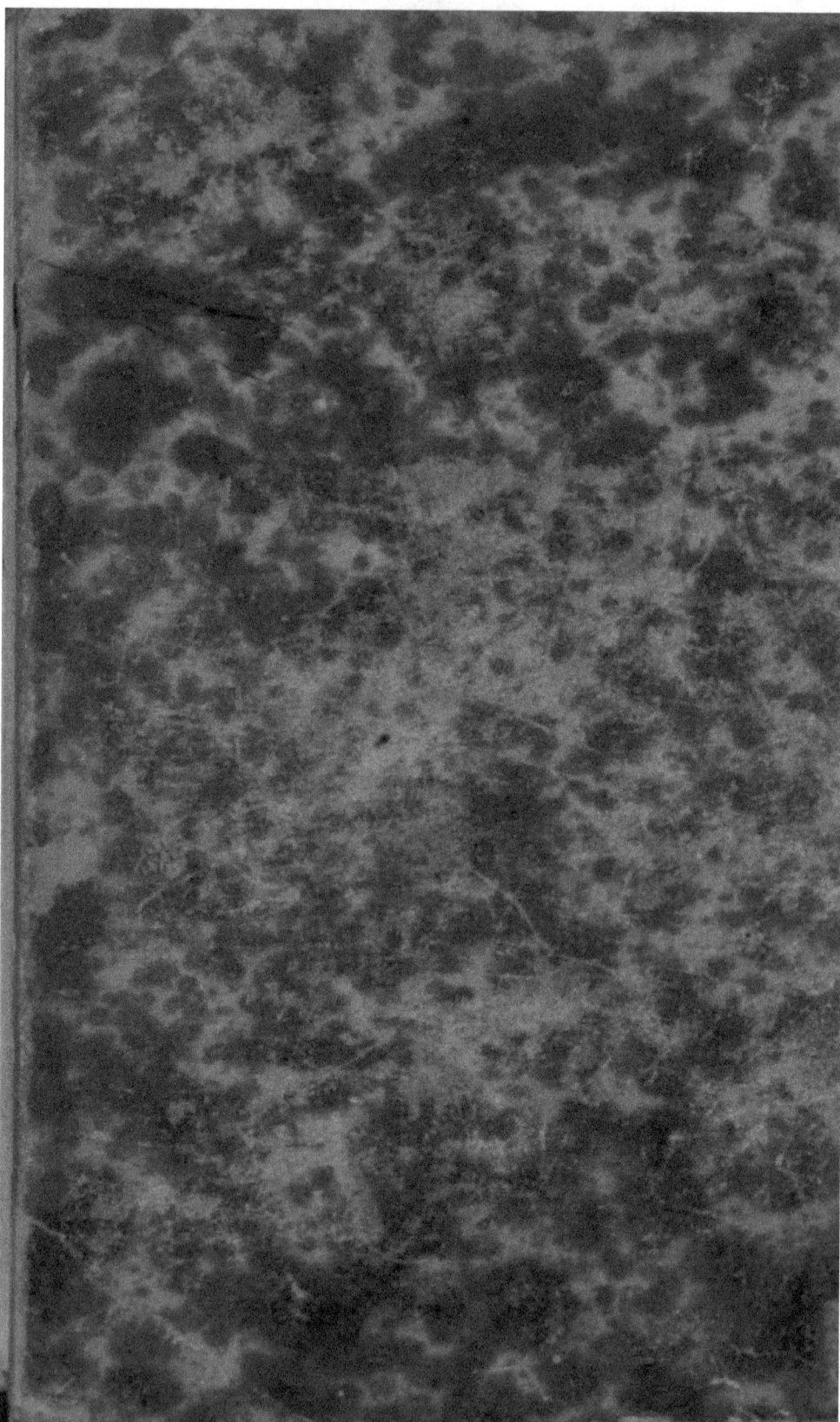

Check Out More Titles From HardPress Classics Series In this collection we are offering thousands of classic and hard to find books. This series spans a vast array of subjects – so you are bound to find something of interest to enjoy reading and learning about.

Subjects:
Architecture
Art
Biography & Autobiography
Body, Mind &Spirit
Children & Young Adult
Dramas
Education
Fiction
History
Language Arts & Disciplines
Law
Literary Collections
Music
Poetry
Psychology
Science
…and many more.

Visit us at www.hardpress.net

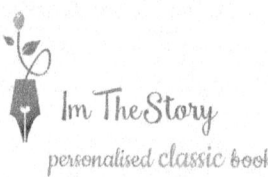

Im TheStory
personalised classic books

"Beautiful gift.. lovely finish. My Niece loves it, so precious!"

Helen R Brumfieldon

★★★★★

UNIQUE GIFT

FOR KIDS, PARTNERS AND FRIENDS

Timeless books such as:

Alice in Wonderland • The Jungle Book • The Wonderful Wizard of Oz
Peter and Wendy • Robin Hood • The Prince and The Pauper
The Railway Children • Treasure Island • A Christmas Carol

Romeo and Juliet • Dracula

Highly Customizable | **Change** Book's Title | **Replace** Characters/names with yours | **Upload** Photo for inside page | **Add** Inscriptions

Visit
Im TheStory.com
and order yours today!